Krishna Bista, *Founding Editor*
Morgan State University, USA

Chris R. Glass, *Editor-In-Chief*
Boston College, USA

Vol. **12** No **3** Nov **2022**

JOURNAL OF INTERNATIONAL STUDENTS

A Quarterly Publication on International Education

Access this journal online at http://ojed.org/jis

Learn about the 12(3) cover art, *Zephyr* (video) by Marc Fornes (France). Zephyr provides an opportunity for connection and camaraderie amidst a bustling microcosm. This issue features articles and authors from Australia, Canada, China, Italy, Korea, Poland, Turkey, the United Kingdom and United States.All 2022 issues will feature cover art from international artists who are part of the Public Art Collection curated by the Texas Tech University System.

DOI: https://doi.org/10.32674/jis.v12i3

This journal is a STAR Scholars Network publication, Baltimore, Maryland.

Print ISSN 2162-3104

Online ISSN 2166-3750

Printed in the United States of America

Disclaimer

Facts and opinions published in *Journal of International Students* (JIS) express solely the opinions of the respective authors. Authors are responsible for their citing of sources and the accuracy of their references and bibliographies. The editors cannot be held responsible for any lacks or possible violations of third parties' rights.

Special Issues

Special Issue | English
**Internationalization for an Uncertain Future:
Emerging Conversations in Critical Internationalization Studies** (2021)
Special Issue Co-Editors:
*Sharon Stein, University of British Columbia, Canada
Dale M. McCartney, University of the Fraser Valley, Canada*

Special Issue | English
Reflection and Reflective Thinking (2020)
Special Issue Co-Editors:
*Georgina Barton, University of Southern Queensland, Australia
Mary Ryan, Macquarie University, Australia*

Special Issue | *Bahasa Indonesia*
International Students and COVID-19 (2020)
Special Issue Co-Editors:
*Handoyo Puji Widodo, King Abdulaziz University, Saudi Arabia
Sandi Ferdiansyah, Institut Agama Islam Negeri, Indonesia and
Lara Fridani, Universitas Negeri Jakarta, Indonesia*

Special Issue | *Chinese*
International Students in China (2020)
Special Issue Co-Editors:
*Mei Tian and Genshu Lu
Xi'an Jiaotong University, China*

Special Issue | English
**Fostering Successful Integration and Engagement
Between Domestic and International Students** (2018)
Special Issue Co-Editors:
*CindyAnn Rose-Redwood and Reuben Rose-Redwood
University of Victoria, Canada*

Special Issue | English
**Role of Student Affairs in International Student
Transition and Success** (2017)
Special Issue Co-Editors:
*Christina W Yao, University of Nebraska-Lincoln, US
Chrystal A. George Mwangi, University of Massachusetts Amherst, US*

Special Issue | English
International Student Success (2016)
Special Issue Editor: *Rahul Choudaha, DrEducation, US*

Emerson is a campus without borders.

We believe producing inspired work requires a global perspective, which is why the Emerson experience isn't limited to one city or even one country. As a global hub of arts and communication in higher education, we strive to provide our students, faculty, and staff with opportunities to connect and collaborate across countries and cultures. From our Global Pathways Programs to our castle in the Netherlands and beyond, we offer more than opportunities for students to study abroad—we provide access to enriching cultural experiences that will guide you on the path to becoming a global citizen.

Our newest global degree programs:

- **Global BA in Business of Creative Enterprises: Australia**
  Our accelerated Global BA in Business of Creative Enterprises (BCE) is powered by a rich management-focused curriculum; immerses students in the life of companies and organizations across two continents through intensive internship programs; and spans venues in **Sydney**, **Boston**, and **Los Angeles**.

- **Global BFA in Film Art**
  Our intercontinental joint Global BFA in Film Art spans venues in **Paris**, **the Netherlands**, and **Boston**. In this one-of-a-kind degree program, students will not only study visual and media arts in the City of Light itself, but will also receive a foundation in the liberal arts and French language.

Learn more at **emerson.edu/global**.

Academic Book Series

Call for Book Proposals

The STAR Scholars Book Series seeks to explore new ideas and best practices related to international student mobility, study abroad, exchange programs, student affairs from the US and around the world, and from a wide range of academic fields, including student affairs, international education, and cultural studies. STAR Scholars publishes some titles in collaboration with Routledge (Taylor & Francis), Springer, Palgrave Macmillan, Open Journals in Education (OJED), Journal of International Students, and other university presses. Scholars interested in contributing a book to our current and future book series are invited to submit a brief proposal directly via this form. All chapters will go through the standard review process before a decision is made. https://www.ojed.org/index.php/gsm/Series

Series Editors
Dr. Chris R. Glass & Dr. Krishna Bista

For questions and submission, email at Krishna.bista@morgan.edu

---

Recently Published Books

1. *Chinese Students and the Experience of International Doctoral Study in STEM*
2. *Developing Intercultural Competence in Higher Education*
3. *International Student Mobility to and from the Middle East*
4. *Inequalities in Study Abroad and Student Mobility*
5. *The Experiences of International Faculty in Institutions of Higher Education*
6. *International Students at US Community Colleges*
7. *Critical Perspectives on Equity and Social Mobility in Study Abroad*
8. *Online Teaching, Learning and Virtual Experiences in Global Higher Education*
9. *International Student Support and Engagement in Higher Education*
10. *Impact of COVID-19 on Global Student Mobility and Higher Education*
11. *Global Higher Education During COVID-19: Policy, Society, and Technology*
12. *COVID-19 and Higher Education in the Global Context*
13. *Reimagining Mobility in Higher Education*
14. *Cross-Cultural Narratives: Stories and Experiences of International Students*
15. *Reimagining Internationalization and International Initiatives at HBCUs*
16. *Delinking, Relinking, and Linking Writing and Rhetorics*
17. *Global Footprints in Higher Education*

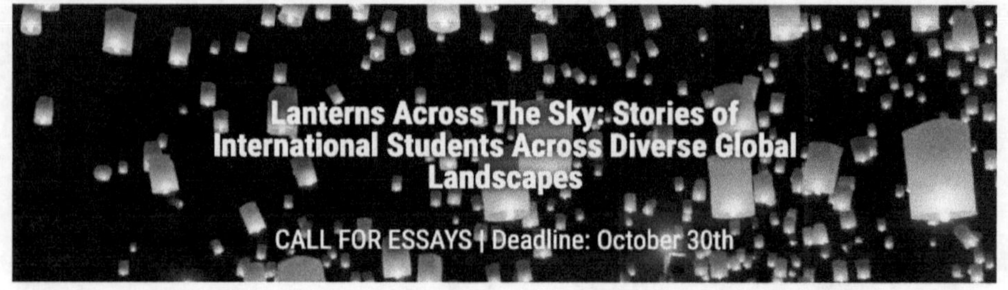

Call for Essays

Everyone has a memorable story of studying or working outside the country of birth. What is your story about studying overseas? What are your cross-cultural experiences from exchange programs or study abroad? Are you a current or former international student? Tell your stories of exploring the words, the world, and the wonders.

Essay Categories

International Student Experience (long-term/degree seeking programs/experiences)
Study Abroad /Exchange Program Experience (short-term/program experience)
Faculty/Staff Experience (International faculty, study abroad mentors, Fulbright scholars)

Languages

You can write your story/essay in any of the following eight languages: Arabic, Chinese, English, French, German, Hindi, Russian, Spanish

Essay Writing Suggestions

Share a story: Focus on moments, encounters, and experiences that shaped your journey as an international student. Tell a story that no one else could tell. Your story can be about friendship, service, freedom, discrimination, injustice, activism, belonging, family, courage, resilience, citizenship, academics, spirituality, parenthood, discovery, inclusion, self-discovery, growth, etc.

Tell your challenges and lessons. Flavor your writing with idioms and figures of speech from your language. Paint the picture. Be concrete about what you have seen in your travels, academic encounters, woes, and wows!

Format Requirements

A story or essay of 1000-1,500 words; Typed in 12-pt size, Times Roman font; double-spaced; 1-inch margins on all sides; includes page numbers. We accept Microsoft Word files only.

More guidelines and sample essays:

https://starscholars.org/lanterns-across-the-sky/

ISSN: 2162-3104 Print/ ISSN: 2166-3750 Online
© *Journal of International Students*
http://ojed.org/jis

Editorial Team

Founder/Executive Editor
Krishna Bista, Morgan State University, USA

Editor-in-Chief
Chris R. Glass, Boston College, USA

Senior Editor
Stephanie K. Kim, Georgetown University, USA

Special Issues Editor
Nelson Brunsting, Wake Forest University

Digital Production Team
Senior Copy Editor*: Joy Bancroft, Emporia State University*
Digital Production Editor, Xi *Lin, East Carolina University*
Editorial Assistant (Digital Production): *Sonali Kathuria, Boston College*

Digital Storytelling Team
Editor, Global Connections, *Györgyi Mihályi, Kent State University*
Director, Social Media: *Sarah Schiffecker, Texas Tech University*
Producer, Global Scholar Stories, *Asuka Ichikawa, Boston College*
Producer, Critical Conversations in International Education, *Mary Ann Bodine Al-Sharif, University of Alabama at Birmingham*

- Dr. Ly Tran, Associate Professor, *Deakin University, Australia*
- Dr. Lydia Andrade, Professor, *University of the Incarnate Word, USA*
- Dr. Stuart Tannock, Senior Lecturer, *University College London, UK*
- Dr. Lien Pham, *Lecturer, University of Technology Sydney, Australia*
- Dr. Janet Ilieva, Founder/Director, *Education Insight, UK*
- Dr. Yingyi Ma, Associate Professor, *Syracuse University, USA*
- Dr. Nicolai Netz, *German Center for Higher Education Research and Science Studies (DZHW), Germany*

Our editorial team is engaged with universities in 20 countries across the world including Australia, Bangladesh, Canada, China, Finland India, Korea, Laos, Mexico, the Netherlands, New Zealand, Portugal, Saudi Arabia, South Africa, Taiwan, Thailand, Turkey, United Kingdom, United States, and Vietnam.

☆ = 2021 *Distinguished Service Award*
★ = *2021 Editor's Choice Award*
◊ = *2021 Excellence in Peer Review Award*

Section Editors

Section Editor (Editorials): Ly Tran, Deakin University
Section Editor (Book Review): Lisa Unangst, Ohio University
Section Editor (Research-in-Context): Jenna Mittelmeier, The University of Manchester
Section Editor (Cross-Border Reflections): Natalie Cruz, Charleston Southern University

Associate Editors

Robert Coelen, University of Groningen (NL)
Kun Dai, Chinese University of Hong Kong (HK)
Carol Griffiths, Girne American University (TR)
Jasper Kun-Ting Hsieh, The University of New South Wales (AU)
Katie Koo, Texas A&M University – Commerce (US)
Masha Krsmanovic, The University of Southern Mississippi (US)
Shu-Wen Lan, National Pingtung Unviersity of Science and Technology (TW)
Charles Mathies, University of Jyväskylä (FI)
Pii-Tuulia Nikula, Eastern Institute of Technology (NZ)
Mohammad Nurunnabi, Prince Sultan University (SA)
Ateeb Ahmad Parray, BRAC James P. Grant School of Public Health (BD)
Thanh Pham, Monash University (AU)
Luísa Helena Ferreira Pinto Pinto, University of Porto (PT)
CindyAnn Rose-Redwood, University of Victoria (CA)
Laura Soulsby, Randolph-Macon College (US)
Melissa Whatley, North Carolina State University (US) ☆
Handoyo Puji Widodo, King Abdulaziz University (SA)
Cora Lingling Xu, Durham University (UK)

Asma Bashir, Beaconhouse National University (PK)
Sushma Basnet, Brunel University (UK)
Amir-Hossein Bayat, Saveh University of Medical Sciences (IR)
Bradley K Beecher, New Mexico State University (US)
Ibrahim Bicak, University of Texas at Austin (US) ◊
Galicia Blackman, University of Calgary (CA) ★
Mary Ann Bodine Al-Sharif, University of Alabama at Birmingham (US) ◊
Shihua Brazill, Montana State University (US)
Mandy Brunson, University of Delaware (US)
Janina Brutt-Griffler, University at Buffalo, The State University of New York (US)
Tram-Anh Bui, Brock University and Ho Chi Minh City University (VN)
Elif Cankaya, Oakwood University at Huntsville (US)
Heather Carmack, University of Alabama (US)
Loredana Carson, California Lutheran University (US)
Shanton Chang, University of Melbourne, Australia (AU)
Bo Chang, Ball State University (US)
Jun Mian Chen, Conestoga College (CA)
Kenneth Chen, University at Albany-SUNY (US)
Baoyan Cheng, University of Hawaii at Manoa (US) ◊
Prashanti Chennamsetti, Texas A&M University (US)
Porshe Chiles, Wake Forest University (US)
Hyun Jin Cho, Purdue University (US)
Courtney Collins, University of Nebraska-Lincoln (US)
John Connolly, University of Texas at Arlington (US)
Shasha Cui, University of Rochester (US)
Kim Dianne Curtin, University of Alberta (CA)
Kimberley Daly, George Mason University (US)
Benjamin Denga, University of Alberta (CA) ★
David Di Maria, University of Maryland - Baltimore County (US)
Dan Dickman, Ivy Tech Community College (US)
Trang Dinh, Rice University(US)
Dely Lazarte Elliot, University of Glasgow (UK)
Omolabake Fakunle, University of Edinburgh (UK)
Mehrdad Falavarjani, University of Saskatchewan (CA) ◊
Xumei Fan, University of South Carolina (US)
Rai Farrelly, University of Colorado - Boulder (US)
Barry Fass-Holmes, University California San Diego (US)
Sarah Fehrman, Purdue University (US)
Amy Fenning, Maryville University (US)
Cesar Augusto Ferrari Martinez, Universidade Federal de Pelotas (BR)
Christine Fiorite, University of Chicago (US) ◊
Steven Fraiberg, Purdue University (US)
Keri Freeman, Queensland University of Technology (AU)
Ann Frkovich, Concordia University Chicago (US)
Yan Gao, University of Victoria (CA)
Jaime Garcia, University of Queensland (AU)
Tiberio Garza, University of Nevada, Las Vegas (US)
Charles Gbollie, Central China Normal University (CN)
Lin Ge, University of Regina (CA)
Danielle Geary, Georgia Tech (US)
Chrystal A. George Mwangi, University of Massachusetts Amherst (US) ◊

Peggy Gesing, Eastern Virginia Medical School (US) ◊
Peter G. Ghazarian, Ashland University (US)
Bianca Gomez, York University (CA)
Ricardo Gonzalez-Carriedo, University of North Texas (US)
Adam Grimm, Michigan State University (US) ◊
Sarah Grosik, University of Pennsylvania (US)
Ning Guo, Saint Louis University (US)
Clarisse Halpern, Florida Gulf Coast University (US)
Karleah Harris, University of Arkansas at Pine Bluff (US)
Catherine Hartman, University of South Carolina (US) ★
Nigel Harwood, University of Sheffield (UK)
Ahdi Hassan,International Association for Technology (TR)
Xuewei He, The George Washington University (US) ◊
Niall Hegarty, St. John's University, United States (US)
Tang Tang Heng, National Institute of Education--Singapore (SG)
Elizabeth Margarita Hernández López, University of Guadalajara (MX)
Andrew Scott Herridge, The University of Southern Mississippi (US)
Sara Hosseini-Nezhad, Eötvös Loránd University (CA)
Ning Hou, St. Cloud State University (US)
Jennifer Hoyte, Florida Southern College (US)
Jing Hua, Troy University (US)
Rong Huang, University of Plymouth (US)
Graham Robert Huether, University of North Texas (US)
Ireena Nasiha Ibnu, Universiti Teknologi MARA(UiTM) (MY) ★
Irene Irudayam, Anna Maria College (US)
Polina Ivanova, Ritsumeikan University (JP)
Laura Jacobi, Minnesota State University at Mankato (US)
Xiushan Jiang, College of Charleston (US)
Shuiping Jiang, Clemson University (IE) ★
Li Jin, DePaul University (US)
Karin Johnson, Texas A&M University (US)
Christopher Johnstone, University of Minnesota (US)
Jae-Eun Jon, Hankuk University of Foreign Studies Seoul Campus (KR)
Alexander Jones, Wheaton College (US)
Jessika Jones, University of Houston (US)
Cebrail Karayigit, Pittsburg State University (US)
Sonali Kathuria, Wake Forest University (US)
Jacob Kelley, Auburn University (US)
Jamshed Khalid, Universiti Sains Malaysia (MY)
David Killick, Leeds Beckett University (UK)
Regine Lambrech, International Education Consulting (US)
Jiva Nath Lamsal, The University of Sydney (AU)
Marleny Leasa, Pattimura University (ID) ★
Sherrie Lee, Tertiary Education Commission (NZ)
Injung Lee, Purdue University Northwest (US)
Anke Li, The Pennsylvania State University (US)
Dan Li, University of North Texas (US)
Jason Li, Wichita State University (US)
Ching-Ching Lin, Touro College (US)
Yang Liu, Beijing Foreign Studies University (CN)
Charles Liu, Michigan State University (US)

Lin Ma, University of Bristol (UK) ★
Kyunghee Ma, University of South Carolina (College of Social Work) (US)
Yingyi Ma, syracuse university (US)
Marc Malone, The University of Kansas (US)
Catia Margarida da Cunha Marques, University of Minho (PT)
Nara M. Martirosyan, Sam Houston State University (US)
Blair Matthews, University of St Andrews (UK)
Elena Maydell, Massey University (NZ)
Dorothy Mayne, University of Illinois Urbana Champaign (US)
Abhijit Mazumdar, Mt. Enterprise High School (US)
Rachel McGee, Nagase/Speaking Partners (US)
Jon L. McNaughtan, Texas Tech University (US)
Megan Mischinski, Wake Forest University (US)
Chi Yun Moon, Texas A&M University (US)
Darlinda Pacheco Moreira, Universidade Aberta (PT)
Heba Mostafa, Saint Louis University (US)
Michael Mu, Queensland University of Technology (AU)
Amirul Mukminin, Jambi University (ID)
Doreen N. Myrie, Jackson State University (US)
Jasvir Kaur Nachatar Singh, La Trobe University (AU)
Atsushi Nagai, Hiroshima University (JP)
Nina Namaste, Elon University (US)
Steve Nerlich, Australian National University (AU)
Bao Trang Thi Nguyen, University of Foreign Languages, Hue University (VN)
Huong Thi Lan Nguyen, Swinburne University of Technology (AU)
Pii-Tuulia Nikula, Eastern Institute of Technology (NZ) ★
Per A. Nilsson, Umeå University (SE)
Yuanlu Niu, University of Arkansas (US)
Conor Nolan, National College of Ireland (IE) ★
Sarah Nutter, University of Victoria (CA) ★
Robert M O'Connell, University of Missouri (US)
Adesola Ogundimu, John Hopkins University (US)
Yakup Öz, Karamanoğlu Mehmetbey University (TR)
Emily-Marie Pacheco, University of Glasgow (UK)
Yolanda Palmer-Clarke, University of Saskatchewan (CA)
Pengfei Pan, Queensland University of Technology (AU) ★
Moses Glorino Rumambo Pandin, Universitas Airlangga (ID)
Astadi Pangarso, Brawijaya University, Telkom University (ID)
Melania Pantelich, Federation University (AU)
Satyanarayana Parayitam, University of Massachusetts Dartmouth (US)
Eunjeong Park, Sunchon National University (KR)
Jerry Parker, Southeastern Louisiana University (US) ◊
Reshma Parveen, University of Queensland (AU)
Kelly A. Pengelly, American University (US)
Bethany Peters, University of Minnesota (US)
Lien Pham, University of Technology Sydney (AU)
Thanh Pham, Monash University (AU)
Huong Le Thanh Phan, Deakin University (AU)
Gareth Phillips, University of Technology, Jamaica (JM)
Bright Phiri, Lovely Professional University (ZM)
Nattavud Pimpa, Mahidol University (TH)

Josef Ploner, University of Hull (UK)
India Plough, Michigan State University (US)
Surendra Pokhrel, Daito Bunka University (NP)
Senel Poyrazli, The Pennsylvania State University - Harrisburg (US)
Bambang Pratolo, Universitas Ahmad Dahlan (ID) ★
Maria Prikhodko, DePaul University (US)
Dana Rad, Aurel Vlaicu University of Arad (RO)
Sophia Glenyse Rahming, Florida State University (US) ◊
Namrata Rao, Liverpool Hope UNiversity (UK) ★
Andres F. Restrepo, Valdosta State University (SK)
Alexandra Reynolds, Université de Bordeaux (FR)
Maureen Rhoden, Independent Researcher (UK) ★
L. Erika Saito, National University (US)
Laura Schaffer Metcalfe, Mesa Community College (US)
Nathaniel H Schierman, Penn State University (US)
Jason Schneider, DePaul University (US)
Lleij Samuel Schwartz, Southern New Hampshire University (US)
Charles J Schwartz, University of Cincinnati (US)
Mary Ann Seow, Past National President of ISANA International Education Association (AU)
Noel L Shadowen, La Salle University (US)
SuYeong Shin, University of Iowa (US)
SuYeong Shin, University of Iowa/University of Utah (US)
Prabin Shrestha, Tri Chandra Multiple Campus (NP)
Anupma Singh, University of Wyoming (US)
Janice Smith, Morgan State Universityt (US)
Adem Soruc, The University of Bath (UK)
Garth Stahl, University of Queensland (AU)
David Starr-Glass, SUNY Empire State College (US) ◊
William Stewart, Hankuk University of Foreign Studies (KR)
Jennifer A. Strangfeld, California State University, Stanislaus (US)
Mengwei Su, Ohio University (US)
Yi Sun, University of Massachusetts Amherst (US)
Manca Sustarsic, University of Hawaii at Manoa (US) ★
Elena K. Taborda, University of Massachusetts Boston (US) ◊
Fujuan Tan, Morehead State University (US)
Bettina Teegen, University of Surrey in England (DE) ★
Eric Terzuolo, American University (US)
Carrie Anne Thomas, The Ohio State University (US) ◊
Mei Tian, Jiaotong University (CN)
Lu Tian, University of Northern Colorado (US)
Ethan Trinh, Georgia State University (US)
Linda Tsevi, University of Ghana (GH)
Siqi Tu, New York University Shanghai (CN)
Haijing Tu, Indiana State University (CA)
Mengwei Tu, East China University of Science and Technology (CN)
Mei-Ling Tung, Saint Louis University (US)
Kandy K. Turner, Widener University (US)
Lisa Unangst, Ohio University (US)
Faith Valencia-Forrester, Griffith University (AU)

Nicole D Vaux, Lindenwood University (US)
Jeanne-Marie Viljoen, University of South Australia (AU)
Louise Michelle Vital, Lesley University (US) ◊
Rong Wang, University of North Carolina at Charlotte (CN) ★
Xingchen Wang, Illinois State University (US)
Xin Wang, Baylor University (US)
Xinxin Wang, University of North Carolina at Chapel Hill (US)
Caroline Wekullo, Texas A&M University (US)
Zhenjie Weng, The Ohio State University (US) ★
Tsung-han Weng, University of Kansas (US)
Nancy Will, University of Washington Seattle (US)
Gloria Wong, Hong Kong University (HK) ★
Jon Woodend, James Cook University (AU) ★
Congcong Xing, Queensland University of Technology (AU) ★
Weiyan Xiong, Lingnan University Hong Kong (HK) ★
Yiying Xiong, Johns Hopkins University (US)
Xing Xu, Sichuan International Studies University (CN)
Jiayi Xu, University of Florida (US)
Fikri Yanda, Universitas Pendidikan Indonesia (ID)
Lili Yang, University of Oxford (UK)
Ruijin Yang, School of International Studies (CN) ◊
HyeJin Tina Yeo, University of Illinois Urbana Champaign (US)
Hyejin Yoon, University of Wisconsin-Milwaukee (US)
Jingran Yu, University of Manchester (CN)
Xi Yu, University of Minnesota-Twin Cities (US)
Roseline Jindori Yunusa Vakkai, De Rose Community Bridge and Holistic Health (US)
Fanyi Zeng, Wake Forest University (US)
Jie Zhang, Guangdong University of Finance (CN)
Xiaoqiao Zhang, Harvard University (US)
Ying Shan Doris Zhang, University of Alberta (CA)
Lin Zheng, University of Portsmouth (UK)

Recent Publications

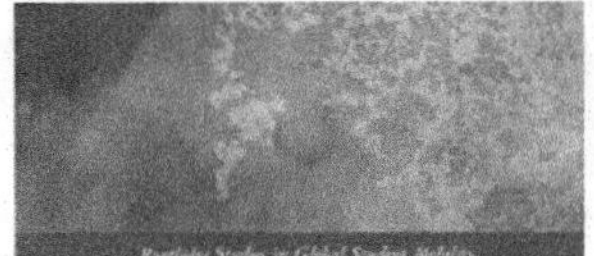

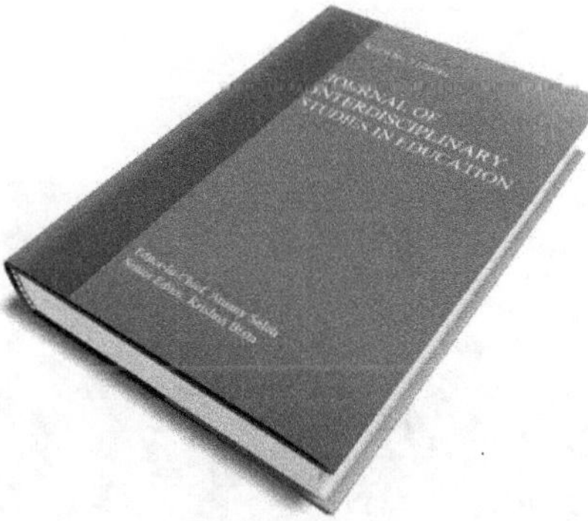

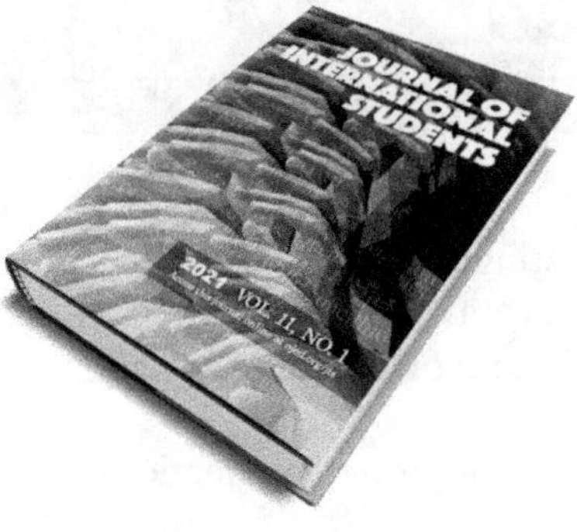

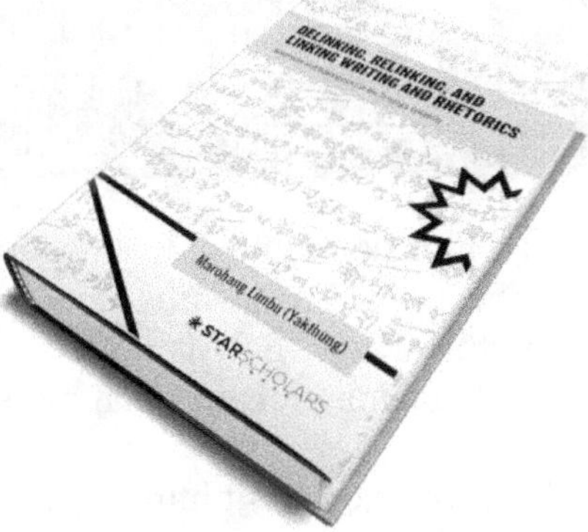

CRITICAL PERSPECTIVES ON EQUITY AND SOCIAL MOBILITY IN STUDY ABROAD
INTERROGATING ISSUES OF UNEQUAL ACCESS AND OUTCOMES
Edited by
Chris Glass and Peggy Gesing

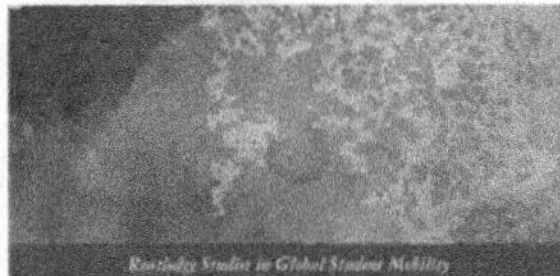

INEQUALITIES IN STUDY ABROAD AND STUDENT MOBILITY
NAVIGATING CHALLENGES AND FUTURE DIRECTIONS
Edited by
Suzan Kommers and Krishna Bista

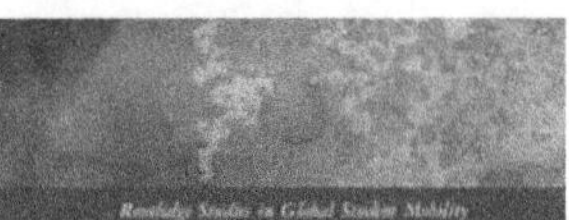

THE EXPERIENCES OF INTERNATIONAL FACULTY IN INSTITUTIONS OF HIGHER EDUCATION
ENHANCING RECRUITMENT, RETENTION, AND INTEGRATION OF INTERNATIONAL TALENT
Edited by
Chris Glass, Krishna Bista and Xi Lin

JOURNAL OF UNDERREPRESENTED AND MINORITY PROGRESS
OJED.ORG / JUMP

JOURNAL OF INTERDISCIPLINARY STUDIES IN EDUCATION

JOURNAL OF INTERNATIONAL STUDENTS
2021 VOL 11, NO 1

DELINKING, RELINKING, AND LINKING WRITING AND RHETORICS
Morohang Limbu (Yakthung)
STARSCHOLARS

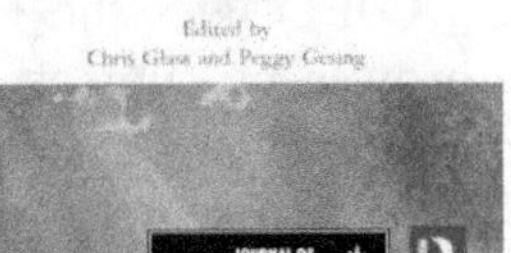

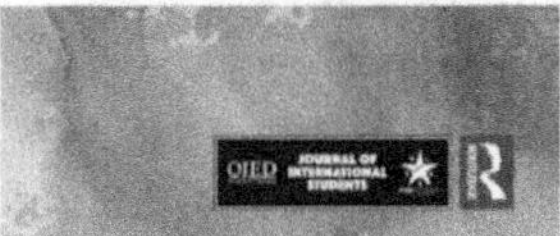

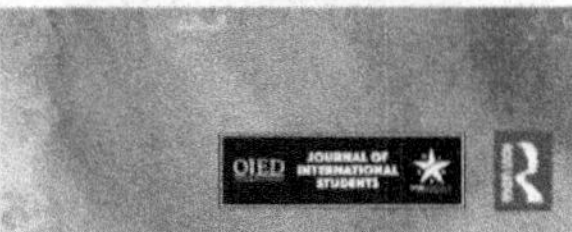

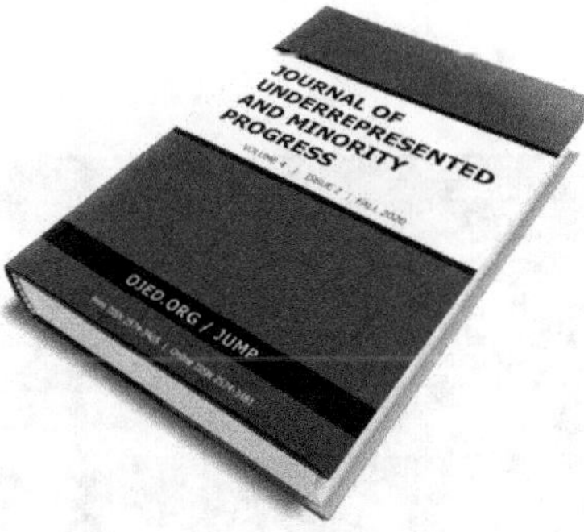

Open Journals in Education (OJED) publishes high quality peer reviewed, open access journals based at research universities. OJED uses the Open Journal System (OJS) platform, where readers can browse by subject, drill down to journal level to find the aims, scope, and editorial board for each individual title, as well as search back issues. OJED journals are required to be indexed in major academic databases to ensure quality and maximize article discoverability and citation. Journals follow best practices on publication ethics outlined in the COPE Code of Conduct. Explore our OJED Journals at www.ojed.org

***

A. Noam Chomsky Global Connections Awards celebrate the power of human connections. The awards recognize distinguished service to the global mission of the STAR Scholars Network. Several individuals with a deep impact on advancing global, social mobility are recognized every year.

For more information, visit https://starscholars.org/global-connections-award/

Indexing

ISSN: 2162-3104 Print/ ISSN: 2166-3750 Online
Journal of International Students
http://ojed.org/jis

SUBJECT: Education- Higher Education/ DEWEY #378

Directory of Open Access Journals, 2011-
EBSCOhost, Education Source, 03/01/2012-
Gale
- o   Academic OneFile, 09/01/2011-
- o   Contemporary Women's Issues, 09/01/2011-
- o   Educator's Reference Complete, 09/01/2011-
- o   Expanded Academic ASAP, 09/01/2011-
- o   InfoTrac Custom, 09/01/2011-

ProQuest
- o   Education Collection, 10/01/2011-
- o   Education Database, 10/01/2011-
- o   Education Database (Alumni Edition), 10/01/2011-
- o   ProQuest Central, 10/01/2011-
- o   ProQuest Central - UK Customers, 10/01/2011-
- o   ProQuest Central (Alumni Edition), 10/01/2011-
- o   ProQuest Central (Corporate), 10/01/2011-
- o   ProQuest Central (US Academic Subscription), 10/01/2011-
- o   ProQuest Central China, 10/01/2011-
- o   ProQuest Central Essentials, 10/01/2011-
- o   ProQuest Central Korea, 10/01/2011-
- o   ProQuest Central Student, 10/01/2011-
- o   ProQuest Research Library, 10/01/2011-
- o   ProQuest Research Library (Corporate), 10/01/2011-
- o   ProQuest Social Sciences Premium Collection, 10/01/2011-
- o   Research Library (Alumni Edition), 10/01/2011-
- o   Social Science Premium Collection, 10/01/2011-

Clarivate Analytics
- o   Web of Science
- o   Emering Sciences Citation Index
- o   Higher Education Abstracts

Source: Ulrichsweb Global Serials Directory

You may access the print and/or digital copies of the Journal of International Students from **686 libraries worldwide** (as of July, 2022).

The Journal of International Students (Print ISSN 2162-3104 & Online ISSN 2166-3750) is a member of the STAR Scholars Network Open Journals in Education (OJED), a OJS 3 platform for high-quality, peer-reviewed academic journals in education.

JIS is a Gold Open Access journal and indexed in major academic databases to maximize article discoverability and citation. JIS follows best practices on publication ethics outlined in the COPE Code of Conduct. Editors work to ensure timely decisions after initial submission, as well as prompt publication online if a manuscript is accepted for publication.

Upon publication articles are immediately and freely available to the public. The final version of articles can immediately be posted to an institutional repository or to the author's own website as long as the article includes a link back to the original article posted on OJED.

None of the OJED journals charge fees to individual authors thanks to the generous support of our institutional sponsors.

For further information

Editorial Office
Journal of International Students
URL: http://ojed.org/jis
E-mail: contact@jistudents.org

The *Journal of International Students* is a Gold Open Access publication thanks to the generous institutional sponsorship of Old Dominion University and publication partnership of Emerson College and American Council on Education.

ISSN: 2162-3104 Print/ ISSN: 2166-3750 Online
2022 Volume 12, Number 3
© *Journal of International Students*
http://ojed.org/jis

CONTENTS

Invited Editorial

Journal of International Students
Volume 12, Issue 3 (2022), pp. i-viii
ISSN: 2162-3104 (Print), 2166-3750 (Online)
ojed.org/jis

Critical Considerations for Optimizing the Support for International Student Engagement

Ly Thi Tran
Deakin University, Australia

Jill Blackmore
Deakin University, Australia

Helen Forbes-Mewett
Monash University, Australia

Diep Thi Bich Nguyen
Deakin University, Australia

Danielle Hartridge
Deakin University, Australia

Renata Aldana
Australian College of Business Intelligence, Australia

INTRODUCTION

Hosting international students enriches the educational, intercultural, social, political, and economic capitals of the host communities. It is therefore a significant privilege and opportunity for education providers and host countries to educate students from other countries. But it is also the host communities' responsibility to nurture an optimal education experience for this cohort, which in turn helps strengthen international education for all. Student engagement is vital for creating a welcoming, caring and positive experience for international students.

International student engagement is often situated in physical and virtual mobilities, in-between spaces, transnational interactions with new educational, socio-cultural environment, and home-host connectedness/disconnectedness. International students' transnational movements and intersections with the new environment shape and re-shape their engagement with space, people, communities as well as cultural and academic practices (Blackmore et al., 2021; Kang & Hwang, 2022; Tran & Gomes, 2017).

International student engagement is often linked with and relies on optimal student experiences across a range of interrelated aspects, including:

- connection between international students and domestic students and communities
- engagement with support services regarding mental health and wellbeing, accommodation, finance, intercultural communication, and language and learning skills
- work-integrated learning (WIL) and employability
- engagement with face-to-face, hybrid and online learning and teaching
- international students' navigation through crises such as, health, financial, natural disaster, geopolitical crises, or war.

COVID-19 has exposed the vulnerabilities of international students as temporary residents and non-citizens in the host society and the de-valuation of this cohort (Tran, 2020). The international discourse shows three main ways in which international students are de-valued: (i) the commercialisation and de-humanisation of international students as tradable commodities, (ii) the essentialisation of international students as a homogenous and deficit group, and (iii) the othering of international students, viewing them as 'others' or 'outsiders' in 'our' country and 'our' education system. However, the pandemic has, at the same time, been a catalyst for the host communities to critically reflect on the support provision for international students and the implications for future pathways, including the role and the expansion of support for this cohort from a range of community groups and organisations beyond the education sector. Based on critical consideration of support provision for international student engagement, this article puts forward practical recommendations for optimising the design and delivery of appropriate, effective, and sustainable support for international students.

The presence of international students, their diverse needs, characteristics, and circumstances have created new challenges, as well as possibilities, for teachers, professional staff and communities to innovate and extend their practices and support provision (Forbes-Mewett & Nyland, 2008; Mahalingappa et al., 2021; Nyland et al., 2013; Tran & Pasura, 2019; Tran & Le, 2018). However, in many cases, staff in education providers and especially members of community organisations had to 'learn on the job' in providing support for international students. Many 'good' practices initiated by individuals or specific groups are ad-hoc and organic rather than being shared, documented, and recognized as common practices across broader levels.

Cultural appropriateness, sustainability and systemic coordination are among critical areas that warrant special attention in designing and delivering effective and sustainable support provision for international student engagement. There is concern about the cultural appropriateness of support services relating to teaching and learning, language and intercultural communication, counselling, and mental health services (Forbes-Mewett & Sawyer, 2015; Tran, 2013). There is also a need to caution against 'one size fits all' in developing international student support services (Darmody et al., 2022; Tran, 2013).

Grouping international and domestic students together does not automatically lead to meaningful engagement (Blackmore et al., 2021; Leask, 2009; Tran, 2013; Tran & Pham, 2016). Proximity of contact alone might just result in surface engagement or superficial interaction between international students and domestic students and communities. International student engagement is most effective when it is built on productive connectedness, which goes beyond simply providing the basic conditions for interaction between international students and Australian students and communities. It is therefore critical to foster real and well-planned opportunities for international and local communities to enrich their mutual understandings and reciprocal learning from the encounter of differences, which forms the basis for long-lasting and meaningful connections.

Over the past decade, support services beyond the education sector targeted international student engagement in work-integrated learning and employability have been on the rise. This might be driven by three main factors: the increased weight international students and families attach to employment outcomes in choosing study destinations; international students have a rising demand for work-integrated learning and employability support but they often find it challenging to secure work placements and internships; universities tend to be reluctant or struggle to arrange WIL because it is expensive and complex, involving partnerships with industry and stakeholders which often take significant time and commitment to develop (Blackmore et al., 2015; Tran & Soejatminah, 2017). While international students' expectations may sometimes need to be managed, they need to be provided with earlier introduction to career planning so that the development of employability and professional portfolios can commence earlier, and work-integrated learning can be beneficial.

The COVID-19 pandemic has forced large-scale shifts to online learning, which presents both challenges and opportunities, with a range of digital technologies being increasingly used to assist not only with online and blended learning, but also with support provision in relation to international students' connectedness, mental health and work-integrated learning (Adachi & Tran, 2022; Humphrey & Forbes-Mewett, 2021). Various innovative practices, capitalising on digital technologies, have been introduced to support international students by education providers in partnership with EdTech companies.

Supporting international students during crises, such as health, financial, natural disaster, geopolitical crises or war, has become a critical area warranting more nuanced understandings. It is crucial to learn and share good practice examples and initiatives in developing effective and sustainable responses to crises of various natures affecting international students, and how this is situated within the institution's immediate and long-term risk management plan.

IMPLICATIONS

We proposed the following recommendations for the host communities to consider in designing and implementing support services for international students:

- Placing international students at the centre in providing student-centred support services should go beyond understanding their needs and characteristics. Rather, it extends to co-designing support resources with them.
- Effective engagement with international students is based on a holistic approach and understanding of how aspects of a cross-border student life are interlinked and inter-dependent on each other, including academic performance, learning outcomes, mental health and wellbeing, employment, accommodation, finance, life plans, and aspirations. It is worthwhile to consider how supporting international students enhances experiences for

all members of the host institutions in designing for optimal student engagement.

- To position international students as a truly integral component of the host communities and create a welcoming environment, it is essential to build mechanisms to engage them not only academically, socially and interculturally, but also mentally and emotionally, especially during hard-hitting crises such as the COVID-19 outbreak or the 2003 SARS epidemic, war or geopolitical crisis, or natural disasters.
- International students tend to be overwhelmed with information, especially during the orientation period, so it is crucial to plan carefully how to clearly and effectively communicate support resources to them.
- There is a critical need to understand international students' help-seeking behaviours and the cultural and social factors impacting on those in designing effective support for international student engagement. A proportion of international students might associate help-seeking or using support services with a sense of losing face or perceptions of their own deficiencies or failures.
- To support international student engagement in the changing context, it is important to build capacity for and up-skill or re-skill staff. It is important to provide sustaining targeted professional development for staff and stakeholders involved in providing support for international students to ensure Australia's commitment to creating a welcoming, empathetic and conducive environment for international students.

To ensure appropriate support for international student engagement, it is crucial to understand enabling and inhibiting factors for support provision for this cohort, and work collectively to create a community of sharing and implementing good practices.

As part of an ongoing commitment to supporting international students, the Australian government funded Deakin University to undertake the Best Practice International Student Engagement Project. This project will identify what successful international student engagement looks like and develop a best practice guide and other resources to encourage and support international student engagement.

If you would like to share an example of good practice and be kept informed of the progress and outcomes of the Best Practice International Student Engagement Project, please send an email to best-practice-ise@deakin.edu.au

REFERENCES

Adachi, C. & Tran, L. (2022). International students are back on campus, but does that spell the end of digital learning? *The Conversation.* https://theconversation.com/international-students-are-back-on-campus-but-does-that-spell-the-end-of-digital-learning-heres-why-it-shouldnt-177545

Blackmore, J., Gribble, C., & Rahimi, M. (2015). Work integrated learning: Employer and international business and accounting students' experiences of Australian universities. *Higher Education, Skills and Work-based Learning,* 5(4), 401-416. http://dx.doi.org/10.1108/HESWBL-04-2015-0015

Blackmore, J., Tran, L., Hoang, T., Chou-Lee, M., McCandless, T., Mahoney, C., Beavis, C., Rowan, L., Hurem, A. (2021). Affinity spaces and the situatedness of intercultural relations between domestic and international students in two Australian schools, *Educational Review.* https://doi.org/10.1080/00131911.2022.2026892

Darmody, M., Groarke, S., & Mihut, G. (2022). Engagement of International Students at Irish Higher Education Institutions. *Journal of International Students*, 12(4), 795-816.

Forbes-Mewett, H., & Nyland, C. (2008). Cultural diversity relocation and the security of international students at an internationalised university. *Journal of Studies in International Education, 12*(2), 181-203. https://doi.org/10.1177/1028315307308136

Forbes-Mewett, H., & Sawyer, A.-M. (2016). International students and mental health. *Journal of International Students*, 6(3), 661–677. https://doi.org/10.32674/jis.v6i3.348

Humphrey, A., & Forbes-Mewett, H. (2021). Social value systems and the mental health of international students during the COVID-19 pandemic. *Journal of International Students*, 11(S2), 58–76. https://doi.org/10.32674/jis.v11iS2.3577

Kang, J., & Hwang, K. (2022). Belonging otherwise: Chinese undergraduate students at South Korean universities. *Globalisation, Societies and Education*, 1-14.

Leask, B. (2009). 'Beside me is an empty chair': The student experience of internationalisation. In E. Jones (Ed), *Internationalisation and the student voice* (pp. 29-43). Routledge.

Mahalingappa, L., Kayi-Aydar, H., & Polat, N. (2021). Institutional and faculty readiness for teaching linguistically diverse international students in educator preparation programs in US universities. *TESOL Quarterly, 55*(4), 1247-1277. https://doi.org/10.1002/tesq.3083

Nyland, C., Forbes-Mewett, H., & Hartel, C. (2013). Governing the international student experience: Lessons from the Australian international education model, *Academy of Management Learning and Education, 12*(4), 656-67. https://www.jstor.org/stable/43698673

Tran, L. T. (2013). *Teaching international students in vocational education and training: New pedagogical approaches*. Camberwell: ACER Press.

Tran, L. T. (2020, August 20). Understanding the full value of international
students.
www.universityworldnews.com/post.php?story=20200820103708349

Tran, L. T., & Gomes, C. (2017). Student mobility, connectedness and identity.
In L. T. Tran & C. Gomes (Eds). *International student connectedness
and identity* (pp.1-11). Dordrecht: Springer.

Tran, L. T., & Le, T.T.T (2018). *Teacher professional learning in international
education.* Basingstoke: Palgrave Macmillan Hong Kong and Australia.

Tran, L. T., & Pasura, R. (2017). Professional development for teachers
working with international students. *Vocations and Learning*, 1-20.
https://doi.org/10.1007/s12186-017-9195-6

Tran, L. T., & Pham, L. (2016). International students in transnational mobility:
Intercultural connectedness with domestic and international peers,
institutions and the wider community. *Compare: A Journal of
Comparative and International Education,* *46*(4), 560–581.
https://doi.org/10.1080/03057925.2015.1057479

Tran, L.T., & Soejatminah S. (2017). Integration of work experience and learning
for international students: From harmony to inequality. *Journal of
Studies in International Education,* *21*(3), 261-277.
https://doi.org/10.1177/1028315316687012

Author Biographies

LY THI TRAN is a Professor in the School of Education, Deakin
University, Australia and an affiliated faculty member of the Centre for
Higher Education Internationalisation, Università Cattolica del Sacro
Cuore, Milan. Her research focuses on international education,
international students, the education-migration nexus, international
graduate employability and Australian student mobility to the Indo-
Pacific. Email: ly.tran@deakin.edu.au

JILL BLACKMORE is Alfred Deakin Professor in Education, Faculty
of Arts and Education, Deakin University, Australia, a Fellow of the
Australian Academy of Social Sciences, and Vice-President of the
Australian Association of University Professors. She researches from a
feminist perspective education policy and governance; international and
intercultural education; and teachers' and academics' work, health, and
wellbeing. Email: jillian.blackmore@deakin.edu.au

HELEN FORBES-MEWETT is Associate Professor of Sociology in the
School of Social Sciences at Monash University. She is Research Lead of
the Monash Migration and Inclusion Centre, Senior Fellow with the
International Education Association of Australia, and Editor in Chief of

the *Journal of Sociology*. Her interdisciplinary background encompasses sociology, psychology, and international business with a focus on international students and vulnerable communities. Email: helen.forbesmewett@monash.edu

DIEP THI BICH NGUYEN is a recent PhD graduate from Deakin University, Australia and a project manager for Best Practice International Student Engagement Project. She has experience in teaching international students and researching academic capacity building in international education, English medium instruction, and graduate employability. Email: diep.nguyen@deakin.edu.au

DANIELLE HARTRIDGE is a practitioner with over 30 years' experience working in international education. She has served as the Deputy Convenor of the International Education Association of Australia's (IEAA) Student Life Network and Convenor of the IEAA Admissions and Compliance Network. Email: danielle.hartridge@deakin.edu.au

RENATA ALDANA is a Colombian international student at Australian College of Business Intelligence, Australia. She is one of the founding members and a student leader of the Oz International Student Hub (OISH). Email: araldanas@gmail.com

Research Article

© *Journal of International Students*
Volume 12, Issue 3 (2022), pp. 565-586
ISSN: 2162-3104 (Print), 2166-3750 (Online)
doi: 10.32674/jis.v12i3.3777
ojed.org/jis

A Study of Chinese Students' Application to UK Universities in Uncertain Times: From the Perspective of Education Agents

Ying Yang[1]
Sylvie Lomer
Miguel Antonio Lim
Jenna Mittelmeier
The University of Manchester, United Kingdom

ABSTRACT

A large number of Chinese applicants use education agents to apply for overseas programs, and agents are one of the most significant influence factors on Chinese international students' choice of overseas programs. However, there is limited research around agents' experiences within the existing information landscape of international higher education. For example, information asymmetries between agents and universities may have an impact on the advice and guidance provided for international applicants. This research investigates agents' practices with in-service Chinese applicants to UK universities in the context of information asymmetry. COVID-19 serves as a backdrop as an illustrative case of a period of high information uncertainty, which has generated severe challenges for the international higher education sector and for Chinese applicants' plans to study overseas. This study reports on the findings from in-depth interviews with 16 Chinese agent consultants undertaken in nine cities across China in the immediate aftermath of the pandemic (May 2020). The findings indicate that education agents attempt to mitigate the information asymmetry and emotionally reassure applicants through a four-step information management process. Our contribution generates a new understanding of the role that education agents play in international students' applications and mobility, voices that are often ignored but

---

[1] Corresponding Author.

essential for international students' decision-making processes and existing university recruitment services.

Keywords: Chinese international student, education agents, information asymmetry, international higher education

INTRODUCTION

On March 11, 2020, COVID-19 was declared a pandemic by the World Health Organization. Soon afterward, in the international higher education sector, most in-person activities on campus were cancelled and the majority of courses were moved online. This resulted in many university staff and faculty working around the clock to deal with the unplanned and unprepared shift to distance teaching and learning. In addition, international students' university applications, including their visa applications and English language tests, were impeded by the high level of uncertainty caused by COVID-19 (Yang *et al.*, 2020). An ongoing QS survey (2020) indicates that, in April 2020, 53% of international offer holders have had their plans to study abroad impacted by uncertainty during COVID-19. Thousands of Chinese international students in the United Kingdom attempted to leave during the spring 2020 semester and, in some cases, even tried to charter airplanes home (The Guardian, 2020). In this sense, COVID-19 can serve as an illustrative case of a period of high information uncertainty. Amid this backdrop, severe challenges for the international higher education sector have been generated (Fischer, 2020). International student mobilities and enrollment in a time of great uncertainty have become top concerns for international higher education providers, policy makers, and researchers.

Indeed, considerable attention has been devoted to exploring the impact of the COVID-19 pandemic on international students' experiences and intentions (QS, 2020; Siczek, 2020; Tran, 2020). However, a scarcity of research investigates these issues from the perspective of education agents, who are key actors in the international student recruitments (Falcone, 2017) and play a significant role in international students' choice of overseas programs (Hagedorn & Zhang, 2011; Yen *et al.*, 2012). This means a number of questions about agents' practices during this period remain, namely: How did education agents interact with students during COVID? How did agents perceive their role in this particular time? Understanding these issues will bring fresh and valuable insights into international students' decision-making processes at times of uncertainty, which identifies insightful implications for international higher education during and beyond COVID-19.

This paper commences by exploring the context of this research, including the marketization of international higher education, information asymmetry in the international higher education market, and education agents. It then illustrates the methodology of this research involving participants and setting, data collection, analysis approach, ethics, and limitation. It ends with key findings and a discussion, and it identifies important implications for international higher education outside COVID-19, along with proposing the future research questions.

THE MARKETIZATION OF INTERNATIONAL HIGHER EDUCATION

In the wake of globalizing neoliberalism, the discourses of marketization emerged within the higher education sector worldwide, which is associated with the exponential growth of international student mobility (Arkoudis *et al.*, 2019). Recent research outlines both demand and supply factors in this particular quasi-market to stimulate international student mobilities (Findlay *et al.*, 2017; Lomer, 2018). From the perspective of the demand side, international students are framed as consumers (Marginson, 2013) who intend to make "rational" economic choices and expect to improve their employability in an increasingly competitive global job market through international higher education (Organisation for Economic Co-operation and Development [OECD], 2020). From the perspective of the supply side, as public funds to higher education were shrunk in many host countries, universities compete for prestige to attract students and expand the recruitment of fee-paying international students as an alternative source of income (Foskett, 2011).

As a result, as in other markets, many intermediaries get involved in the international higher education market, such as education agents who provide recruitment services for both international students and universities (Findlay et al., 2017). The size of the education agent sector in China (Zhang & Fumasoli, 2019) and growth in recent years is also an indicator of overt marketization. This particular quasi-market displays characteristics that are distinct from a pure market system led by the relationship between seller and buyer on the basis of the price mechanism (Tomlinson, 2018). For example, higher education (HE) is a post-experience and an invisible product whose value is reflected via long-term impact (Tomlinson, 2018) with limited opportunity of repeat purchase (Foskett, 2011) or exchange. Competition in this market is not oriented by "orthodox economic bottom lines" (Marginson, 2013, p. 357), but it is constrained by government intervention, though economic rewards coincide with success in this competition. In this sense, the considerations of both international students (buyers) and overseas universities (sellers) in this special market context are, by their very nature, more complicated.

INFORMATION ASYMMETRY IN THE INTERNATIONAL HIGHER EDUCATION MARKET

In neoliberal terms, information for consumers to make decisions about purchases is a key prerequisite for a pure market. Government agencies and the media produce information with the intention of guiding students to make comparable judgments, such as institutional rankings and league tables. Many governments require the publication of institutional metrics, programs, curricula, services, tuition fees, and so on; they seek to make the information transparent through the audit and inspection of governments or quangos (Foskett, 2011). However, in fact, such measurements and metrics have limitations, such as a lack of transparency of how to weigh those indicators. In some domestic contexts, such as the United Kingdom, information is associated with teaching satisfaction; for instance, the Teaching Excellence Framework omits international students' perspectives (Hayes, 2019).

One continuing issue is whether international students, as potential consumers, can access and understand sufficient information to help them make choices. For international students, geographic distance and language barriers may hinder acquiring enough information about higher education abroad (Coffey, 2014), as well as likely cultural differences. Some international students encounter great information asymmetries before their arrival, leading to apparent deficits in preparedness for their course (Marginson et al., 2010; Sá & Sabzalieva, 2018). Therefore, there is an issue of information asymmetry between potential international students and universities abroad.

Information asymmetry is a concept drawn from economic literature that explains, as Stiglitz (2003) describes, how some information is initially possessed by one party involved in a purchase rather than all the parties involved. Issues arise among actors in specific markets (Akerlof, 1970; Rothschild & Stiglitz, 1976; Spence, 1973), which are likely to lead to adverse selection (Akerlof, 1970), meaning that potential buyers are unhappy if they perceive that sellers possess more information, resulting in the potential to feel "cheated," and therefore they decide not to buy the product.

Applied to international HE, in the rational decision-making process, pronounced information asymmetry is likely to give rise to adverse selection where international students will not choose to go abroad for study if they do not have sufficient knowledge of courses and universities. On the other hand, however, in the less rational decision-making process, to some extent, information gaps contribute to the formation of a fad of study abroad. Constrained by limited information, some international students may base their choices simply on the current trend of studying abroad and/or personal feelings. In addition, Wankhade and Dabade (2006) differentiate between two kinds of information asymmetry. One is general information asymmetry, referring to potential buyers lacking full information about products in the particular market. The second is product information asymmetry, such that sellers do not effectively depict their product to the potential consumer. In the international HE market, typically universities (sellers) set out their information on websites, such as admission requirements, course description, and tuition fees. However, this information may be difficult for international students to interpret, for example, students still feel confused about how to prepare documents up to admission criteria (Hagedorn & Zhang, 2011). Therefore, there is significant general information asymmetry in the international market.

To address information asymmetry, in pure markets, Akerlof (1970) suggests that counteracting institutions could mitigate quality uncertainty effectively, such as product guarantees, brand names, and chains. Subsequently, using "signals" such as education credentials (Spence, 1973) and "screening mechanism"

(Rothschild & Stiglitz, 1976) are also identified as effective approaches to filling information gaps. In practice, however, there does not appear to be much research indicating a uniform institution or effective measures to resolve these issues in the international HE market so far.

EDUCATION AGENTS

In recent years, education agents have emerged as an active part of international recruitment and university applications (Collins, 2012; Nikula, 2020). Agents are organizations and/or individuals who provide a range of services in exchange for a fee from their service users, including overseas higher education institutions and/or students who will study or are studying abroad (Krasocki, 2002; Nikula & Kivistö, 2018). Recent research indicates that a large number of universities in top host countries, such as the United Kingdom, Australia, New Zealand, and Canada, rely heavily on agents' services to secure advantageous positions in the competition of international student recruitment (Nikula, 2020; Raimo et al., 2014). At the same time, a large quantity of international students, especially from China, use agents to apply to overseas programs (Hagedorn & Zhang, 2011; Universities UK, 2017). In this regard, education agents are listed as one of the top five factors influencing undergraduate international students' choice of study destination (Universities UK, 2017). Therefore, the role of education agents cannot be overlooked in the studies of the international higher education market.

Applications to programs at the postgraduate level involve similar steps within most universities in the popular host countries. They accept applications via their individual application system and require similar application documents for international applicants, including online application forms, academic transcripts, reference letters, English language test scores, and personal statement (motivation letter). Some programs may have their specific requirement, such as scores of GMAT[2] or GRE.[3] Finally, the application results will be released on the due date or on the rolling basis. Hagedorn and Zhang (2011) suggest that lots of Chinese international students who use agents possess less knowledge about the application processes, universities in other countries, as well as visa application, which results in difficulties in choosing programs to apply to. Preparing the application documents is another typical dilemma, particularly writing personal statements that is new to them. Completing application forms makes some students frustrated because of the repetitive information collection. Further, preparing standardized English language tests is also challenging, as it is hard to achieve the necessary English language entry requirement in a short time (Hagedorn & Zhang, 2011).

---

[2] Graduate Management Admission Test.

[3] Graduate Record Examination.

Education agents provide an attentive "one-stop shop" for potential international students (Hagedorn & Zhang, 2011; Pimpa, 2003; Robinson-pant & Magyar, 2018), which can be categorized into five main services:

1. Providing full-range information regarding countries, cities, institutions, application documents, etc.;

2. Advising services on selecting countries, institutions, or programs;

3. Assisting with applications, including preparing personal essays, references, and certificates; filling in application forms; and tracking application status;

4. Visa-processing services, including document translation, interview training, filling in visa application forms, and making visa appointments;

5. Pre-arrival services, such as pre-departure training, alumni connections, pick-up and drop-off services, accommodation application, and deposit payment.

In China, since the early 2000s, the Ministry of Education has promoted market-based education reform aiming at diversifying education revenues and improving the quality of education, in keeping with many of the global trends toward neoliberal practices. In this context, international education in both the public and private sectors sprang up within China, along with the burgeoning trend of study abroad (Liu, 2020). More and more prospective Chinese international students, struggling with information gaps about overseas education, reached out to the third-party education agents for help, such that the industry of education agencies mushroomed in China's market (Ma, 2020). The Chinese Bureau of Supervision and Administration of Foreign Affairs in Education [CBSAFA] (2019) reports that there are 555 registered private education agents across 30 provinces in China. However, there are no systematic data about the number of agents of different types. Individual agents or agencies, analogous to school counselors in the international divisions of China's school (Ma, 2021), organize their work by dividing labor into two key roles: communicators and processors (Yang *et al.*, 2020). Communicators, similar to navigators, are primarily responsible for promoting overseas universities and advising about the choices of schools and programs alongside informing about the application progress. Processors, in contrast, similar to nannies, take care of every detail of application operations, visa processing, and pre-arrival services.

Education agents' services play a significant role in bridging the information asymmetry gap between students and universities. However, despite their utility, there are concerns and criticism related to some agents' unethical practices, such as providing students with false or inaccurate information, overpromising students, breaching the bribery registration, forging documents, writing personal letters on behalf of students, and so on. These issues may give rise to issues such as accepting unqualified students, which may damage the image of institutions or the host country as a high-quality education destination by definition (Nikula & Kivistö, 2018; Raimo Humfrey & Huang, 2014).

Currently, during the ongoing COVID-19 pandemic, various discussions, concerns, and uncertainties arise among key actors of the international HE market. We assume that information asymmetries have been exacerbated alongside such a great uncertainty in this particular market. In light of the widespread use of education agents among Chinese applicants and the great influence of education agents on Chinese applicants' choice of programs in the United Kingdom, we aimed at exploring education agents' practices during the COVID-19 crisis. Therefore, this research aims at using information asymmetry to investigate education agents' practices with their in-service students, who were in the process of applying to UK universities during the pandemic. We had two research questions:

- How did education agents work for their in-service students during the COVID-19 crisis?
- How did education agents perceive the impact of their practices on their in-service students during the COVID-19 crisis?

Building on these two questions, we explored a new information landscape where education agents play an important mediating role in the relationship between Chinese students and UK universities.

METHODOLOGY

Participants and Setting

Our research aim was to develop deeper insights into the practices of education agents during a period of great uncertainty. As such, the approach for collecting data involved semi-structured interviews. Given travel restrictions during the pandemic, all interviews took place online by using video calls. As the primary researcher previously worked as an education agent, we initially approached participants within this existing network; then, we relied on a snowball method to recruit other agent consultants who worked at different education agencies. Between May 1 and 15, 2020, 16 agent consultants who were specifically responsible for UK cases participated in this research, including 13 communicators and 3 processors (see Table 1). They were from 16 different education agencies located in 10 cities across China. Among these education agencies, 14 agencies were large enterprises (i.e., agencies with branches located in different cities); two agencies were small companies (i.e., agencies without branches consisting of several members).

Table 1: Snowball recruitment

Item	Description	Method of data collection	Number	Total
Agent consultant	Communicator	Online interview	13	16
	Processor		3	

Data Collection Process

The interview questions were developed in reflection of the literature, based on the steps that in-service students go through with agent consultants after signing the service contract (Yang, 2019). During the interviews, participants were asked questions about their work modes, consulting services, application services, students' inquiries and concerns, information sources, and delivery, particularly in light of the COVID-19 crisis. The interviews were conducted in Chinese and audio-recorded, lasting approximately 1.5 hrs each time.

Analysis Approach

Throughout the interviews, nearly all the participants categorized their professional roles across four themes: tracking application statuses, forwarding information, counseling, and processing follow-up work. As we wished to develop a reflective understanding of experiences within each of these categories between interview participants, thematic analysis (Braun & Clarke, 2006) was used to analyze the data. In the first phase, familiarization with the data was developed by transcribing all interviews and conducting multiple in-depth readings. In the second phase, initial codes were developed to categorize key and recurring concepts. There were 38 codes generated in total. In the third phase, the main themes were developed by collating the coded lines and/or paragraphs in an additional in-depth read of the data. In the fourth phase, with the concepts of information asymmetry and information management in mind, the developed themes were reviewed several times by checking the codes in detail, new extracts were included, and similar codes were integrated. In the fifth phase, the four themes—"finding information," "confirming information," "interpreting and selecting information," and "elaborating and communicating the selected information"—were identified and finalized, based on the steps of participants' information processing and management. Then, all the relevant codes were reorganized and assigned to the corresponding themes. Finally, based on the four themes, agents' information practices with in-service students during the COVID-19 crisis were examined through the lens of information asymmetry.

Ethics

The invitation letter, consent form, and information sheet of the research project were emailed to each participant. After receiving participants' consent, each interview was scheduled. In the course of the interviews, none of the questions were seen as personally sensitive or controversial topics. All the personal identifiable information had been anonymized or deleted.

Limitations

First, this research solely investigated education agents' reflections on their work practice with students and UK universities during the COVID-19 crisis; this influences the understanding of the actual effect of their practices on both their in-service students and UK universities. Second, the length and type of work experience in this industry is likely to influence perceptions, and precisely how these experiences shape agents' perceptions could not be explored in sufficient detail here. We recommend that future work extrapolates from this insight and incorporates this into the sampling strategy and research design.

FINDINGS AND DISCUSSION

This research finds that the information asymmetry between many Chinese applicants (potential buyers) and UK universities (sellers) was heightened during the COVID-19 crisis. Education agents attempted not only to mitigate the asymmetries through four-step information management but also to reassure their in-service students. Because the themes and processes are complex, we have introduced the data and interpreted it briefly in this section, before extending this into the conceptual framework in the final section.

Information Asymmetry Heightened

Participants' accounts indicate that applications for pre-sessional language courses, which is supposed to be the most important area of work in spring, became particularly burdensome.

The majority of Chinese applicants had not yet taken an English language test or did not have satisfactory English language scores when applying for the programs abroad (by the end of 2019). The IELTS test centers closed in mainland China after the COVID-19 outbreak in January 2020, which directly impacted many Chinese applicants' plans to take the test in February, causing great anxiety. Many students had no idea about how to overcome these obstacles and turned to agents with inquiries about English language tests and pre-sessional courses early in the COVID-19 crisis.

> Since February, lots of my students have been panicking, because there is no place for the IELTS test in April. The whole industry stayed in a panic because of no place for English tests. Students can't take English

language tests. UK universities did not release any policy to deal with this issue at that point. That was a time of panic. (Communicator 3)

Students' applications were impeded by the uncertainty caused by the COVID-19 pandemic for a significant period. Students did not know how UK universities would deal with this situation, as UK universities did not give prompt responses, which enlarged the information asymmetry. As a result, their university applications were temporarily stalled.

> Now the volume of inquiries from in-service and post-service students increases sharply. They inquired mainly about whether UK universities would reopen this fall or what to do next in terms of IELTS language tests. … lots of questions are around this. (Communicator 5)

> Particularly in April, there has been a constant stream of inquiries and confirmations about UK university policies from my in-service students. (Communicator 10)

Again, it shows that in uncertain times, for many Chinese applicants, the information gap regarding intended programs appears to be heightened, which can be characterized as general information asymmetry (Wankhade & Dabade, 2006). At the same time, students as potential buyers intend to confirm information and expect more information before making decisions, which chimes with Akerlof's information asymmetry theory (1970), which states that buyers tend to use the market statistics to measure the value of the goods, although the sellers have richer knowledge of their goods.

Moreover, during the COVID-19 crisis, UK universities appeared to lack information about their prospective international students. The participants reflected that UK universities contacted their offer holders more frequently and closely than earlier. Various surveys regarding offer holders' plans for the coming academic year were received by their in-service students continuously while these students were invited to join university welcome WeChat groups during the pandemic.

> A few students have received calls from UK universities. … Asked them whether to come if classes were postponed to the spring term. It's indicated UK universities are taking measures to know their students' plans now. They may be concerned that universities cannot reopen in September. (Processor 2)

> I feel that UK universities recognised that Chinese students may not go to the UK. So, lots of them launched surveys in which there are four or five options for each question. These surveys were directly sent to students' university email boxes. (Processor 4)

> UK universities worried about the shortage of students this year and the surplus of students next year like us. Last week, British Council did some surveys for UK universities and also collected our views on these

issues … I felt UK universities appeared more anxious than us" (Communicator 4)

In line with product information asymmetry (Wankhade & Dabade, 2006), UK universities (sellers) themselves were uncertain about their policies and services and could not release their information explicitly. Further, as university services and policies were entwined with international students' choices, it seems that UK universities needed their prospective students' information to inform decisions and policies. In this sense, during the COVID-19 crisis, there appeared to be a reciprocal information asymmetry and even information absence between UK universities and prospective international students, which differs from the one-way information asymmetry identified in previous literature.

Strategies That Education Agents Adopted During the COVID-19 Crisis

Confronting the heightened information asymmetry depicted earlier, education agents employed a four-step information management approach (see Figure 1): (1) for in-service students in four steps of information management: (1) finding information; (2) confirming information; (3) selecting information; and (4) communicating information. In this way, agents attempted to mitigate information asymmetry as much as possible, apart from comforting their in-service students.

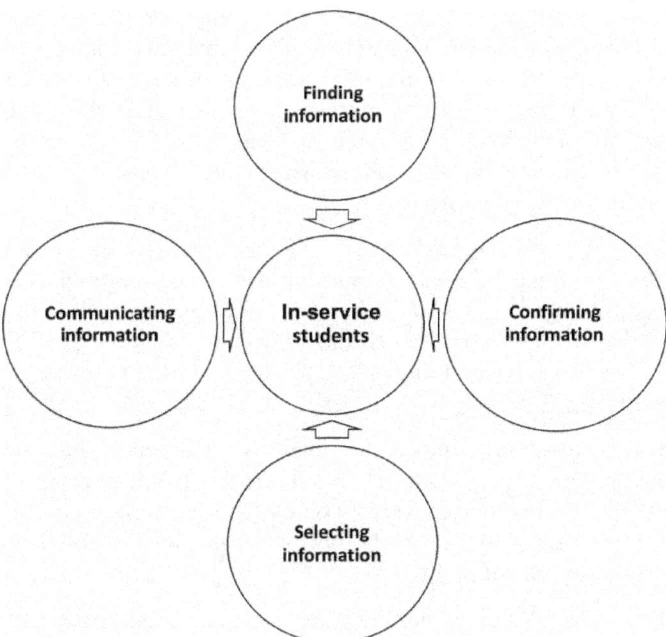

Figure 1: Education Agents Service during the COVID-19 Crisis.

1) Finding information

During the COVID-19 crisis, education agents proactively took measures to understand their in-service students' needs while managing students' applications.

Interviews indicate that communicators made regular calls to their in-service students to understand students' learning status and any changing thoughts on study-abroad plans. They made notes of each student's test plans and checked up their study progress whenever necessary. Some participants said during the interviews that they were required to call their students at least once every two or three days, or once a week. By contrast, some participants argued that it should depend on the progress of students' cases and characteristics. On some occasions, frequent contacts could be counterproductive, annoying students. The approach to checking could be flexible.

> When I saw the students' WeChat moments saying delicious food, good sleep, travel to some town, I know they must take effective precautions and protect themselves well. In contrast, as for the moments about cancelling flights, I would become alert and search for the flight information … (Processor 4)

Education agents, as noted earlier, similar to nannies, kept a close eye on their students' progress and learned their students' needs during the COVID-19 crisis, thereby providing feasible solutions in a timely manner. Therefore, education agents have access to in-depth information of students during uncertain times.

Participants described a common practice to manage in-service students' applications: checking through the work-in-progress form, which captured and consolidated information about each stage of each student's application. It was an essential tool to follow up on progress and help students consult admission offices for further information when necessary.

> It took me much time to update the work-in-progress form every single day. The first thing I did every morning was to read through the form and sort out urgent cases. Whether the offer has expired? If so, how could I deal with it? Argue with the admission office to get the offer back? Seriously, everything was possible during the pandemic. (Processor 4)

In addition, a common view among participants was that universities in the United Kingdom had regular times when they would update application statuses, which updates of the work-in-progress forms would highlight. If necessary, they would follow up with admission offices before students asked them to do so. For example, Processor 5 mentioned,

> Like I have four students applying for the same programme, three of whom have received the results. I would be sensitive to how many students did not receive the result at this point. I would email the university to inquire about the status before students ask me.

Students may not get a sense of the timing of university applications, which is likely to influence necessary decision making or steps to be taken in a timely manner. In this regard, education agents help students to fill this knowledge gap and recognize the particular points in time in terms of university applications, which contributes to progressing students' applications.

2) Confirming information

Participants reflected that during the COVID-19 crisis, information associated with admission requirements and policies of UK universities spread far and wide. Education agents confirmed the validity of the information as soon as they received it. As for information from social media or other students, education agents would contact the university admission offices for confirmation. For the information directly emailed by universities or circulated by university representatives, education agents would not verify it, but they may ask for further information to clarify the guidance.

> Our first priority is to ensure information accuracy. ... But the information I circulated must be 100% correct and important. In terms of timeliness, it is at most one-day lag. ... Delivering accurate information helps build up students' trust in you rather than causing complaints. (Communicator 2)

> Information on the internet really influences my work. For example, XX university lowers the admission requirement for some programmes as a result of COVID 19. You know, some information may be for specific purposes on certain platforms. Students cannot tell the news is true or not. (Communicator 4)

> For example, students sent me a screenshot of information on an unknown website or official account of a cyber celebrity. I would contact admission offices to confirm the information. (Communicator 4)

In such uncertain times, the proliferation of information caused confusion as inaccurate or false information conflicted with accurate updates. Education agents help students to ignore any misleading information by confirmation of guidance with universities.

3) Selecting information

Due to the pressure generated by a large amount of information and uncertainty, education agents evaluated and selected only the most relevant information to send to their students. This included information from the universities where their students applied or decided to do their in-service studies.

> For example, if student A decided to go to university A and his other offers expired, then I would only deliver the information of university A to him. However, if the student applied for five universities and only

> had an IELTS test score of 5, which was ineligible for the pre-sessional courses of any five universities, I would inform him of the language policies of the five universities while watching any possible alternatives for him. (Processor 4)

> At present, a large amount of application information is out there. This easily causes pressures to students. I'll tell them the most relevant and important. (Communicator 1)

Education agents appear to evaluate the importance of information, and to filter overwhelming information and select only key points. The interviewed participants highlighted that they would also provide comments and opinions on the key information. In addition, if any information was likely to negatively influence students' motivation for studying abroad, they neither disseminated it nor even brought it up of their own accord. However, they would discuss this information in their own words if students raised such questions with them.

> I never spread any information that likely lowers students and their parents' motivation or expectation of study abroad or makes them panic on my initiative, because of my role. But I would respond to these issues when they ask me. (Communicator 11)

This also demonstrates that education agents are trying to cut off conduits of commentary and/or subjective negative information about overseas education. In this sense, education agents may guide students and their parents to think about overseas education in a particular direction that is not being driven by the consideration of students' best interests. Precisely, students and their parents potentially receive only part of the information, and may be misled by the incomplete picture, which echoes the public's concern on agents' unethical practices (Raimo et al., 2014).

4) Communicating information

One key strategy during the COVID-19 crisis, particularly for large enterprises, was to maintain consistent broadcast information updates. They continued holding regular webinars and online education fairs, and they carefully posted and circulated "generally valuable information" through WeChat moments and WeChat client groups. In participants' words, valuable information refers to policies released by UK universities, measures being taken by the UK government, as well as reports published by important organizations such as British Council. This sort of "generally valuable information" supplements the specific information targeting in-service students, contributing to students' access to market information.

For in-service students on an individual basis, during the COVID-19 crisis, education agents typically elaborated on the selected information one to one via WeChat or phone; then, they edited formal notices, briefly translating the original information into Chinese and underlining the deadlines and related requirements; and finally, they delivered them by email or WeChat. Agents proposed possible options for specific issues and detailed their pros and cons, respectively, as well. Some participants argued in the interviews that they had to consider their own livelihood and should lead students to make the decision to study abroad; we characterize these as "hard sellers," who were typically financially motivated. While communicating with students, they would emphasize the value of study abroad and potential opportunities emerging in the pandemic, to encourage students to study abroad.

> Absolutely, we should direct students towards particular ways by addressing the temporality of this pandemic. It will be gone sooner or later. You still need to move forward … your plan may be delayed for one and a half year at most…it is not a big thing as opposed to your whole life. (Processor 2)

By contrast, other participants addressed that they solely explained the issues in detail and fully respected students' considerations or decisions, and they would not ask them to make any decision in this unusual time, as they felt that current issues and decisions involved students' health and safety, about which they should be very cautious. These agents can be characterized as "information providers," who are motivated more by students' welfare and agency.

> I always believe my job is to tell students the possible routes and risks before their decision-making themselves. They are not idiots. … We needn't to do more and actually we are not able to get involved that much. (Communicator 9)

This suggests that education agents have different perceptions of their work, which may influence their strategies of guiding students to interpret the information. For the financial-motivated agents, they are very likely to solely convey positive information and even exaggerate the value of overseas education, to influence students' understanding of the situation and decision making. In contrast, other agents appear less interest-led and adopt an ostensibly neutral position in transmitting information. Although this research does not point out agents' reflections on their possibly misleading behaviors, as mentioned earlier, the information delivered by agents is likely to be oriented toward producing desired outcomes rather than increasing students' understanding of UK universities, which creates opportunities for agents' unethical conduct.

Frequently, however, participants reported feeling at a loss, unable to answer many questions raised by students and their parents. In terms of advice on studying abroad, agents felt themselves less capable during the pandemic than earlier.

> They continuously asked questions about universities' policies, like the open date of schools, whether the admission office is open. We didn't know either. The main thing we did was to reassure them by telling them that UK universities must take measures very soon and encouraging them to prepare the tests at home. (Communicator 1)

> This year, as a result of COVID-19, students might worry about more issues than before that we did not know, decide or predict either. Therefore, under this condition, the only thing we can do is to comfort them. Perhaps they just needed comforts. They were very anxious during that period. (Communicator 9)

The information that education agents possessed in a quickly changing situation was also limited, which constrained their potential to circulate valid information from universities to their students. In this case, they tried to chat with students and spread positivity to reassure students and retain their positive attitudes toward study abroad.

Apart from delivering information to in-service students, education agents also helped students reflect issues to UK universities in the hope of getting solutions.

> We wrote emails for our students to universities about IELTS problems. Meanwhile, we also explained to students that universities needed time to discuss these issues. There is a procedure. We needed patience to wait for universities' replies. (Communicator 3)

Agents' active contacts with UK universities are helpful to inform universities of their prospective students' problems and situations to implement timely solutions. Further, while waiting for universities' responses, agents explained the universities' situations and arranged feasible work for students, which actually also helped fill in the students' information gap on what universities were doing during the pandemic. In this sense, we highlight a significant role that education agents play in reciprocally circulating information between Chinese applicants and UK universities. During this process, however, education agents may not have consistently or fully expressed students' concerns, as they may not have fully reported on universities' policies or the decisions that students would react negatively to. Education agents could, therefore, invisibly influence the decisions of both students and universities.

IMPLICATIONS AND CONCLUSIONS

This section connects education agents' information practices during the COVID-19 crisis to the conceptual framework of information asymmetry, and it explores a different role of education agents in prospective Chinese students' applications to UK universities in uncertain times. In the context of the international higher education market, information asymmetry (Akerlof, 1970) assumes that prospective Chinese students are very likely to choose not to study in the United Kingdom, when they do not have enough information about their intended programs.

Our research demonstrates that it was reciprocal information asymmetry and even information absence that occurred between UK universities and Chinese applicants during the pandemic. The majority of agents' in-service students, indeed, had not at this point made a decision to study or not for the coming academic year. We discuss education agents' four steps of information management, which reveals the agents' efforts to bridge the information gap between both parties and to enable their in-service students to get access to their university places. Our findings contribute to previous literature related to education agents by unfolding a new picture of their information practices and outlining different positions within the information landscape for agents, Chinese applicants, and UK universities during a time of great uncertainty (see Figure 2).

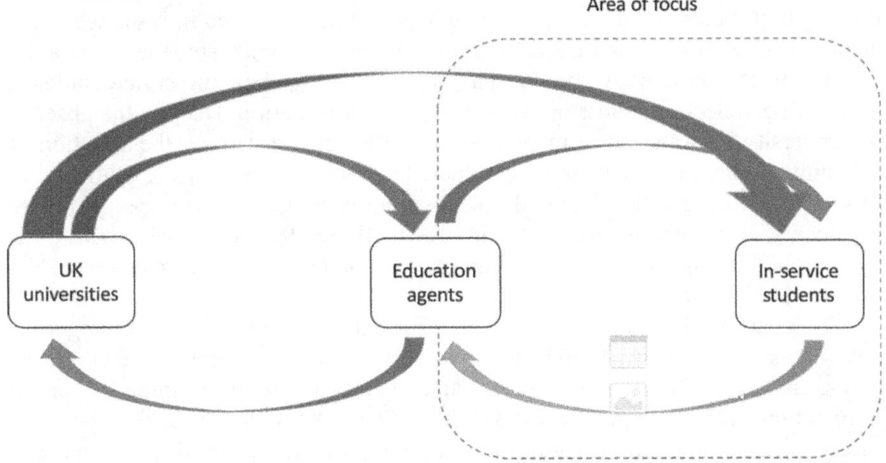

Figure 2: Information Landscape Within and Between UK Universities, Educations Agents, and Service Students During the COVID-19 Crisis.

The COVID-19 pandemic created increasing uncertainty about UK universities for international applicants. The included questions were about when universities would reopen, the format courses would take, how travel would work, how language could be assessed, how rules and norms for socialization would work, and what a university experience would look like. Confirmed information was in high demand for many Chinese applicants, which led them to reach out to their agents for advice. Many in-service students tended to rely on agents to contact UK universities. In the meantime, education agents discerned that UK universities were uncertain about their policies and services for the forthcoming academic year and also needed much information about their prospective students' intended plans. At times, UK universities bypassed agents and proactively approached their prospective students by themselves in the forms of surveys and emails, while still keeping in touch with their agents. It is clear that students and universities were in need of others' information during the pandemic, but both parties did not appear to get in touch with each other effectively.

In this case, as Figure 2 indicates, during the COVID-19 crisis, education agents played a profound role as information brokers in managing flows between their in-service students and UK universities, particularly in information circulation with their in-service students. This differs from previous research showing that education agents primarily provide operational application services for their students (Raimo et al., 2014; Thomson et al., 2014). Through proactively seeking students' information and continuously receiving inquiries, education agents acquired students' information in a prompt and timely manner. At the same time, agents delivered students' information to UK universities in an attempt to access further inside information or possible solutions. In effect, agents did receive UK universities' responses and the latest policies, but this sort of information was often still inexplicit and subject to continuous revision, as the university policies and decisions were developed and changed in response to the changing COVID-19 pandemic. In their interactions with students, education agents selectively conveyed university information to their in-service students, confirming, selecting, and communicating this information. Despite the absence of university information in many cases, agents kept explaining the situation of UK universities to their in-service students to temporarily reassure students. In this way, information continued to flow between UK universities, Chinese applicants, and education agents during the COVID-19 crisis. The design of this study relied on agents' own accounts of their practices, which may understate unethical behaviors.

This case study creates insights into information flow within and among three key actors in the international higher education market during the COVID-19 crisis, namely students, universities, and agents. It identifies three important implications for this specific market beyond COVID-19. First, the issues of information lag and gap are built into the international higher education market, which should draw the close attention of international higher education providers and policy makers, as it has caused temporary suspensions of university applications in uncertain times. Second, UK universities' decisions and policies largely depend on prospective international students and vice versa, which points to the significance of effective connections between UK universities and international students, especially in the time of great uncertainties. Above all, this research highlights the value of education agents in filling in the information gap and circulating information between prospective international students and UK universities in this particular market. However, the information circulated to students by education agents is selective and filtered, which is potentially problematic. For example, agents may only transmit information in their interest to students, which would mislead students' decision making. Agents are also likely to partially reflect the students' situation to universities, resulting in inappropriate decisions made by universities. In light of this, future research could cast light on the context of China's neoliberal education, how Chinese international students and universities perceive these practices, and how education agents interpret information they possess and select information for their service users (including prospective Chinese international students and universities overseas).

REFERENCES

Akerlof, G. A. (1970). The market for lemons: Quality uncertainty and the market mechanism. *Quarterly Journal of Economics, 84*, 488–500. https://doi.org/10.2307/1879431

Arkoudis, S., Dollinger, M., Baik, C., & Patience, A. (2019). International students' experience in Australian higher education: Can we do better?. *Higher Education, 77*(5), 799–813. https://doi.org/10.1007/s10734-018-0302-x

Braun, V., & Clarke, V. (2006). Using thematic analysis in psychology. *Qualitative Research in Psych*ology, 3(2), 77–101. 10.1191/1478088706qp063oa

British Universities' international Liaison Association (BUILA). (2020). A route to a UK quality framework with education agents. https://www.ukcisa.org.uk/Research--Policy/Policy-and-lobbying/A-Partnership-for-Quality-a-route-to-a-UK-quality-framework-with-education-agents

Chinese Bureau of Supervision and Administration of Foreign Affairs in Education. (2019, June 26). *List of self-funded overseas education services agents (自费出国留学中介服务机构名单)*. http://jsj.moe.gov.cn/news/1/147.shtml

Coffey, R. N. (2014). *The influence of education agents on student choice making in the Canadian postsecondary search process.* PhD. Michigan State University.

Collins, F. L. (2012). Organizing student mobility: Education agents and student migration to New Zealand. *Pacific Affairs, 85*(1), 137–160. https://doi.org/10.5509/2012851137

Falcone, S. (2017). International student recruitment: Trends and challenges. *Journal of International Students, 7*(2), 246–256. https://doi.org/10.32674/jis.v7i2.379

Findlay, A. M., McCollum, D., & Packwood, H. (2017). Marketization, marketing and the production of international student migration. *International Migration, 55*(5), 1–26. https://doi.org/10.1111/imig.12330

Fischer, K. (2020). Confronting the seismic impact of COVID-19: The need for research. *Journal of International Students, 10*(2), 211. https://doi.org/10.32674/jis.v10i2.2134

Foskett, N. (2011). Markets, government, funding and the marketisation of UK higher education. In R. Scullion, M. Molesworth and E. Nixon (Ed.), *The marketisation of higher education and the student as consumer* (pp. 25–38). Routledge.

Hagedorn, L. S., & Zhang, L. Y. (2011). The use of agents in recruiting Chinese undergraduates. *Journal of Studies in International Education, 15*(2), 186–202. https://doi.org/10.1177/1028315310385460

Hayes, A. (2019). *Inclusion, epistemic democracy and international students: The teaching excellence framework and education policy.* Palgrave Macmillan.

Krasocki, J. (2002). Education UK: Developing the UK's International Agent Network. *Promotions and Partnerships (ECS).* The British Council.

Liu, S. (2020). *Neoliberalism, globalization, and "elite" education in China: Becoming international*. Routledge.

Lomer, S. (2018). UK policy discourses and international student mobility: The deterrence and subjectification of international students. *Globalisation, Societies and Education, 16*(3), 308–324. https://doi.org/10.1080/14767724.2017.1414584

Ma, Y. (2020). *Ambitious and anxious: How Chinese college students succeed and struggle in American higher education*. Columbia University Press.

Ma, Y. (2021). Educating the elites: School counselors as education nannies in Urban China. *Comparative Education Review, 65*(3), 493–512. https://doi.org/10.1086/714869

Marginson, S. (2013). The impossibility of capitalist markets in higher education. *Journal of Education Policy, 28*(3), 353–370.

Marginson, S., Nyland, C., Sawir, E., & Forbes-Mewett, H. (2010). *International student security*. Cambridge University Press.

Nikula, P. T. (2020). Education agent standards in Australia and New Zealand–Government's role in agent-based international student recruitment. *Studies in Higher Education, 47*(4), 1–16. https://doi.org/10.1080/03075079.2020.1811219

Nikula, P. T., & Kivistö, J. (2018). Hiring education agents for international student recruitment: Perspectives from agency theory. *Higher Education Policy, 31*(4), 535–557. https://doi.org/10.1057/s41307-017-0070-8

Organisation for Economic Co-operation and Development (2020). What is the profile of internationally mobile students? https://www.oecd-ilibrary.org/sites/974729f4-en/index.html?itemId=/content/component/974729f4-en

Pimpa, N. (2003). The influence of peers and student recruitment agencies on Thai students' choices of international education. *Journal of Studies in International Education, 7*(2), 178–192. https://doi.org/10.1177/1028315303007002005

QS. (2020, April 16). *How international students are responding to COVID-19*. https://www.qs.com/how-international-students-are-responding-to-covid-19/

Raimo, V., Humfrey, C., & Huang, I. Y. (2014). *Managing international student recruitment agents: Approaches, benefits and challenges*. The British Council.

Robinson-Pant, A., & Magyar, A. (2018). The recruitment agent in internationalized higher education: Commercial broker and cultural Mediator. *Journal of Studies in International Education, 22*(3), 225–241. https://doi.org/10.1177/1028315318762485

Sá, C. M., & Sabzalieva, E. (2018). The politics of the great brain race: Public policy and international student recruitment in Australia, Canada, England and the USA. *Higher Education, 75*(2), 231–253. https://doi.org/10.1007/s10734-017-0133-1

Siczek, M. (2020). International student agency in the face of a global health crisis. *Journal of International Students, 10*(4), vii–ix. https://doi.org/10.32674/jis.v10i4.2424

Spence, A. M. (1973). Job market signalling. *Quarterly Journal of Economics, 87*, 355–374. https://doi.org/10.2307/1882010

Stiglitz, J. E. (2003). Information and the change in the paradigm in economics, Part 1. *The American Economist, 47*(2), 6–26. https://doi.org/10.1177/056943450304700202

Rothschild, M. E. & Stiglitz, J. E. (1976). Equilibrium in competitive insurance markets. *Quarterly Journal of Economics, 90*, 629–649. https://doi.org/10.2307/1885326

The Guardian. (2020, March 27). *Students try to flee UK by chartered plane for 'safer' China'.* https://www.theguardian.com/education/2020/mar/27/students-try-to-flee-uk-by-chartered-plane-for-safer-china

Thomson, A., Hulme, R., Hulme, M., & Doughty, G. (2014). Perceptions of value: Assessing the agent/commission model of UK higher education recruitment in Africa. *Africa Review, 6*(2), 105–120. https://doi.org/10.1080/09744053.2014.914638

Tomlinson, M. (2018). Conceptions of the value of higher education in a measured market. *Higher Education, 75*(4), 711–727. https://doi.org/10.1007/s10734-017-0165-6

Tran, L. T. (2020). Teaching and engaging international students: People-to-people connections and people-to-people empathy. *Journal of International Students, 10*(3), XII–XVII. https://doi.org/10.32674/jis.v10i3.2005

Universities, U.K. (2017). *The UK's Competitive Advantage 2017.* https://www.universitiesuk.ac.uk/policy-and-analysis/reports/Documents/International/UUKi-Competitive-advantage-2017.pdf

Wankhade, L., & Dabade, B. M. (2006). Analysis of quality uncertainty due to information asymmetry. *International Journal of Quality & Reliability Management, 23*(2), 230–241. https://doi.org/10.1108/02656710610640961

Yang, Y. (2019). *The effect of education agents on Chinese undergraduates' motivations to study PGT programmes in the UK.* Present at China and Higher Education conference, The University of Manchester, UK, 9–10 December.

Yang, Y., Mittelmeier, J., Lim, M. A., & Lomer, S. (2020). Chinese international student recruitment during the COVID-19 crisis: Education agents' practices and reflections. *HERE@Manchester.* https://www.research.manchester. ac. uk/portal/en/publications/chinese-international-student-recruitment-during-the-covid19-crisis(be489a37-107c-480e-82c4-4583bc3dfeeb).html

Yen, D. A., Yang, Hsiao-Pei, S., & Cappellini, B. (2012). Ranking gives power: Relationships between UK universities and Chinese agents. *Journal of General Management, 38*(1), 23–44. https://doi.org/10.1177/030630701203800102

Zhang, M., & Fumasoli, T. (2019). *Scale and scope of Chinese education recruitment agents: A mapping exercise.* Presented at China and Higher Education conference, Manchester, UK, 9–10 December.

YING YANG is a PhD candidate doctoral researcher in the Manchester Institute of Education at The University of Manchester. Her research interests focus on internationalization of higher education, international students' motivations, mobilities, and experiences, as well as international student recruitment. Email: ying.yang-3@manchester.ac.uk

Dr SYLVIE LOMER is a senior lecturer in Policy and Practice in the Manchester Institute of Education at the University of Manchester. Her research interests focus on international higher education, specifically the policies, pedagogies, and recruitment practices related to international students in the United Kingdom. Email: sylvie.lomer@manchester.ac.uk

Dr MIGUEL ANTONIO LIM is a senior lecturer in Education and International Development in the Manchester Institute of Education at the University of Manchester. His research expertise focuses on internationalization strategies in higher education and higher education policies, particularly in East and Southeast Asia. Email: miguelantonio.lim@manchester.ac.uk

Dr JENNA MITTELMEIER is a lecturer in International Education in the Manchester Institute of Education at the University of Manchester. Her area of research expertise focuses on international students' transition experiences and broader aspects of internationalization in higher education. Email: jenna.mittelmeier@manchester.ac.uk

Research Article

© *Journal of International Students*
Volume 12, Issue 3 (2022), pp. 587-606
ISSN: 2162-3104 (Print), 2166-3750 (Online)
doi: 10.32674/jis.v12i3.3964
ojed.org/jis

International Undergraduates' Academic Resilience During Onset of the Coronavirus Pandemic's Educational Disruptions as Evidenced by Term Grade Point Averages

Barry Fass-Holmes
University of California, San Diego, USA

ABSTRACT

How did international undergraduates perform academically during onset of the coronavirus pandemic's educational disruptions? The present study addresses this question by testing the hypothesis that an American public university's entire population of international undergraduates who were enrolled throughout academic year 2019–2020 would struggle academically (term grade point averages [GPA] below 2.0) to a greater extent in spring 2020 (coinciding with the pandemic's onset) than in fall 2019 and winter 2020 (pre-pandemic). Five different analyses of GPAs yielded disconfirmatory, counterintuitive evidence; for example, the hypothesis leads to the prediction that the number and percentage of international undergraduates who struggled academically should increase in spring 2020 compared to that in fall 2019 and winter 2020 terms. This report's results are consistent with these international undergraduates' resilience and their institution's beneficial support. The reasons for ruling out alternative explanations (widespread cheating, instructors' leniency, and grade inflation) are discussed.

Keywords: COVID-19, GPA, international undergraduates, pandemic, resilience, stress, transfer shock

International students' learning environment while attending American postsecondary institutions during academic year (AY) 2019–2020 included an extraordinary, new condition—the novel coronavirus (COVID-19) pandemic. In response to the COVID-19 pandemic, American postsecondary institutions (including the present report's) canceled in-person classes and examinations for spring and summer 2020, implemented online-only finals and instruction, and/or closed their campus (Burke, 2020; Redden, 2020; Smalley, 2020). The institutions' responses resulted in major disruptions of students' instructional/learning continuity, housing, interpersonal interactions, finances, graduation plans, and other hallmarks of their education (Dickerson, 2020; Gallagher et al., 2020; Krahmer et al., 2020; Lederer et al., 2021; Osaze, 2021). These disruptions were consistent with the acknowledged characteristics of stressors—arousing, aversive, and unpredictable or uncontrollable conditions (Kim & Diamond, 2002).

The pandemic's educational disruptions might jeopardize international undergraduates' academic performance while attending American postsecondary institutions. These students could be particularly susceptible to the disruptions; they previously had to contend with a host of impactful learning environment conditions (discussed below), which would have little (if any) bearing on domestic counterparts. Addition of the pandemic's disruptions to the preexisting conditions might reasonably be expected to result in international undergraduates experiencing academic struggles. Consequently, the present study's purpose was to explore this expectation by analyzing international undergraduates' academic performance during AY 2019–2020. This study exploits COVID-19's educational disruptions to investigate these students' academic performance as indicated by various analyses of mean grade point averages (GPAs) earned before and during the pandemic's onset at an American West Coast public university (where the AY has three terms rather than two semesters). The historically extensive range of international student support services and programs at this university, in combination with its reputation of academic excellence, has attracted a dramatic influx of these students during the past decade (Fass-Holmes & Vaughn, 2018) and resulted in one of the 10 largest international student populations nationwide (Open Doors, 2020). As reported below, analyses of several measures of change in the international undergraduates' term GPAs at this university unexpectedly revealed decreases during the academic term coinciding with the pandemic's disruptions rather than expected increases (or vice versa). These changes are interpreted as evidence of the students' resilience.

The present study's primary objective was to test the hypothesis that the university's international undergraduates would struggle academically (administratively defined as GPA below 2.0) to a greater extent in spring 2020 (SP20), coinciding with the onset of COVID-19's educational disruptions and stressors, than during the two preceding terms (fall 2019 [FA19] and winter 2020 [WI20]). Although reports about the coronavirus pandemic's impact on student mobility and institutional finances already have appeared in the literature (e.g., Martel, 2020; NAFSA: Association for International Educators [NAFSA: AIE],

2020), research on international students' academic performance had not appeared by the time of this report's review. The present findings would be the first ones focusing specifically on international undergraduates' academic performance during the AY coinciding with onset of the pandemic's educational disruptions.

A secondary objective was to measure the degree to which international undergraduates who previously entered the university as transfer students (TRAN) struggled academically during SP20 compared with their counterparts who previously entered as first-time students (NFRS). This objective was based on previous reports of "transfer shock" (defined as a "severe drop in performance upon transfer" from one postsecondary institution to another; Hills, 1965, p. 202), which could be another stressor specifically affecting this undergraduate subgroup's academic performance. Consequently, the present results have been disaggregated by applicant type rather than treating undergraduates as a single, homogeneous group (Krsmanovic, 2021).

The following specific questions and related hypotheses, regarding the university's entire international undergraduate population who previously entered as NFRS or TRAN and enrolled throughout AY 2019–2020, were addressed in this study:

1. How many and what percentage earned GPAs below 2.0 (struggled academically) during each term in AY 2019–2020? Hypothesis: If these students struggled academically to a greater extent in SP20 (coinciding with the pandemic's onset) than in the two preceding terms, then the numbers and percentages who earned GPAs below 2.0 in SP20 should exceed the corresponding values in FA19 and/or WI20.

2. What were their mean GPAs during each term in AY 2019–2020? Hypothesis: If these students struggled academically to a greater extent in SP20 than in the two preceding terms, then their mean GPAs in FA19 and/or WI20 should exceed their corresponding value in SP20.

3. What was their change in GPA between successive terms, in particular between fall term (FA19) and SP20; or between WI20 and SP20? Hypothesis: If these students struggled academically to a greater extent in SP20 than in the two preceding terms, then the change in their mean GPAs between FA19 or WI20 and SP20 should be a negative value.

4. How many and what percentage earned an improved GPA in each successive term? Hypothesis: If these students struggled academically to a greater extent in SP20 than in the two preceding terms, then few and a low percentage of them should have an improved GPA in SP20 relative to FA19 and/or WI20.

5. How many and what percentage earned a worse GPA in each successive term? Hypothesis: If these students struggled academically to a greater extent in SP20 than in the two preceding terms, then many and a high percentage of them should have a worse GPA in SP20 relative to FA19 and/or WI20.

Relevant events during AY 2019–2020 to keep in mind for this report were as follows: The university's administration first informed its students about the coronavirus on January 22, 2020; WI20 final examinations were administered online beginning March 14, three days after the pandemic's declaration. On March 20, the governor of the university's state issued a stay-at-home order, and the campus closed except for critical functions. WI20 ended on March 21; SP20 began on March 25, coinciding in its entirety with the pandemic's educational disruptions and stressors. March 29 was the deadline for all students who could safely leave the campus to do so, and SP20 ended on June 12.

THEORETICAL CONTEXT

Challenge vs. Stress

The term "challenge" has been used in the educational research literature to describe the learning environment conditions that international students typically experience while attending American postsecondary institutions (e.g., Banjong, 2015; Gautam et al., 2016; Henneberry, 2019; Misra et al., 2003; Perry, 2016; Zhang-Wu, 2018). Examples of "challenging" conditions include acculturation (Yan & Berliner, 2013), American academic integrity standards (Bista, 2011) and teaching methods (Ota, 2013; Roy, 2013), campus climate (Ota, 2013), discrimination (Ota, 2013), English language (Jin & Schneider, 2019; Ota, 2013; Sherry et al., 2010; Yan & Berliner, 2013), family expectations (Ota, 2013; Yan & Berliner, 2009), finances (Sherry et al., 2010; Yan & Berliner, 2013), homesickness and/or loneliness (Ota, 2013; Sherry et al., 2010), mandatory compliance with federal immigration regulations (Urias & Yeakey, 2009), neo-racism (Lee, 2020), social norms (Ota, 2013; Sherry et al., 2010), and travel/visa restrictions (U.S. Department of State, 2021).

An alternative interpretation of international students' learning environment conditions is that they could be experienced as stressors. The concept of stressor implies stimulating or arousing conditions that an individual perceives as aversive and unpredictable or uncontrollable (Fink, 2017; Kim & Diamond, 2002). If international students attending American institutions do perceive their learning environment conditions as aversive and unpredictable or uncontrollable, they could be experiencing stress (e.g., Misra et al., 2003; Yan, 2017) and risk negative impacts on their learning (e.g., Vogel & Schwabe, 2016).

The research literature on stressors includes many theoretical categorizations. Relevant examples include (but are not limited to) Berry's (1997) stress-coping framework that divides stressors into individual (micro)- and group (macro)-level sources (Yan, 2017; Yan & Berliner, 2009, 2011, 2013); Alharbi and Smith's

(2018) division of stressors into categories (acculturative, English-language proficiency, perceived discrimination, loneliness, and academic) on the basis of a literature review; and Henneberry's (2019) nine areas of stress (academic, language, financial, family, social, logistic, religious, dietary, and identity stressors) that reflect their sources. The following more simplistic categorization provides a context for the present study.

Stressors simplistically could be divided into *institution-specific* stimulating or arousing conditions that a student perceives as aversive and unpredictable or uncontrollable versus *institution-independent* ones. Institution-specific stressors are ones that originate from within the institution and differ between institutions; American academic integrity standards are an example because they originate from each institution's administration and differ between institutions regarding their associated policies, communications, etc. (Fishman, 2016). Institution-independent ones originate from sources other than the institution and are relatively generalized across institutions; family expectations are an example because they originate outside of the institution and generally occur across institutions due to their association with students' parents (Ota, 2013; Yan & Berliner, 2009). Accordingly, international students' conditions described in the research literature as challenges could be recategorized as follows: Institution-specific stressors include academic integrity standards, campus climate, discrimination (i.e., institutionally systemic), neo-racism (i.e., institutionally systemic), and teaching methods; institution-independent stressors include acculturation, discrimination (i.e., societal), English language, family expectations, finances, homesickness, loneliness, mandatory compliance with federal immigration regulations, neo-racism (i.e., societal), social norms, and travel/visa restrictions.

The above distinctions between institution-specific vs. institution-independent stressors, and between stressors vs. challenges are relevant in the present report because of the likelihood that the coronavirus pandemic's educational disruptions were stressors. To the extent that international undergraduates attending American postsecondary institutions did perceive the aforementioned learning environment conditions as stressors (Yan, 2017; Yan & Berliner, 2009, 2011, 2013), the educational disruptions associated with the COVID-19 pandemic's onset (Lederer et al., 2021) also would be perceived as stressors (e.g., Xia & Duan, 2020). Students would have perceived the pandemic's disruptions as stressors because of their stimulating or arousing, aversive, and unpredictable or uncontrollable conditions (Dickerson, 2020; Gallagher, 2021; Gallagher et al., 2020; Krahmer et al., 2020; Osaze, 2021). Stressfulness is further suggested by stakeholders' documented concerns about the pandemic having a negative impact on students' learning and development (e.g., Engzell et al., 2021; Lederer et al., 2021) and by studies showing negative impacts on students' mental health (Ma & Miller, 2020; Onyema et al., 2020). Some of the pandemic's disruptions would qualify as institution-specific stressors (e.g., campus closure communications and process) since they originate from the students' institution and differ between institutions; others would qualify as institution-independent stressors (e.g., travel bans/restrictions) since they originate from a source other than the institution and are relatively generalized across institutions (Smalley, 2020).

Interpreting international students' learning environment conditions as stressors (rather than as challenges) has implications for the student development theory, specifically Nevitt Sanford's challenge and response principle underlying postsecondary institutions' efforts to promote learning. He described "challenge" as follows:

> This approach to developing the individual grows out of the belief that people do not change unless they encounter a situation to which they cannot adapt with the use of devices already present. … It is the job of the change-inducing institution to present the person to be changed with a succession of new challenges which will stimulate the desired responses. … It is the teacher's task to find a way to reach these students, challenge them, jolt them out of their ruts, so that they will revise their ways of looking at things and thus be required to generate new perspectives and systems of response. … By creating a little anxiety in [the student] we open him to learning. (Sanford, 1966, pp. 44–45)

The above quotation implies that Sanford defined "challenges" as strategies or approaches that teachers would use to "jolt [students] out of their ruts," to promote change in their responses, and, consequently, to promote student learning and development. If the challenge (teacher's strategy/approach) is so overwhelming that students have difficulty coping, the teacher would need to offer support (Sanford, 1966). If the challenge (teacher's strategy/approach) instead is too weak, the teacher would not have stimulated the desired responses. In other words, too much or too little challenge results in the absence of student learning and development (Chaves, 2006; McCallum, 2015). Sanford's support principle is relevant to the present study, because beneficial institutional support has the potential to promote international undergraduates' resilience and academic success during the pandemic's onset (cf, Robbins et al., 2018).

Most (if not all) of the aforementioned learning environment conditions experienced by international students studying in America are tangential to teachers' strategies/approaches for challenging students to promote their learning and development. If Sanford's challenge concept signifies teachers' strategies or approaches to promote students' learning and development, it could be considered a teacher-specific condition of students' learning environment. The research literature's challenges are different, because they reside outside of teachers' purview. These non-teacher-specific conditions of international students' learning environment consequently should be described as something other than "challenges," to distinguish them from Sanford's concept. Describing them instead as *stressors* in the present report accomplishes this distinction.

METHOD

This study was based on an American West Coast public university (its AY has three terms rather than two semesters) that afforded the following educationally significant and distinct advantages: 1) It has historically provided a broad range of student support services and programs plus additional ones specifically tailored for international students that were enhanced during the pandemic's onset; 2) these support services and programs, plus the university's strong reputation for academic excellence, have combined to attract one of the 10 largest international student populations nationwide (Open Doors, 2020); and 3) previous studies' results on this university's undergraduate population's academic performance (Dorado & Fass-Holmes, 2016; Fass-Holmes, 2016; Fass-Holmes & Vaughn, 2014, 2015) were available for potential comparison.

The entire international (F-1 or J-1 visa; U.S. Department of State, n.d.) undergraduate population attending this university in AY 2019–2020 comprised the study's participant pool (N = 5,026; NFRS = 3,761, TRAN = 1,265). Demographic data plus GPAs for all international undergraduates who initially enrolled at the university before or during FA19 were extracted from the student information system using structured query language programs (Fass-Holmes & Vaughn, 2014, 2015). The resulting records contained unique ID, term GPAs, applicant type (NFRS vs. TRAN), field of study, home country, and visa. These records were organized in a spreadsheet file with quality controls that precluded double-counting students with multiple records.

Records belonging to the university's entire population of international undergraduates who were enrolled for each of the three terms of AY 2019–2020 were identified and included in the study (N = 3,970; NFRS = 3,101, TRAN = 869); counterparts without enrollment in at least one term were excluded. This method ensured that data belonging to the exact same students were used in comparing GPAs between terms. An additional control consisted of identifying and deleting records with 0.00 term GPAs, which resulted from taking all classes in that term on pass/fail option; only authentic 0.00 term GPAs (i.e., F in all letter-graded classes within the term) were included. Confidentiality was ensured by carrying out procedures approved by the Institutional Review Board, and using encryption on a locked-down computer.

Descriptive statistical analyses consisted of calculating counts, percentages, means, and standard deviations on term GPAs earned by the university's entire population of international undergraduates who were enrolled in FA19, WI20, and SP20. In the calculations of percentages, the denominator was a total value appropriate for the data category in question; for example, the denominator for calculating the percentage of TRAN with term GPA <2.0 in SP20 was the total number of enrolled TRAN in SP20. These analyses were disaggregated by AY 2019–2020's terms, to facilitate calculations of GPA changes between terms.

RESULTS

Demographics

The university's entire population of international undergraduates who were enrolled in FA19, WI20, and SP20 included 3,970 F-1 or J-1 students; 3,101 had previously entered the university as NFRS and 869 as TRAN (the vast majority having transferred from community colleges). These students' top five home countries were China ($N = 2{,}771$; 69.8% of the population), India ($N = 228$; 5.7%), South Korea ($N = 182$; 4.6%), Taiwan ($N = 145$; 3.6%), and Hong Kong ($N = 87$; 2.2%). Their top five fields of study were Social Sciences ($N = 1{,}299$), Engineering ($N = 900$), Physical Sciences (including Mathematics; $N = 837$), Biological Sciences ($N = 362$), and Multidisciplinary Studies ($N = 251$).

Research Question 1—Term GPAs Below 2.0

In FA19, 3.2% ($N = 100$) of the university's entire population of international undergraduates who had previously entered as NFRS and were enrolled in FA19, WI20, and SP20 earned GPAs below 2.0 (administratively defined as "academically struggling"). In WI20, 2.3% ($N = 71$) earned GPAs below 2.0; in SP20, 2.1% ($N = 64$). The majority of these students, 69.0%, came from China, 10.0% from South Korea, and 8.0% from India. The largest percentages had a major in Social Sciences (29.0%), Physical Sciences (25.0%), or Engineering (20.0%).

In FA19, 8.7% ($N = 76$) of the university's entire population of international undergraduates who had previously entered as TRAN and were enrolled in FA19, WI20, and SP20 earned GPAs below 2.0 (academically struggling). In WI20, 4.7% ($N = 41$) earned GPAs below 2.0; in SP20, 3.3% ($N = 29$), which was 57.1% and significantly (Z test of independent proportions [http://vassarstats.net/propdiff_ind.html]; $Z = -2.193$, $p < .05$) higher than NFRS' corresponding value (2.1%). The majority of these students, 57.9%, likewise came from China, 18.4% from India, and 7.9% from Indonesia (none from South Korea). The largest percentages of these students had a major in Social Sciences (43.4%), Multidisciplinary Studies (22.4%), or Physical Sciences (18.4%).

These results indicate that less than 10% of the university's entire population of international undergraduates who were enrolled throughout AY 2019–2020 earned term GPAs below 2.0, and that the percentage who previously entered the university as TRAN and struggled academically was roughly double the corresponding percentage of NFRS. Contrary to what might reasonably be expected, and opposite to what the research hypothesis would predict, the number and percentage of these students who struggled academically decreased from FA19 and WI20 to SP20. They struggled academically to a lesser extent during onset of the pandemic's educational disruptions and stressors than during the immediately preceding terms.

Research Question 2—Mean GPAs

Figure 1 shows the mean GPAs and their changes between the three terms of AY 2019–2020, disaggregated by applicant type (NFRS in Figure 1A vs. TRAN in 1B) and by FA19 academic performance (term GPA below 2.0 in gray bars vs. at or above 2.0 in black). The university's entire population of international undergraduates who previously entered as NFRS and were enrolled in FA19, WI20, and SP20 earned somewhat higher mean GPAs than TRAN counterparts in each of the three terms, regardless of whether they academically struggled (<2.0) or succeeded (≥2.0) in FA19. The mean GPA difference between these two applicant type groups was less than half of a letter grade in each term; that is, less than the difference between C and C- or between C and C+.

Figure 1 additionally shows a 90.1% improvement in mean GPA in WI20 (before the pandemic's onset) and a further 14.6% improvement in SP20 (coinciding with the pandemic's onset)—from D+ to B-; and from B- to ~B+, respectively—by the university's entire population of international undergraduates who 1) previously entered as NFRS, 2) were enrolled in FA19, WI20, and SP20, and 3) academically struggled in FA19. The counterparts who academically succeeded in FA19 improved their mean GPA (B+) by 10.1% (A-) in WI20, and they improved by an additional 3.2% (A-) in SP20. TRAN counterparts who academically struggled in FA19 improved their mean GPA (~D+) by 107.9% (~B-) in WI20, and they improved by an additional 19.3% (~B) in SP20. The counterparts who academically succeeded in FA19 (B) improved by 13.4% (B+) in WI20, and they improved by an additional 4.6% (~A-) in SP20.

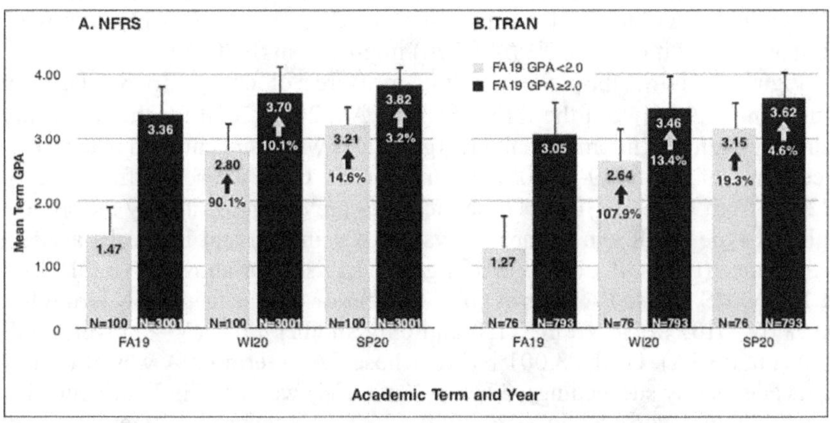

Figure 1: Mean Term GPA of International Undergraduates (Disaggregated by Applicant Type and Fall 2019 Academic Performance).

Note: Error bars represent standard deviations. Values at the top of each bar represent the value of the mean term GPA. Percentage values beneath the arrows represent the change from the previous term's mean GPA, and the arrows indicate the change's direction. Values at the bottom of each bar represent the number of international undergraduates. Abbreviations: NFRS = first-time students; TRAN = transfer students; FA19 = fall 2019; WI20 = winter 2020; SP20 = spring 2020.

The results in Figure 1 indicate that the direction of change in SP20's mean GPAs relative to FA19 and WI20 was the exact opposite of what the research hypothesis would have predicted for the university's entire population of international undergraduates who were enrolled throughout AY 2019–2020. These students counterintuitively showed an improvement in SP20 (coinciding with the pandemic's onset), whereas the research hypothesis would have predicted a worsening. The present results, therefore, disconfirm the research hypothesis that these students would struggle academically (term GPA below 2.0) to a greater extent during SP20 than during the preceding two terms.

Research Questions 3–5—Changes in GPAs Between Terms

Figure 2 shows additional measures of change in GPA between the three terms of AY 2019–2020: the percentages and counts of the university's entire population of international undergraduates who were enrolled in each of the three terms of AY 2019–2020 and whose mean GPA improved from FA19 to WI20 or from FA19 to SP20. These measures are disaggregated by the students' applicant type (NFRS in Figure 2A vs. TRAN in 2B) and by FA19 academic performance (term GPA below 2.0 in gray bars vs. at or above 2.0 in black). Of the 100 NFRS whose FA19 term GPA was below 2.0 (academically struggling), 87.0% ($N = 87$) improved in WI20 and only another 1.1% ($N = 1$) improved in SP20. Of the 3,001 NFRS whose FA19 term GPA was at or above 2.0 (academically succeeding), 51.1% ($N = 1533$) improved in WI20 and an additional 42.6% ($N = 605$) improved in SP20. Of the 76 TRAN whose FA19 term GPA was below 2.0, 93.4% ($N = 71$) improved in WI20 and only another 1.4% ($N = 1$) improved in SP20. Of the 793 TRAN whose FA19 term GPA was at or above 2.0, 51.8% ($N = 411$) improved in WI20 and an additional 53.7% ($N = 220$) improved in SP20.

Figure 3 shows the corresponding measures of change (percentages and counts) in GPA between the three terms of AY 2019–2020 for the university's entire population of international undergraduates who were enrolled in each of the three terms of AY 2019–2020 and whose mean GPA worsened from FA19 to WI20 or from FA19 to SP20. These measures are disaggregated by the students' applicant type (NFRS in Figure 3A vs. TRAN in 3B) and by FA19 academic performance (term GPA below 2.0 in gray bars vs. at or above 2.0 in black). Of the 100 NFRS whose FA19 term GPA was below 2.0 (academically struggling), 10.0% ($N = 10$) worsened in WI20 and only another 1.0% ($N = 1$) worsened in SP20 (Figure 3A). Of the 3,001 NFRS whose FA19 term GPA was at or above 2.0 (academically succeeding), 37.8% ($N = 1,134$) worsened in WI20 but 61.6% ($N = 700$) fewer worsened in SP20. Of the 76 TRAN whose FA19 term GPA was below 2.0, 6.6% worsened in WI20 and 19.7% ($N = 1$) fewer worsened in SP20 (Figure 3B). Of the 793 TRAN whose FA19 term GPA was at or above 2.0, 44.9% ($N = 356$) worsened in WI20 and 64.4% ($N = 229$) fewer worsened in SP20.

Figures 2 and 3 indicate that larger numbers and percentages of the university's entire population of international undergraduates who previously had entered as NFRS or TRAN and were enrolled throughout AY 2019–2020 had improved GPAs in SP20 (coinciding with the pandemic's onset) than in FA19 and WI20. In addition, smaller numbers and percentages of these students who were enrolled throughout AY 2019–2020 had worse GPAs in SP20 than in FA19 and WI20. The opposite results would have been predicted—smaller numbers and percentages of students with improved GPAs, larger numbers and percentages of students with worse ones. The directionality of these results counterintuitively disconfirms the research hypothesis that the university's entire population of international undergraduates who were enrolled throughout AY 2019–2020 would struggle academically (term GPA below 2.0) to a greater extent during SP20 than during the preceding two terms. Instead, these students struggled academically to a lesser extent during onset of the pandemic's educational disruptions and stressors.

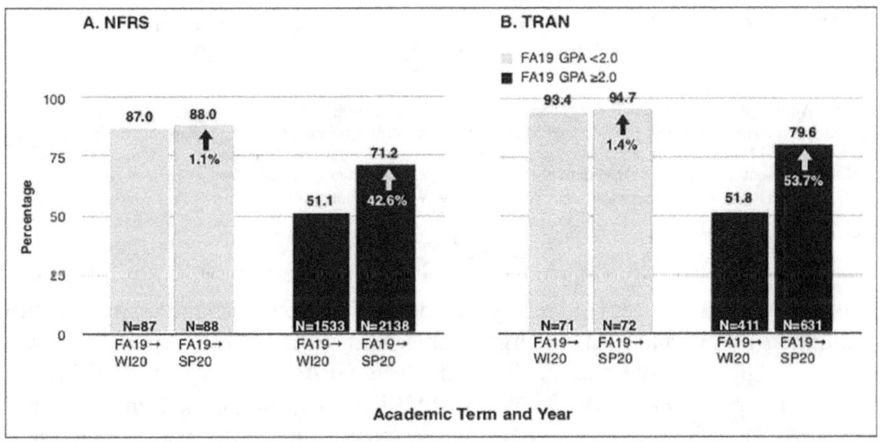

Figure 2: Percentages and Counts of International Undergraduates Whose Mean Term GPA Improved Between Terms (Disaggregated by Applicant Type and Fall 2019 Academic Performance).

Note: Values above each bar represent the percentage of international undergraduates whose term GPA improved from FA19 to WI20 or SP20. Percentage values beneath the arrows represent the change from the FA19 mean GPA, and the arrows indicate the change's direction. Values at the bottom of each bar represent the number of international students. Abbreviations: NFRS = first-time students; TRAN = transfer students; FA19 = fall 2019; WI20 = winter 2020; SP20 = spring 2020.

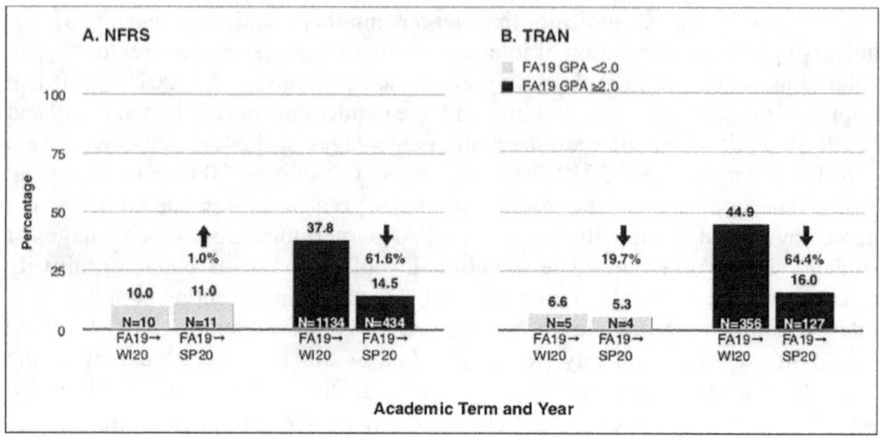

Figure 3: Percentages and Counts of International Undergraduates Whose Mean Term GPA Worsened Between Terms (Disaggregated by Applicant Type and Fall 2019 Academic Performance).

Note: Values above each bar represent the percentage of international undergraduates whose term GPA worsened from FA19 to WI20 or SP20. Percentage values beneath the arrows represent the change from the FA19 mean GPA, and the arrows indicate the change's direction. Values at the bottom of each bar represent the number of international undergraduates. Abbreviations: NFRS = first-time students; TRAN = transfer students; FA19 = fall 2019; WI20 = winter 2020; SP20 = spring 2020.

DISCUSSION

This study's primary objective was to determine how the university's entire population of international undergraduates who were enrolled throughout AY 2019–2020 performed academically (using term GPAs as an indicator) during the coronavirus pandemic's onset. The hypothesis, based on the likelihood that the pandemic's educational disruptions were stressors (Fink, 2017; Kim & Diamond, 2002) that could negatively impact learning (e.g., Vogel & Schwabe, 2016), was that these students would struggle academically to a greater extent in SP20 than in FA19 and/or WI20. Confirmation of this hypothesis would suggest that the pandemic's educational disruptions and stressors (institution-specific and/or institution-independent ones) negatively impacted these students independently of or synergistically with other stressors that they experienced while studying in America. A second objective was to measure the degree to which the university's entire population of international undergraduates who were enrolled throughout AY 2019–2020 and previously entered the university as TRAN struggled academically in SP20. If these students showed evidence of greater academic struggling in SP20 than their NFRS counterparts, it could indicate that transfer shock negatively impacted TRAN during the pandemic's educational disruptions and stressors.

These two objectives were accomplished by descriptive statistical analyses of GPAs earned by the university's entire population of international undergraduates who were enrolled throughout AY 2019–2020. The analyses counterintuitively yielded evidence disconfirming each of the five research questions' hypothesis; contrary to what might reasonably be expected, these students struggled academically to a lesser extent during onset of the pandemic's educational disruptions than during the immediately preceding terms. The evidence additionally indicates that the university's entire population of international undergraduates who previously entered as TRAN and were enrolled throughout AY 2019–2020 struggled academically to a statistically greater extent than their NFRS counterparts, although less than 10% of each subgroup struggled.

The present findings' directionality supports the conclusion that the university's entire population of international undergraduates who were enrolled throughout AY 2019–2020 did not struggle academically to a greater extent in SP20 (during the pandemic's institution-specific and/or institution-independent stressors) than in FA19 and WI20; instead, these students struggled academically to a lesser extent. These findings are the first to provide evidence of international undergraduates showing improvement (rather than worsening) of academic performance during onset of the coronavirus pandemic, and they are educationally meaningful for researchers and administrators alike. They indicate that these students generally succeeded academically in SP20, despite the pandemic's disruptions and stressors. Their academic success could have been attributable (at least in part) to their having devoted more time or effort to studying, using translation software to facilitate their understanding of course content, exam questions, etc., and/or using other coping strategies during the pandemic's onset (Ferdiansyah et al., 2020; Xia & Duan, 2020; Yan, 2017). Further research is needed to learn more about these students' coping strategies.

What other explanation(s) could account for these counterintuitive, disconfirmatory findings? One candidate is that they constitute an outlier and are not truly representative. This explanation is unlikely because the present findings replicate and extend previous ones showing similarly low percentages of academically struggling international undergraduates during previous fall terms at the same university (Fass-Holmes, 2016; Fass-Holmes & Vaughn, 2014, 2015). Other candidate explanations include increased cheating, grade inflation, and/or instructors' sympathetic grading (Fass-Holmes, 2017; Pattison et al., 2013) during SP20 compared with FA19 and WI20. These explanations would require unreasonable stretching to compellingly account for the present findings' specific patterns. For instance, faculty and teaching assistants (TAs) would have needed to administer final examinations with ineffective and/or insufficient safeguards against cheating (contrary to established policies) to produce the present results' patterns. They also would have needed to expend time and effort determining which students in their classes were international NFRS or TRAN, then use the determinations to inflate or sympathetically assign grades accordingly to yield the present findings' patterns. These explanations consequently seem highly improbable considering that faculty and TAs also had to endure the pandemic's disruptions and stressors. Additional research will be required, however, to conclusively resolve these other explanations' validity.

The more parsimonious explanation (cf, Borowski, 2012) is that these students showed evidence of resilience ("attitudes and behaviours which are associated with an individual's ability to recover from adversity and also to actively adapt in the face of these adversities and stress … an essential capacity for a student to fully thrive within [higher education]"; Robbins et al., 2018, p. 44) and effective institutional support (Glass et al., 2021) during the pandemic's onset. Although SP20's learning environment conditions most likely did include stressors (Kim & Diamond, 2002), the university's international undergraduates evidently adapted to remote learning and other educational disruptions more successfully than researchers and educators might have expected (Dhawan, 2020; Lee et al., 2021; Onyema et al., 2020; Serhan, 2020). This is not to say that every student resiliently succeeded academically during the pandemic's onset. However, the percentages who did struggle academically are remarkably low (less than 10%), considering their extraordinary learning environment conditions.

This study's second objective was to measure the degree to which the university's entire population of international undergraduates who were enrolled throughout AY 2019–2020 and previously had entered as TRAN struggled academically in SP20 compared with their NFRS counterparts. It tested the hypothesis that if the former students showed evidence of greater academic struggling in SP20 than the latter, then transfer shock could have had an additional negative impact during the pandemic's onset. The present results are consistent with this hypothesis: 1) The percentage of academically struggling TRAN in SP20 significantly exceeded the corresponding percentage of NFRS; and 2) TRAN's mean GPAs were below NFRS' corresponding values in SP20 (and the preceding two terms). These findings replicate and extend previous ones comparing the university's TRAN and NFRS on measures of academic achievement, retention, graduation, and time to degree (Dorado & Fass-Holmes, 2016; Fass-Holmes, 2016). Although the difference between percentages of TRAN and NFRS who struggled academically in SP20 was statistically significant, both subgroups' values were below 10%; instead, both largely succeeded academically.

Two noteworthy limitations should be kept in mind. First, the present study used a single university's entire international undergraduate population that was enrolled throughout AY 2019–2020 (except students taking all classes pass/fail). Replications analyzing other postsecondary institutions' data (including community colleges for the first objective) are needed to evaluate generalizability. Second, the university's response to the pandemic might have varied between faculty, TAs, and/or departments; some could have adapted more efficiently and effectively to the pandemic's disruptions than others. This issue requires further investigation, identifying the best practices that optimize adaptation.

This report's results have implications for education policy and practice, specifically regarding the decisions about development and/or delivery of international undergraduates' support programs and services. A deficit view that international undergraduates necessarily and collectively struggle academically because of their English language incompetency or linguistic inferiority to their domestic counterparts (Jin & Schneider, 2019; Zhang-Wu, 2018) could lead administrators to implement support programs and services for all (or at least a substantial percentage of) international undergraduates. To the extent that any institution's existing beneficial supports promote international undergraduates' academic success (term GPAs at or above 2.0) during the pandemic's disruptions and stressors, their administrators can focus instead on additional programs and/or services designed specifically and cost effectively for those students who need them most rather than for the entire population.

In conclusion, this report contributes the research literature's first evidence of international undergraduates showing improvement (rather than worsening) of academic performance during onset of the coronavirus pandemic. The counterintuitive direction of change in SP20 GPAs relative to the immediately preceding two terms disconfirms the present study's hypothesis that international undergraduates should struggle academically to a greater extent in SP20 than in FA19 and/or WI20. This hypothesis is based on the likelihood that the pandemic's educational disruptions were stressors (Fink, 2017; Kim & Diamond, 2002) and put these students at a risk of negative impact on their learning (e.g., Vogel & Schwabe, 2016). Instead, the university's entire population of international undergraduates who were enrolled throughout AY 2019–2020 struggled academically to a lesser extent in SP20 than in FA19 and/or WI20. (e.g., Vogel & Schwabe, 2016). The present findings are indicative of these students' resilience during onset of the pandemic's stressful educational disruptions.

REFERENCES

Alharbi, E. S., & Smith, A. P. (2018). Review of the literature on stress and wellbeing of international students in English-speaking countries. *International Education Studies, 11*(6), 22–44. https://doi.org/10.5539/ies.v11n6p22

Banjong, D. N. (2015). International students' enhanced academic performance: Effects of campus resources. *Journal of International Students, 5*(1), 132–142. https://doi.org/10.32674/jis.v5i2.430

Berry, J. W. (1997). Immigration, acculturation, and adaptation. *Applied Psychology: An International Review, 46*(1), 5–68. https://doi.org/10.1111/j.1464-0597.1997.tb01087.x

Bista, K. (2011). Academic dishonesty among international students in higher education. In J. Miller & J. Groccia (Eds.), *To improve the academy: Vol. 30. Resources for faculty, instructional, and organizational development* (pp. 159–172). Jossey-Bass. https://doi.org/10.1002/j.2334-4822.2011.tb00655.x

Borowski, S. (2012). *The origin and popular use of Occam's razor.* https://www.aaas.org/origin-and-popular-use-occams-razor

Burke, L. (2020, March 9). *Colleges move online amid virus fears.* Inside Higher Ed. https://www.insidehighered.com/news/2020/03/09/colleges-move-classes-online-coronavirus-infects-more

Chaves, C. (2006). Involvement, development, and retention. Theoretical foundations and potential extensions for adult community college students.

Community College Review, 34(2), 139–152. https://doi.org/10.1177/0091552106293414

Dhawan, S. (2020). Online learning: A panacea in the time of COVID-19 crisis. *Journal of Education Technology, 49*(1), 5–22. https://doi.org/10.1177/0047239520934018

Dickerson, C. (2020, April 26). *'My world is shattering': Foreign students stranded by coronavirus.* The New York Times. https://www.nytimes.com/2020/04/25/us/coronavirus-international-foreign-students-universities.html

Dorado, D. A. L., & Fass-Holmes, B. (2016). Academic achievement and demographics of international undergraduates. In K. Bista & C. Foster (Eds.), *Exploring the social and academic experiences of international students in higher education institutions* (pp. 227–252). IGI Global. https://doi.org/10.4018/978-1-4666-9749-2.ch013

Engzell, P., Frey, A., & Verhagen, M. D. (2021). Learning loss due to school closures during the COVID-19 pandemic. *Proceedings of the National Academy of Sciences, 118*(17), e2022376118. https://doi.org/10.1073/pnas.2022376118

Fass-Holmes, B. (2016). International undergraduates' retention, graduation, and time to degree. *Journal of International Students, 6*(4), 933–955. https://doi.org/10.32674/jis.v6i4.327

Fass-Holmes, B. (2017). International students reported for academic integrity violations: Demographics, retention, and graduation. *Journal of International Students, 7*(3), 644–669. https://doi.org/10.5281/zenodo.570026

Fass-Holmes, B., & Vaughn, A. A. (2014). Are international undergraduates struggling academically? *Journal of International Students, 4*(1), 60–73. https://doi.org/10.32674/jis.v4i1.497

Fass-Holmes, B., & Vaughn, A. A. (2015). Evidence that international undergraduates can succeed academically despite struggling with English. *Journal of International Students, 5*(3), 228–243. https:// doi.org/10.32674/jis.v5i3.418

Fass-Holmes, B., & Vaughn, A. A. (2018). International students reported for academic integrity violations—Is English deficiency a predictor variable? In K. Bista (Ed.), *Global perspectives on international student experiences in higher education. Tensions and issues* (pp. 157–177). Routledge. https://doi.org/10.4324/9781315113456

Ferdiansyah, S., Supiastutik, & Angin, R. (2020). Thai students 'experiences of online learning at Indonesian universities in the time of the COVID-19 pandemic. *Journal of International Students, 10*(S3), 58–74. https://doi.org/10.32674/jis.v10iS3.3199

Fink, G. (2017). Stress: Concepts, definition and history. *Reference Module in Neuroscience and Biobehavioral Psychology,* 3–9. https://doi.org/10.1016/B978-0-12-809324-5.02208-2

Fishman, T. (2016). Academic integrity as an educational concept, concern, and movement in US institutions of higher learning. In T. Bretag (Ed.), *Handbook of academic integrity* (pp. 7–21). Springer. https://doi.org/10.1007/978-981-287-079-7

Gallagher, H. L., Doherty, A. Z., & Obonyo, M. (2020). International student experiences in Queensland during COVID-19. *International Social Work, 63*(6), 815–819. https://doi.org/10.1177/0020872820949621

Gallagher, J. (2021). *Compounding stress: The pandemic's effects on mental health.* International Educator. https://www.nafsa.org/ie-magazine/2021/4/6/compounding-stress-pandemics-effects-mental-health

Gautam, C., Lowery, C. L., Mays, C., & Durant, D. (2016). Challenges for global learners: A qualitative study of the concerns and difficulties of international students. *Journal of International Students, 6*(2), 501–526. https://doi.org/10.32674/jis.v6i2.368

Glass, C. R., Godwin, K. A., & Matross Helms, R. (2021). *Toward greater inclusion and success: A new compact for international students.* https://www.acenet.edu/Documents/Intl-Students-Monograph.pdf

Henneberry, D. (2019). International students: A population facing significant stress. *American Journal of Biomedical Science & Research, 3*(2), 142–143. https://doi.org/10.34297/AJBSR.2019.03.000650

Hills, J. R. (1965). Transfer shock: The academic performance of the junior college transfer. *Journal of Experimental Education, 33*(3), 201–215. https://doi.org/10.1080/00220973.1965.11010875

Jin, L., & Schneider, J. (2019). Faculty views on international students: A survey study. *Journal of International Students, 9*(1), 85–97. https://doi.org/10.32674/jis.v9i1.268

Kim, J. J., & Diamond, D. M. (2002). The stressed hippocampus, synaptic plasticity and lost memories. *Nature Reviews. Neuroscience, 3*(6), 453–462. https://doi.org/10.1038/nrn849

Krahmer, S. M., McManus, G., & Sharma, R. (2020, March 4). *Ensuring instructional continuity in a potential pandemic.* Inside Higher Ed. https://www.insidehighered.com/advice/2020/03/04/preparing-instructional-continuity-advent-covid-19-pandemic-opinion

Krsmanovic, M. (2021). The synthesis and future directions of empirical research on international students in the United States: The insights from one decade. *Journal of International Students, 11*(1), 1–23. https://doi.org/10.32674/jis.v11i1.1955

Lederer, A. M., Hoban, M. T., Lipson, S. K., Zhou, S., & Eisenberg, D (2021). More than inconvenienced: The unique needs of U.S. college students during the COVID-19 pandemic. *Health Education & Behavior, 48*(1), 14–19. https://doi.org/10.1177/1090198120969372

Lee, J. J. (2020). Neo-racism and the criminalization of China. *Journal of International Students, 10*(4), i–vi. https://doi.org/10.32674/jis.v10i4.2929

Lee, K., Fanguy, M., Lu, X. S., & Bligh, B. (2021). Student learning during COVID-19: It was not as bad as we feared. *Distance Education, 42*(1), 164–172. https://doi.org/10.1080/01587919.2020.1869529

Ma, H., & Miller, C. (2020). Trapped in a double bind: Chinese overseas student anxiety during the COVID-19 pandemic. *Health Communication.* https://doi.org/10.1080/10410236.2020.1775439

Martel, M. (2020). *COVID-19 effects on U.S. higher education campuses: Academic student mobility to and from China. Institute of International Education.* https://www.iie.org/COVID19-Effects-on-US-Higher-Education-Campuses.

McCallum, C. M. (2015). Turning graduate school aspirations into enrollment: How student affairs professionals can help African American students. *The New York Journal of Student Affairs, 15*(1), 1–18. https://commons.library.stonybrook.edu/nyjsa/vol15/iss1/2

Misra, R., Crist, M., & Burant, C. J. (2003). Relationships among life stress, social support, academic stressors, and reactions to stressors of international students in the United States. *International Journal of Stress Management, 10*(2), 137–157. https://doi.org/10.1037/1072-5245.10.2.137

NAFSA: Association for International Educators. (2020). *Fall 2020 survey: Financial impact of COVID-19 on international education.* fasthttps://www.nafsa.org/policy-and-advocacy/policy-resources/fall-2020-survey-financial-impact-covid-19-international-education

Onyema, E. M., Eucheria, N. C., Obafemi, F. A., Sen, S., Atonye, F. G., Sharma, A., & Alsayed, A. O. (2020). Impact of coronavirus pandemic on education. *Journal of Education and Practice, 11*(13), 108–121. https://doi.org/10.7176/JEP/11-13-12

Open Doors (2020). *2020 fast facts.* https://opendoorsdata.org/fast_facts/fast-facts-2020/

Osaze, O. (2021, March 1). *Living through the pandemic as an international student.* Inside Higher Ed. https://www.insidehighered.com/views/2021/03/01/congress-should-include-international-students-any-government-covid-19-relief

Ota, A. (2013). *Factors influencing social, cultural, and academic transitions of Chinese international ESL students in U.S. higher education* [Doctoral dissertation, Portland State University]. Portland State University PDX Scholar. http://pdxscholar.library.pdx.edu/cgi/viewcontent.cgi?article=2050&context=open_access_etds

Pattison, E., Grodsky, E., & Muller, C. (2013). Is the sky falling? Grade inflation and the signaling power of grades. *Educational Researcher, 42*(5), 259–265. https://doi.org/10.3102/0013189x13481382

Perry, C. J. (2016). Comparing international and American students' challenges: A literature review. *Journal of International Students, 6*(3), 712–721.

Redden, E. (2020, April 20). *Colleges move summer classes online; some consider tuition reductions, technology fee waivers.* Inside Higher Ed. https://www.insidehighered.com/news/2020/04/10/colleges-move-summer-classes-online-some-consider-tuition-reductions-technology-fee

Robbins, A., Kaye, E., & Catling, J. C. (2018). Predictors of student resilience in higher education. *Psychology Teaching Review, 24*(1), 44–52. https://doi.org/10.32674/jis.v6i3.352

Roy, S. R. (2013). Educating Chinese, Japanese, and Korean international students: Recommendations to American professors. *Journal of International Students, 3*(1), 10–16. https://doi.org/10.32674/jis.v3i1.514

Sanford, N. (1966). *Self & society: Social change and individual development.* Atherton.

Serhan, D. (2020). Transitioning from face-to-face to remote learning: Students' attitudes and perceptions of using Zoom during COVID-19 pandemic. *International Journal of Technology in Education and Science, 4*(4), 335–342. https://doi.org/10.46328/ijtes.v4i4.148

Sherry, M., Thomas, P., & Chui, W. H. (2010). International students: A vulnerable population. *Higher Education, 60,* 33–46. https://doi.org/10.1007/s10734-009-9284-z

Smalley, A. (2020, July 27). *Higher education responses to coronavirus (COVID-19). National Conference of State Legislatures.* https://www.ncsl.org/research/education/higher-education-responses-to-coronavirus-covid-19.aspx

U.S. Department of State. (n.d.). *Directory of visa categories.* https://travel.state.gov/content/travel/en/us-visas/visa-information-resources/all-visa-categories.html

U.S. Department of State. (2021). *COVID-19 travel restrictions and exceptions.* https://travel.state.gov/content/travel/en/us-visas/visa-information-resources/covid-19-travel-restrictions-and-exceptions.html

Urias, D., & Yeakey, C. C. (2009). Analysis of the U.S. student visa system: Misperceptions, barriers, and consequences. *Journal of Studies in International Education, 13*(1), 72–109. https://doi.org/10.1177/1028315307308135

Vogel, S., & Schwabe, L. (2016). Learning and memory under stress: Implications for the classroom. *NPJ Science of Learning, 1,* 16011. https://doi.org/10.1038/npjscilearn.2016.11

Xia, M., & Duan, C. (2020). Stress coping of Chinese international students in face of COVID19 pandemic: Cultural characteristics. *International Journal of Mental Health Promotion, 22*(3), 159–172. https://doi.org/10.32604/IJMHP.2020.011117

Yan, K. (2017). Chinese international students' stressors and coping strategies in the United States. In R. Maclean & L. P. Symaco (Eds.), *Education in the Asia-Pacific region: Issues, concerns and prospects, volume 37* (pp. 1–145). Springer. https://doi.org/10.1007/978-981-10-3347-6

Yan, K., & Berliner, D. C. (2009). Chinese international students' academic stressors in the United States. *College Student Journal, 43*(4), 939–960.

Yan, K., & Berliner, D. C. (2011). An examination of individual level factors in stress and coping processes: Perspectives of Chinese international students in the United States. *Journal of College Student Development, 52*(5), 523–542. https://doi.org/10.1353/csd.2011.0060

Yan, K., & Berliner, D. C. (2013). Chinese international students' personal and sociocultural stressors in the United States. *Journal of College Student Development, 54*(1), 62–84. https://doi.org/10.1353/csd.2013.0010

Zhang-Wu, Q. (2018). Chinese international students' experiences in American higher education institutes: A critical review of the literature. *Journal of International Students, 8*(2), 1173–1197. https://doi.org/10.32674/jis.v8i2.139

BARRY FASS-HOLMES, Ph.D., is the SEVIS Coordinator for the International Student Center at San Diego State University. His research interests include international students' academic achievement and integrity. Email: bfassholmes@sdsu.edu

Research in Context

© *Journal of International Students*
Volume 12, Issue 3 (2022), pp. 607-612
ISSN: 2162-3104 (Print), 2166-3750 (Online)
doi: 10.32674/jis.v12i3.3835
ojed.org/jis

Korean Female Graduate Students' Experiences in the United States: Recognizing and Addressing Their Challenges

Jung Eun Hong
*Department of Natural Sciences,
University of West Georgia, USA*

ABSTRACT

The unique experiences of Korean female graduate students (KFGS) in the United States (US) have not received much attention or been discussed, although Korea has been one of the leading countries sending students to the United States. By examining literature regarding the experiences of KFGS studying and living in the United States, this paper reports the challenges they face (e.g., racial and gender discrimination, the model minority stereotype, and multiple roles as students and as wives and/or mothers) and the ways in which they respond to those challenges. This paper also urges one to conduct more research on the lives of KFGS to make them visible and heard in U.S. academia.

Keywords: coping strategies, discrimination, female students, graduate students, international students, model minority

In general, the United States (U.S.) is an inequitable place for higher education for women in terms of their college experiences and career outcomes, although women outpace men regarding the overall degrees granted (Dua, 2007). Prior studies reported the inequalities that women of color face in academia, but the voices of female Asian scholars have been relatively unheard in U.S. higher education because of a dearth of studies identifying and understanding their challenges and needs in the higher education system (Green & Kim, 2005; Yoon & Kim, 2018). Only a few studies have explicitly explored international female

Asian graduate students in the United States and reported their struggles as women, racial and ethnic minorities, and international students (e.g., Le et al., 2016; Liu et al., 2016). However, among other ethnic groups, the unique experiences of Korean female graduate students (KFGS) in the United States have not been much discussed although Korea was ranked as the third leading country in terms of sending students to the United States in 2019 and 2020, after China and India (Institute of International Education [IIE], 2020; Lim, 2019). Further, the increase in anti-Asian violence and harassment during the COVID-19 pandemic has made Asian women in the United States especially vulnerable (Stop AAPI Hate, 2021). Thus, there is a need to increase the visibility of and discussions about the life experiences of Asian women in the United States. The purpose of this paper is to examine literature[1] regarding the experiences of KFGS studying and living in the United States. This paper focuses particularly on reporting their challenges and the ways in which they respond to those challenges.

THE STATUS OF KOREAN WOMEN IN KOREA

Korea's traditional culture, strongly influenced by Confucianism, has shaped a patriarchal society, where Korean women must adhere to strict gender roles, a patrilineal family system, and a hierarchical social structure (Shim, 2001). Although Korean women have experienced improved social status (e.g., obtainment of equal rights, education opportunities, and greater social engagement) through modernization and globalization, such rapid social changes have not been able to completely erase the Confucian ideology in contemporary Korean society (Shim, 2001). Korean women continue to have limited career mobility compared with Korean men (Park & Shahiri, 2015). Small numbers of women are in leadership positions at major corporations and organizations, but often they are paid lower salaries than men who are at the same educational level (Park & Shahiri, 2015). Employed, married Korean women also frequently have dual roles in paid labor and domestic work as housewives and mothers (Yoon & Kim, 2018). Gender inequality is not much different in Korean academia because there are fewer career opportunities for female scholars.

Many KFGS choose to leave Korea to pursue graduate degrees in other countries because female Korean scholars often face traditional gender disparities in the academic job market (Green & Kim, 2005; Yoon & Kim, 2018). According to the Korean Education Statistics Service [KESS] (2020), female professors comprised only 27% of the total full-time faculty members in 2020. Most female scholars work in short-term, contract-based, non-tenure-track positions (Yoon &

---

[1] Papers reporting the experiences of KFGS, Korean female scholars, and other international female graduate students in the United States were reviewed.

Kim, 2018). Prior studies have reported that several KFGS decided to study in the United States because there were fewer professional career opportunities for women and insufficient recognition of women's abilities in Korea (e.g., Green & Kim, 2005; Lim, 2019; Yoon & Kim, 2018). However, KFGS experience additional challenges and different environmental pressures in the United States.

KFGS' CHALLENGES AND COPING STRATEGIES

The frequently identified difficulties for KFGS are language barriers and isolation, which are common issues for all international students (Green & Kim, 2005; Lim, 2019). Both are primary stressors for most international students because they are closely associated with academic success, psychological well-being, and social adjustment (Yeh & Inose, 2003). Often, students who were actively engaged in class in their home countries consider themselves inferior students in the United States because of a lack of English proficiency, and this may cause psychological stress (Yeh & Inose, 2003). Language barriers may also prevent students from interacting with their American peers and from being involved in cultural and social activities (Yeh & Inose, 2003). Moreover, international students often feel lonely and isolated because they have a low level of social support and engagement in the United States, which may significantly affect their quality of life (Yeh & Inose, 2003). In addition to these issues, there are other challenges that specifically KFGS face more than other international students.

In general, female Asian international students have "triple minority statuses as women, racial minorities, and foreigners" (Liu et al., 2016, p. 412). Racial and gender discrimination has, as expected, been identified as a challenge by KFGS in the United States (Green & Kim, 2005; Lim, 2019). Several KFGS reported that they had faced racial and gender stereotypes as Asian women (Green & Kim, 2005; Lim, 2019). KFGS are often considered and judged as stereotypical Asian women, who are submissive, dependent, unprofessional, cute, and quiet (Green & Kim, 2005). Other studies conducted with Chinese and Japanese female international students reported similar findings (e.g., Bonazzo & Wong, 2007; Hsieh, 2006). These stereotypical images negatively affect not only students' daily lives but also their academic lives, such as their relationships with faculty members, classmates, undergraduate students whom they teach, and people whom they meet in professional settings such as conferences (Green & Kim, 2005).

KFGS must also deal with the model minority stereotype of Asian Americans, according to which all Asian Americans are hard workers, academically high-achieving students, and harsh instructors (Green & Kim, 2005). Coined by Petersen (1966), the "model minority" refers to the success of Asian immigrants in the United States, and it suggests that other minority groups should aspire to be like them. Clearly, this label cannot represent all Asian minority groups. In particular, it negatively affects students because of people's expectations of them as academic high achievers. The model minority myth becomes a burden on KFGS as well; some students feel pressurized to maintain the image of smart, hardworking Asian students (Green & Kim, 2005). In addition, this widespread stereotype tends to overlook or even hide any discrimination and challenges that Asian women face in academia (Green & Kim, 2005).

KFGS' experiences seem to differ depending on their marital status. Married KFGS often have different motivations behind coming to the United States and experience additional difficulties compared with unmarried students. Some decide to study in the United States to stay with their husbands, who are pursuing academic degrees or work (Yoon & Kim, 2018). These married female students often struggle to balance their roles as students with their roles as wives and/or mothers because Korean women are unexceptionally responsible for housework and childcare (Yoon & Kim, 2018). Another situation is that of married Korean women coming to the United States with their children to obtain their own graduate degrees and improve their children's English fluency while their husbands stay in Korea alone (Lee, 2013). These women have difficulties playing dual roles as full-time graduate students and single, primary caregivers; however, they also feel some relief because they do not have to deal directly with traditional domestic obligations to their husbands and in-laws (Lee, 2013).

To cope with these challenges, KFGS have found helpful approaches for themselves because people naturally develop strategies to manage or overcome difficulties during the acculturation process (Green & Kim, 2005; Lim, 2019; Park et al., 2017). For example, students develop a support system by engaging in Korean or other Asian communities and attending extracurricular activities, social events, or a church regularly (Green & Kim, 2005; Lim, 2019). They also maintain supportive relationships with their academic advisors, family members in Korea, and classmates (Green & Kim, 2005).

RECOMMENDATIONS FOR HIGHER EDUCATION ADMINISTRATORS AND RESEARCHERS

Most higher education institutions in the United States have been offering various support programs for their international students (e.g., language, health and wellness, cultural adaptation, immigration, and accommodations support) (Le et al., 2016). However, some university programs are not very helpful for many international graduate students because the programs do not meet these students' specific needs; most support programs last for a short term and are more suitable for undergraduates (Lim, 2019). International student service providers and researchers need to do more research on students' various needs based on their race, ethnicity, culture, gender, age group, marital status, parenting, and degree program. Universities should also provide systematic, culturally responsive training for faculty members, particularly master's and doctoral student advisors, because their relationships with international graduate students are crucial to the students' academic achievement and successful acculturation (Le et al., 2016).

For KFGS specifically, there should be more studies on them because KFGS should no longer be "invisible and unheard" in U.S. academia (Green & Kim, 2005, p. 493). Recommended topics may include the mental health impact of anti-Asian racism on KFGS and the implications for their social lives and career plans;

tensions between KFGS and Korean Americans; and Generation Z KFGS' perspectives on traditional gender roles. More stories of KFGS need to be told, and their voices should be heard.

REFERENCES

Bonazzo, C., & Wong, Y. J. (2007). Japanese international female students' experience of discrimination, prejudice, and stereotypes. *College Student Journal, 41,* 631–640. https://link.gale.com/apps/doc/A169306807/AONE?u=anon~86c4a23c&sid=googleScholar&xid=73335ffa

Dua, P. (2007). Feminist mentoring and female graduate student success: Challenging gender inequality in higher education. *Sociology Compass, 1,* 594–612. https://doi.org/10.1111/j.1751-9020.2007.00042.x

Green, D. O. N., & Kim, E. (2005). Experiences of Korean female doctoral students in academe: Raising voice against gender and racial stereotypes. *Journal of College Student Development, 46,* 487–500. https://doi.org/10.1353/csd.2005.0048

Hsieh, M. H. (2006). Identity negotiation among female Chinese international students in second-language higher education. *College Student Journal, 40,* 870–884. https://link.gale.com/apps/doc/A156364421/AONE?u=anon~951efac2&sid=googleScholar&xid=d818d406

Institute of International Education. (2020). International scholars: Leading places of origin. https://opendoorsdata.org/data/international-students/leading-places-of-origin/

Korean Education Statistics Service (2020). Number of full-time/non full-time teachers by establishment and position. https://kess.kedi.re.kr/eng/stats/school?menuCd=0102&cd=4996&survSeq=2020&itemCode=01&menuId=m_010206&uppCd1=010206&uppCd2=010206&flag=A

Le, A. T., LaCost, B. Y., & Wismer, M. (2016). International female graduate students' experience at a midwestern university: Sense of belonging and identity development. *Journal of International Students, 6,* 128–152. https://doi.org/10.32674/jis.v6i1.485

Lee, J. Y. (2013). *South Korean "New Wild Geese" mothers studying in the US: Balancing between studenthood and motherhood* (Master thesis, University of Kansas). http://hdl.handle.net/1808/14540

Lim, Y. (2019). *The acculturation experiences of South Korean international female graduate students: A phenomenological study* (Doctoral dissertation, Saint Louis University). https://www.proquest.com/dissertations-theses/acculturation-experiences-south-korean/docview/2247080336/se-2?accountid=15017

Liu, T., Wong, Y. J., & Tsai, P. C. (2016). Conditional mediation models of intersecting identities among female Asian international students. *The Counseling Psychologist, 44,* 411–441. https://doi.org/10.1177%2F0011000016637200

Park, H., Lee, M. J., Choi, G. Y., & Zepernick, J. S. (2017). Challenges and coping strategies of East Asian graduate students in the United States. *International Social Work, 60*, 733–749. https://doi.org/10.1177%2F0020872816655864

Park, K., & Shahiri, H. (2015). Over-education and job mobility among young Korean female graduates. *Asian Women, 31*, 55–78. http://www.e-asianwomen.org/xml/04994/04994.pdf

Petersen, W. (1966, January 6). Success story, Japanese-American style. *New York Times Magazine*. https://timesmachine.nytimes.com/timesmachine/1966/01/09/356013502.html?pageNumber=180

Shim, Y. H. (2001). Feminism and the discourse of sexuality in Korea: Continuities and changes. *Human Studies, 24*, 133–148. https://doi.org/10.1023/A:1010775332420

Stop AAPI Hate. (2021). Stop AAPI hate national report. https://stopaapihate.org/wp-content/uploads/2021/04/Stop-AAPI-Hate-National-Report-210316.pdf

Yeh, C. J., & Inose, M. (2003). International students' reported English fluency, social support satisfaction, and social connectedness as predictors of acculturative stress. *Counselling Psychology Quarterly, 16*, 15–28. https://doi.org/10.1080/0951507031000114058

Yoon, H., & Kim, H. (2018). Career–family strategies and spatial mobility among South Korean women scholars. *Asian and Pacific Migration Journal, 27*, 101–120. https://doi.org/10.1177%2F0117196818760863

JUNG EUN HONG, Ph.D., is an associate professor in the Department of Natural Sciences at the University of West Georgia. Her research interests include geography and GIS education, global understanding and citizenship, diversity in higher education, and qualitative methods. Email: jhong@westga.edu

Research Article

© *Journal of International Students*
Volume 12, Issue 3 (2022), pp. 613-632
ISSN: 2162-3104 (Print), 2166-3750 (Online)
doi: 10.32674/jis.v12i3.3954
ojed.org/jis

Perceived Social Support and Well-Being of International Students at an Italian University

Sabrina Cipolletta[1,2]
Arianna Mercurio
Department of General Psychology,
University of Padua, Italy

Rachele Pezzetta
IRCCS San Camillo Hospital, Italy

ABSTRACT

The present study aims at exploring international students' well-being in relation to their perception of social support and dispersion of dependency on various resources. The participants were 139 international students at an Italian university who completed the WHO-5 Well-being Index, Symptom Checklist 90-R, Multidimensional Scale of Perceived Social Support, and Dependency Grids. The results show that higher well-being is correlated with higher support and lower distress and that higher dispersion of dependency was associated with higher perceived support. International students who seek professional psychological help also report lower well-being, higher distress, and fewer resources compared with those who do not seek psychological support. Further, coming from collectivist cultures (rather than individualist ones) as well as being a long-term (rather than short-term) student was mostly associated with higher distress and less perceived support. These results suggest that counseling services for international students should help them find new sources of social support.

[1] Corresponding author.

[2] The authors have no conflicts of interest to declare.

Keywords: dispersion of dependency, international students, social support, well-being

According to the Institute of International Educations (IIE, 2020), the number of international students has been more than one thousand starting from 2015 till date, with a peak in international mobility between 2010 and 2015, growing annually from +2,9% to +10%. The most recent data available for Italy show that in 2018–2019 there were about 89,000 international students, most of whom were from Asia (26,313), outside the European Union (20,453), and inside the European Union (19,624) (Naldi, 2020). According to the United Nations Educational, Scientific and Cultural Organization (UNESCO) Institute of Statistics (2020), international students are defined as those "who have crossed a national or territorial border for the purpose of education and are now enrolled outside their country of origin" (para. 1). They can be grouped as long-term or short-term international students, with the former studying in full-time programs and the latter participating in exchange programs, such as Erasmus, lasting from 3 months to 1 year (O'Reilly et al., 2015).

International students are at a greater risk of developing psychological distress (including at a clinical level) compared with domestic students because they are distanced from their main social resources; consequently, they face problems related to the sense of belongingness, loneliness, and acculturative stress (Brunsting et al., 2019; Poyrazli et al., 2004). In addition, they are highly exposed to linguistic, academic, interpersonal, financial, and intrapersonal stressors that can influence their psychological and physical well-being, thus leading to depression, loneliness, homesickness, and psychosomatic symptoms (Mori, 2000). Moreover, students with low levels of belonging to a university who experience a lower sense of coherence as well as less academic and social integration are also the ones who are more likely to seek professional support (e.g., psychologist, social worker, clergy), rather than informal help (e.g., family members, friends; Swanbrow Becker et al., 2018). Therefore, it is crucial to investigate the relationship between social support and well-being in international students and also in relation to their search for professional help. First of all, we will clarify and analyze the construct of social support in relation to well-being. Further, we will revise social support through the lens of personal construct psychology (Kelly, 1955) to gain a more comprehensive view that might inform psychological interventions.

THE CONSTRUCT OF SOCIAL SUPPORT

Social support is a multidimensional construct that refers to the availability of concrete and psychological resources that are perceived or received from interpersonal relationships (Rodriguez & Cohen, 1998). Cohen (1988) distinguished between *structural support*, which quantitatively measures social networks' integration and strength, and *functional support*, which qualitatively evaluates social networks' functions (e.g., tangible, emotional, informational, or appraisal). However, factorial analyses of various assessment instruments showed that social support measures are often independent; these analyses provided indexes of various aspects of the construct related to the way in which social support is defined (Barrera, 1986).

The lack of a comprehensive definition of *social support* and the lack of a fully explicative model of its links with physical and mental health complicate the establishment of a strong construct validity (Sarason & Sarason, 2009). Two models have been proposed to describe the effects of social support on health: the main-effect model, which states that social support promotes health-eliciting positive psychological states, higher self-esteem, and environmental control (Cohen & Syme, 1985); the stress-buffering model, in which social support buffers the harmful effects of stress before or at the beginning of the psychophysiological reaction (Cohen & Wills, 1985). However, so far, these models have reached mixed or partial validation.

Previous studies have shown that the lack of social support can have an effect on a medical level (Uchino, 2006; Wang et al., 2005), with higher levels of support predicting better prognosis and lower mortality (Brummett et al., 2001). Likewise, some authors have found that social support had direct effects on reducing depression or improving well-being in older people (Oxman et al., 1992) and in various clinical conditions (Ambrosio et al., 2019; Fatima & Jibeen, 2019; Thompson et al., 2017). However, other authors found only indirect and mixed indirect–direct effects of social support in reducing psychological distress and improving well-being (Kagee et al., 2018; Kurtović & Ivančić, 2019).

These results also provide a confusing picture of the role of social support in well-being due to the use of different tests to measure the construct (Fatima & Jibeen, 2019; Thompson et al., 2017; Wang et al., 2005); these tests are sometimes not standardized (e.g., Berkman et al., 1992) and make results difficult to compare and generalize. Further, different studies (Berkman et al., 1992; Brummett et al., 2001; Fatima & Jibeen, 2019; Horsten et al., 2000) indicate different components (structural or functional, emotional or tangible) of social support as the determinants of well-being.

SOCIAL SUPPORT AND INTERNATIONAL STUDENTS

For international students, social support is a fundamental resource by which they cope with acculturative stress and its consequences, such as depression, anxiety, and somatic symptoms (Jou & Fukada, 1997; Lee et al., 2004; Ra & Trusty, 2017; Zhang & Goodson, 2011). Some studies (Aldawsari et al., 2018; Berger et al., 2018; Brisset et al., 2010; O'Reilly et al., 2010) have considered well-being the result of the positive effect of social support on loneliness (Lin & Kingminghae, 2014) or stress (O'Reilly et al., 2015). Other studies exploited international students' life satisfaction in relation to functional support (Yusoff, 2012) or to their need for support, information, and feedback (Bektaş et al., 2009). Several studies (Atri et al., 2007; Dao et al., 2007; Meghani and Harvey, 2016; Nahidi et al., 2018; Sümer et al., 2008) underlined the positive effects of the various components of social support to reduce anxiety and depression, whereas other studies focused more on the supportive role of different types of social ties. Nabavi and Bijandi (2018) found that family and friends are the ones who mostly moderate the effect of loneliness. Other studies (Bektaş et al., 2009; Lin & Kingminghae, 2014; Mak et al., 2015; Poyrazli et al., 2004) underlined that international students engage mostly with compatriots or other international students and avoid meeting locals, thereby lowering the protective role of social ties.

Previous studies (Hofstede, 2001) have also pointed out how the culture of origin could determine a different attitude toward engaging in social relationships and building social ties, which could influence the well-being and perceived support. Students from collectivist cultures (e.g., Africa, Asia, and South America) are likely to define themselves as aspects of groups, to focus on the context rather than the content in communicating, to search for relationships with ingroup members, compared with students from individualist cultures (e.g., Europe and North America) (Triandis, 2001). Moreover, students from collectivistic countries show more lack of support and distress compared with other subgroups (Poyrazli et al., 2004; Sawir et al., 2008; Yeh & Inose, 2003).

A sparse number of studies has analyzed the influence of the length of stay on the perception of social support and well-being. O'Reilly et al. (2015) found that long-term students perceived more instrumental support and had more ties with locals than the short-term students; however, they did not perceive more well-being. Other authors (Aldawsari et al., 2018; Kim et al., 2019) also found greater stress and a lower autonomy in long-term international students.

PERSONAL CONSTRUCT PSYCHOLOGY

In the context of this complex research field, personal construct psychology (Kelly, 1955) can be a useful perspective to incorporate different aspects of social support and to combine them in a unique measure. According to this perspective, the constructs of dependency are the earliest regularities that we form in our life, linking our survival to caregivers who can satisfy our needs (Kelly, 1969). Kelly (1969) replaced the usual contraposition between autonomy and dependency with the concept of dispersion of dependency, which means that a person can refer to different resources to satisfy their needs (dispersed dependency) or can concentrate it in one or a few resources (undispersed dependency). In this context, a small number of resources and an undispersed dependency suggest a poor social network and social support: If a person relies on a few resources and these resources are not available when he or she needs help, then the person will not be able to receive any support (Walker, 1997, 2005). Previous studies have investigated the dispersion of dependency in several domains (Cipolletta et al., 2012, 2013, 2017, 2019a, 2019b; Cipolletta & Amicucci, 2017; Laso Ortiz et al., 2015; Powell, 2013; Smith et al., 1991; Talbot et al., 1991) and in relation to social network (Mitchell & Latchford, 2010; Stevens & Walker, 1996) and social support (Cipolletta et al., 2019a). However, so far, no study has investigated dependency in the international students and its relationship with social support and well-being.

The Dependency Grid (Fransella et al., 2004; Kelly, 1955) is a measure developed to assess the dispersion of dependency; it can be considered useful in the study of the role of social support for international students' well-being because it can provide information on how students differentiate among the resources and receive support from them. This knowledge can help in designing tailored intervention strategies.

STUDY AIM

The aim of the present study is to investigate the relationships between the dispersion of dependency, perceived social support, well-being, and distress in a sample of international students at the University of Padua (UniPD; Italy) who sought or did not seek professional help from the institutional Psychological Assistance Service (PAS). The following hypotheses informed the study:

1. International students referred to PAS have lower well-being, higher distress, and lower perceived support; they rely on fewer resources; and they have lower dependency than the international students who did not seek help from the service (non-PAS students).
2. International students who are short-term students at the university experience higher well-being and less distress than long-term students at the university do.
3. Students from collectivist cultures experience higher distress and a smaller support network than students from individualist cultures do.
4. Higher dispersion of dependency and perceived support correlates with lower distress and higher well-being.
5. A broader social network correlates with lower distress and higher perceived support.

MATERIALS AND METHODS

Participants

Between March 2019 and January 2020, we recruited 139 long- and short-term international students at University of Padova. The students were recruited through university classes and residences, Facebook groups, and PAS. The PAS provides free-of-charge counseling and psychotherapy to international students at the University of Padova. This psychological support aims at helping students facing a range of issues that affect their ordinary life or academic studies. International students can have information on this service from the university website and can also benefit from other services offered by the university, such as a psychiatric service, a welcome office, and master's degree students (called "buddies") who will welcome and support them during their stay.

The inclusion criteria for this study were: being a short-term or long-term international student at UniPD (bachelor, master, or doctorate); being in Italy for educational purposes. An a priori power analysis using G*Power3 (Faul et al., 2007) showed moderate correlations ($p = 0.3$) in a normal bivariate model with a significance of $\alpha = .05$ and found that a sample of 115 participants was necessary to achieve a power of .95.

The sample of 139 students with a mean age of 24.39 years (SD = 3.78) included 85 females and 54 males. From the total sample, 43 sought psychological help from PAS and 43 were short-term students (Erasmus), among whom there were 10 PAS and 33 non-PAS. On average, the participants had been in Italy for 1.4 years ($M = 15.60$ months; $SD = 22.15$) and had planned to stay 2.4 years ($M = 28.36$ months; $SD = 25.16$). Regarding their academic degree programs, 49 were undergraduate students, 75 were master's degree students, eight were PhD students, and seven students' programs were unknown. Regarding the division in individualist and collectivist cultures as defined in the literature (Hofstede, 2001; Triandis, 2001), 69 students came from individualist cultures and 67 from collectivist ones (thus we excluded three people from the analyses that considered the culture of origin because they had dual citizenship). The participants were mostly enrolled in psychology (35%), economics and political sciences (20%), agricultural sciences and veterinary medicine (11%), biology (9%), and engineering (6%) programs.

Data Collection

Besides sociodemographic details, data from the following four questionnaires were collected with the standardized English version.

The WHO-5 Well-being Index (WHO-5; World Health Organization [WHO], 1998) is a five-item, 6-point Likert scale instrument ranging from 0 (*at no time*) to 5 (*all the time*) that assesses the percentage of perceived mental well-being. The score is obtained by multiplying the sum of the responses by 4 (raw score). For raw scores less than 13 (poor perceived well-being), the WHO recommends checking for depression, but we did not proceed with this step because our research did not have a clinical purpose.

The Symptom Checklist 90-R (SCL-90-R; Derogatis, 1983) is a 90-item, 5-point Likert scale (ranging from *not at all* to *extremely*) that uses a self-report inventory to evaluate the severity of externalizing and internalizing distress symptoms along 10 dimensions: somatization (SOM), obsessive-compulsiveness (O-C), interpersonal sensitivity (I-S), depression (DEP), anxiety (ANX), hostility (HOS), phobic anxiety (PHOB), paranoid ideation (PAR), psychoticism (PSY), and sleep disturbance (SLEEP). The questionnaire also has three general indexes: Global Severity Index (GSI: intensity of general distress level), Positive Symptoms Total (PST: self-reported symptoms), and Positive Symptom Distress Index (PSDI: intensity of distress levels for recognized symptoms). The mean score for each scale (scores ≥ 1 are of interest) was calculated, except PST, whose range is 0–90.

The Dependency Grid (DG; Fransella et al., 2004; Kelly, 1955) is a list of 23 problematic situations (e.g., a time when the participant felt frightened, lonely, or was in poor health). Participants listed, in columns, the people who were important to them (the interviewer added "self" as the final resource in the grid) and indicated the person or the people (including themselves) to whom they would go for help in each situation.

The number of people listed indicates the potential breadth of the participants' social networks. The number of resources selected indicates those in whom the participants can effectively confide. The total number of crosses gives a measure of the total dependency. The uncertainty column index (UCI) shows the distribution of dependency among various resources. The uncertainty column coefficient (UCC) indicates the discrimination among resources. Proportions of 0–1 are used as measures of dispersion. High indexes ($\approx$1) and low coefficients ($\approx$0) indicate a dilated distribution (Walker, 1997) with reliance on all the resources for everything. Low indexes ($\approx$0) and high coefficients ($\approx$1) show a constricted distribution (Walker, 1997) with reliance on a few resources for everything. Finally, the dependency percentages corresponding to specific resources and themselves indicate whom the participants rely on for help.

The Multidimensional Scale of Perceived Social Support (MSPSS; Zimet et al., 1988) is a validated 12-item, 7-point Likert scale (1 = *very strongly disagree*, 7 = *very strongly agree*) that assesses perceived emotional support over three dimensions: friends (SSfr), family (SSfam), and significant others (SSso), with four items for each dimension. In addition, a global (SStot) score was obtained by calculating each scale's mean score (1–2.9 indicates poor support, 3–5 indicates moderate support, and 5.1–7 indicates high support).

For each instrument, the researcher emphasized that the questions did not have right or wrong answers, but rather depended on one's personal experience. Each participant completed the questionnaires in the order just cited without variation.

Data Analysis

We analyzed DGs with the Gridstat software and the whole data set with SPSS Statistics 25 and R, after first applying the Shapiro–Wilk normality test (finding a distribution that was not normal but that did not have severe violations) and calculating Cronbach's α coefficients for every instrument to assess the test's reliability. We carried out descriptive analyses and *t* tests paired with Bonferroni corrections to verify differences. To test the study hypotheses, we performed planned comparisons to verify the effects of PAS on well-being, distress (PSDI, PSI, and GSI), chosen resources, and total dependency. In addition, we performed comparisons to verify the effects of both length of stay (short- or long-term students) and culture of origin (collectivist or individualist) on distress (PSDI, PSI, and GSI) and perceived social support (SStot). We calculated exploratory Pearson (*r*) and Spearman (rho) correlations to explore the association between variables of interest. Finally, to investigate whether students could be grouped according to their dispersion of dependency, we grouped the perceived support and distress levels as well as data considering nine variables of interest (%well-being, GSI, PST, number of chosen resources, dependency on self, dependency on a significant other, UCI, UCC, and SStot) with a hierarchical cluster analysis (Ward method). Univariate ANOVA with Bonferroni post hoc correction was used to evaluate the degree to which the variables' indexes weighed on the cluster formations and differentiated a cluster from another. A chi-square test was subsequently applied in cases of distribution among the identified clusters to verify whether significant differences occurred due to sociodemographic variables (being a PAS client, gender, length of stay, and culture).

RESULTS

Cronbach's α proved that the instruments have good reliability for MSPSS (SStot: 0.88; SSfam: 0.86; SSfr and SSso: 0.84), WHO-5 (%well-being: 0.85), and SCL-90-R (PAR: 0.85; O-C: 0.87; I-S: 0.85; DEP: 0.90; ANX: 0.87; HOS, PHOB and PAR: 0.81; PSY: 0.79; and SLEEP: 0.72). Descriptive analysis showed that 46% of international students reported a WHO-5 raw score of less than 13, which indicates poor well-being and a need for further evaluation. For the SCL-90-R, the PSDI and GSI indexes had values higher than 1, which is considered of clinical interest. The mean number of resources indicated in the DG was 10.01 ($SD = 2.83$) with concepts, things, animals, groups, and activities specified as resources by 18 students. The DG also showed a high dispersion of dependency (UCI) but was mainly indiscriminate (UCC). Dependency on self was higher than the participants' dependency on their fathers was, $t(136) = 6.97, p < .001$, although it was not different from their dependency on their mothers, after correction, $t(136) = 2.41, p = .17$. However, dependency on a significant other (mostly a partner or a friend) was higher than their dependency on their mothers, $t(136) = 7.46, p < .001$, fathers, $t(136) = 13.19, p < .001$, and self, $t(136) = -3.76, p < .001$. SStot was generally high, with the scores being higher than 5. Nevertheless, SSos was higher than SSfam was, $t(138) = 2.43, p < .02$, whereas the other comparisons did not survive post hoc correction.

As illustrated in Table 1, planned comparisons showed that PAS clients generally had lower well-being, higher PST, and higher GSI compared with non-PAS clients. PAS clients also showed fewer "chosen" resources compared with non-PAS clients. Comparisons based on the length of stay showed that short-term students had lower distress scores (PSDI, PST, and GSI) and higher SStot scores compared with long-term students. Students from collectivist cultures showed higher PST and GSI and lower SStot compared with those from individualist countries.

Table 1: Planned Comparisons on the Variables of Interest. Only Significant Results Are Shown

Dependent variable	Independent variable	*M*	*SD*	*df*	*t*	*p*
% well-being	PAS	43.35	20.17	137	−3.52	0.001
	non-PAS	55.96	19.24			
PST	PAS	53.02	17.55	137	−3.07	0.003
	non-PAS	42.52	19.07			
PSDI	PAS	2.29	0.54	137	−5.35	<0.001
	non-PAS	1.78	0.51			

Dependent variable	Independent variable	M	SD	df	t	p
GSI	PAS	1.40	0.70	137	−4.38	<0.001
	non-PAS	0.90	0.59			
chosen res.	PAS	7.60	2.31	137	4.06	<0.001
	non-PAS	9.72	3.02			
PST	short-term	40.86	16.90	137	−2.04	0.04
	long-term	48.00	19.90			
PSDI	short-term	1.76	0.48	137	−2.64	0.01
	long-term	2.03	0.59			
GSI	short-term	0.85	0.57	137	−2.48	0.01
	long-term	1.15	0.68			
SStot	short-term	5.90	0.80	137	2.00	0.049
	long-term	5.55	1.00			
PST	coll	50.47	18.48	134	3.22	0.002
	ind	40.31	18.35			
GSI	coll	1.19	0.67	134	2.62	0.001
	ind	0.90	0.63			
SStot	coll	5.45	1.03	134	−2.82	0.006
	ind	5.89	0.81			

Note: coll: collectivist; ind: individualist; PAS: clients who seek help at the Psychological Assistance Service; non-PAS: clients who did not seek help at the Psychological Assistance Service.

Pearson correlational analysis (Table 2) showed that well-being had moderate negative correlations with distress (GSI, PST, and PSDI) and positive correlations with social support measures (SSso, SStot, SSfam, and SSfr). In addition, %well-being had a weak positive correlation with the dispersion of dependency (UCI) and a negative correlation with UCC. DG measures (i.e., number of dependencies, chosen resources, UCI, and concentration of dependencies, which is a part of the number of indicated resources and UCC) had significant positive correlations with MSPSS measures (SSso, SSfam, SSfr, and SStot) and negative correlations with distress indexes (GSI, PST, and PSDI). Both UCI and UCC had significant positive and negative correlations with distress measures (GSI, PST, and PSDI), but they had weaker correlations than some dependency indexes had (i.e., number of chosen resources, total number of dependencies, and the concentration of dependencies). SCL-90-R measures (GSI, PST, and PSDI) had significant negative correlations (mostly moderate) with MSPSS indexes.

Table 2: Pearson Correlations Between Dependency Grid Measures (DG), Perceived Support (MSPSS), Well-being (WHO-5), and Distress (SCL-90-R)

		MSPSS				WHO-5	SCL-90-R		
	Dependent variable	SSso	SSfam	SSfr	SStot	% well-being	GSI	PST	PSDI
WHO-5	% well-being	-	-	-	-	-	−.56***	−.47***	−.54***
DG	TOT dependency	.41***	.27***	.37***	.44***	.13	−.17*	−.28***	−.15
	%dependency	.45***	.29***	.40***	.47***	.12	−.09	−.19**	−.07
	indicated res.	.09	.11	.08	.12	.09	−.17*	−.18*	−.16
	chosen res.	.20*	.22**	.15	.25**	.17	−.27***	−.28 ***	−.25**
	UCI	.31***	.46**	.18*	.42***	.21*	−.24**	−.22**	−.20*
	UCC	−.48***	−.29**	−.45***	−.50**	−.19*	.17*	.20*	.16
MSPSS	SSso	-	-	-	-	.29***	−.38***	−.33***	−.36***
	SSfam	-	-	-	-	.34***	−.33***	−.28***	−.27***
	SSfr	-	-	-	-	.18*	−.37***	−.35***	−.33***
	SStot	-	-	-	-	.35***	−.45***	−.40***	−.40***

** p<.05 ** p≤.01 ***p≤.001*

Lastly, the cluster analysis highlighted a distribution in three clusters (Figure 1) of 31, 90, and 17 students, respectively, who, according to univariate ANOVA results, differed more for %well-being, $F(2, 135) = 28.71$, $p < .001$, GSI, $F(2, 135) = 101.41, p < .001$, PST, $F(2, 135) = 59.26, p < .001$, number of chosen resources, $F(2, 135) = 18.46, p < .001$, UCI, $F(2, 135) = 41.49, p < .001$, UCC, $F(2, 135) = 44.02; p < .001$, dependency on a significant other, $F(2, 135) = 11.46$, $p < .001$, dependency on self, $F(2, 135) = 4.28, p = .016$, and SStot, $F(2, 135) = 46.70, p < .001$.

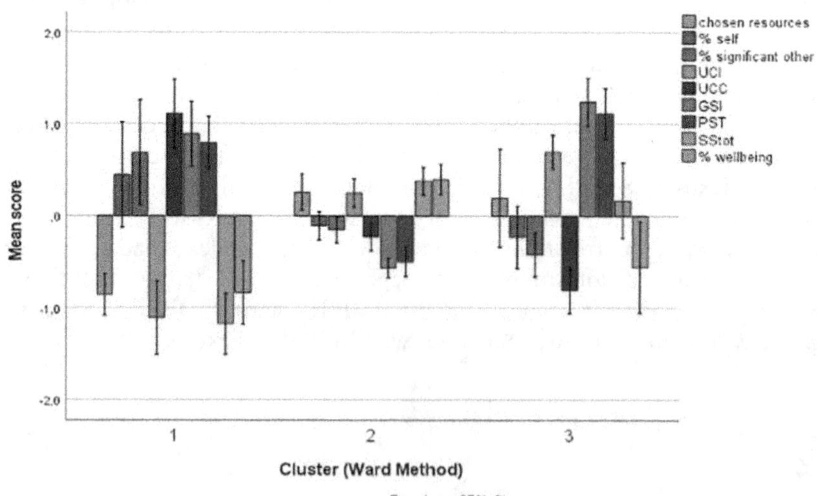

Figure 1: Distribution in the Three Clusters of the Standardized Variables Derived from WHO-5, SCL-90-R, DG, and MSPSS.

Bonferroni post hoc analysis (Table 3) showed that Cluster 1, compared with the other two clusters, had a smaller support network, lower UCI, and higher UCC, with the dependency more concentrated on a significant other and self, accompanied by lower perceived social support. At the same time, Cluster 1 reported lower well-being than Cluster 3 did and higher distress (GSI and PST) than Cluster 2 did. Clusters 2 and 3 did not significantly differ for the support network's breadth, reliance on self, reliance on a significant other, and UCI. Students in Cluster 2 differed from those in Cluster 3 because they had higher UCC and lower distress (GSI and PST) but had lower well-being. Regarding the distribution of participants' characteristics among clusters, chi-square analysis showed that PAS students, X^2 (2, 138) = 10.63, p = 0.005, were mostly distributed in Cluster 1 (48.4%) and Cluster 3 (47.1%), compared with Cluster 2 (21.1%), and that students in Cluster 2 were more often short-term students (37.38%) than students in Clusters 1 and 3 (16.1% and 17.6%, respectively), X^2(2, 138) = 6.60, p = 0.037.

Table 3: Bonferroni Post Hoc Analysis on the Standardized Variables Constituting the Three Clusters. Only Significant Comparisons Are Reported

Dependent variable	Cluster	M	SD	I-J	Std error	95% CI Lower limit	Upper limit	p
% well-being	1	−0.84	0.94	−1.23	0.18	−1.66	−0.81	<.001
	3	0.40	0.79					
PST	1	0.80	0.76	1.30	0.15	0.91	1.70	<.001
	2	−0.50	0.75					
GSI	1	0.89	0.96	1.48	0.13	1.14	1.77	<.001
	2	−0.57	0.49					
Chosen res.	1	−0.86	0.62	−1.11	0.19	−1.57	−0.67	<.001
	2	0.26	0.94					
% self	1	0.45	1.56	0.57	0.20	0.06	1.05	=.021
	2	−0.11	0.74					
% signif. Other	1	0.69	1.56	0.84	0.19	0.37	1.31	<.001
	2	−0.16	0.67					
UCI	1	−1.11	1.09	−1.36	0.17	−1.76	−0.96	<.001
	2	0.25	0.73					
UCC	1	1.11	1.02	1.34	0.16	0.95	1.74	<.001
	2	−0.23	0.73					
SStot	1	−1.18	0.90	−1.56	0.16	−1.98	−1.16	<.001

Dependent variable	Cluster	M	SD	I-J	Std error	95% CI Lower limit	Upper limit	*p*
	2	0.38	0.72					
Chosen res.	1	−0.86	0.62	1.12	0.19	−1.70	−0.40	<.001
	3	0.19	1.04					
% signif. Other	1	0.69	1.56	1.11	0.28	0.43	1.79	<.001
	3	−0.43	0.46					
UCI	1	−1.11	1.09	−1.81	0.24	−2.39	−1.23	<.001
	3	0.70	0.36					
UCC	1	1.11	1.02	1.92	0.24	1.34	2.49	<.001
	3	−0.81	0.49					
SStot	1	−1.18	0.903	−1.34	0.23	−1.91	−0.77	<.001
	3	0.17	0.804					
% well-being	2	0.40	0.79	0.96	0.22	0.41	1.50	<.001
	3	−0.56	0.97					
PST	2	−0.50	0.75	−1.62	0.19	− 2.08	−1.15	<.001
	3	1.11	0.53					
GSI	2	−0.57	0.49	−1.81	0.17	−2.21	−1.41	<.001
	3	1.24	0.51					
UCC	2	−0.23	0.734	0.575	0.21	0.07	1.08	=.019
	3	−0.81	0.49					

DISCUSSION

The aim of this study was to investigate international students' well-being in relation to their perceptions of social support and differentiation of resources (dispersion of dependency). Results showed that international students perceived their well-being as poor compared with the general population, confirming that they are potentially highly vulnerable to developing clinical psychological distress (Mori, 2000). Moreover, international students relied more often on another significant person (mostly a partner or a friend), rather than on their mothers, fathers, or selves and did not discriminate among resources. This result suggests that family in general might be less often considered when seeking help and support, probably because of their physical distance, as well as suggesting that international students indiscriminately seek help from one person or another.

Our expectation that seeking professional psychological help is associated with less perceived support and well-being, poor dispersion of dependency, and higher distress was confirmed. PAS clients showed lower well-being, higher distress, and fewer resources compared with non-PAS clients. Results showed that students coming from collectivist cultures (i.e., Asia, Africa, or South America; for example, students coming from Vietnam, Iran, Venezuela) into an individualist one (i.e., Italy) generally perceived higher psychological distress and less perceived support than those coming from individualist cultures (i.e., Europe and North America) did. This finding is in line with previous literature and is likely due to greater cross-cultural differences (Atri et al., 2007; Bektaş et al., 2009; Dao et al., 2007; Jou & Fukada, 1997; Meghani & Harvey, 2016; Nahidi et al., 2018; Zhang & Goodson, 2011). In relation to the length of stay, short-term students experienced lower distress and higher social support than long-term students did, and they had a greater ability to disperse their dependency. These results expand the current literature (O'Reilly et al., 2015) and are in line with previous findings that pointed out that long-term students show higher stress (Kim et al., 2019). This could be due to a greater difficulty in adapting to a new environment (such as acculturation difficulties) and to the physical distance from their country of origin and support network when the situation lasts longer and/or the perspective is that it will last longer (Aldawsari et al., 2018; Kim et al., 2019). However, further studies should investigate whether this result might be due to different psychological profiles of those who decide to move to another country for shorter rather than longer periods or whether those who leave for longer periods already experience higher levels of distress before leaving.

This study's hypotheses about the relationships between the dispersion of dependency, the breadth of network and social support, psychological distress, and well-being were confirmed. Specifically, greater well-being and lower distress were associated with higher perceived social support (mostly globally and from the family) and higher dispersion of dependency. In line with previous literature (Cipolletta et al., 2019a; Laso Ortiz et al. 2015; Powell, 2013; Talbot et al. 1991), DG measures confirmed their relationship with social support and distress measures and suggested that when someone has a higher number of resources and a higher dispersion of dependency, they perceive greater social support and less distress. Results also confirmed the association between social support and well-being pointed out by previous studies (Atri et al., 2007; Nahidi et al., 2018; Sümer et al., 2008). Although family support was lower than the support of significant others was and had weaker relationships with distress and dispersion than the other kinds of support had, it showed a strong relationship with well-being, suggesting that this could still be an important aspect to consider in psychological interventions for international students.

Finally, the cluster analysis confirmed the expected differentiation of participants based on their dispersion of dependency, levels of perceived support, distress, and well-being. The students grouped in the first cluster were mostly students who sought help from the psychological service, with a lower number of resources, a concentration of the dependencies on themselves and on a significant other, low social support, lower levels of well-being, and higher levels of distress. The second cluster comprised mostly short-term students who did not seek help from the psychological service and who showed a higher number of resources with a higher discrimination among them, higher levels of well-being, and lower levels of distress. Finally, the third group was mainly composed by students who sought help from the psychological service, who had a high dispersion of dependency but were mainly undifferentiated, that is, they tended to use the resources without discrimination. The third group showed lower well-being and higher levels of distress than the second group. These results suggest that the distribution of dependency may make a difference in well-being: Those with undispersed dependencies, both constricted (Cluster 1) and dilated (Cluster 3), perceived more distress and less well-being than those who mostly dispersed their dependency and differentiated their resources (Cluster 2) did. The fact that short-term and non-PAS students were mostly grouped in Cluster 2 suggests that these students distributed their dependency more on different resources than long-term students did, and that this behavior probably enabled them to maintain their well-being and not ask for professional support.

Limitations and Future Directions

A limitation of our study is that it is cross-sectional; thus, over a period of time, we cannot predict the degree to which social support and dispersion of dependency can be beneficial to distress and well-being. Future studies could address this issue by investigating students' distress before and after the therapeutic intervention, with follow-up meetings after a defined period. In addition, we did not consider whether students sought professional psychological help externally from PAS, whether students had ever relied on psychological support services, or whether they had ever had experiences abroad; all such information could be helpful in drawing students' profiles and in predicting their well-being. Future studies could also investigate whether the physical proximity of the people identified as "significant others" can have an impact on the levels of students' well-being. Also, the social support network of international students could be potentiated by planning specific programs according to the students' length of stay.

CONCLUSIONS

The results of this study showed that the breadth of social networks, the dispersion of dependency, and perceived support identify the associated constructs and that these are useful to understand international students' well-being. Moreover, DG proved to be a useful tool to integrate the information derived by a standardized scale of social support and to provide additional information on students' social ties by differentiating among resources to whom students refer for help. Overall, the results of this study highlight how different aspects such as length of stay, culture of origin, and the search for professional help play a fundamental role in international students' well-being.

All these aspects should be taken into consideration while planning personalized intervention strategies. Psychological interventions should be aimed at promoting well-being by forming groups to share acculturation/enculturation strategies, by reducing the potential cultural stigma associated with seeking psychological help, by guaranteeing counseling services that are accessible and sensible to cultural differences, particularly for students from collectivist cultures, and by encouraging international students to explore the territory and make new social ties.

REFERENCES

Aldawsari, N. F., Adams, K. S., Grimes, L. E., & Kohn, S. (2018). The effects of cross-cultural competence and social support on international students' psychological adjustment: Autonomy and environmental mastery. *Journal of International Students, 8*(2), 901–924. https://doi.org/10.32674/jis.v8i2.120

Ambrosio, L., Portillo, M. C., Rodriguez - Blazquez, C., Rojo, J. M., Martinez - Martin, P., & EC-PC Validation Group (2019). Influencing factors when living with Parkinson' s disease: A cross - sectional study. *Journal of Clinical Nursing, 28*(17–18), 3168–3176. https://doi.org/10.1111/jocn.14868

Atri, A., Sharma, M., & Cottrell, R. (2007). Role of social support, hardiness, and acculturation as predictors of mental health among international students of Asian Indian origin. *International Quarterly of Community Health Education, 27*(1), 59–73. https://doi.org/10.2190/IQ.27.1.e

Barrera, M. (1986). Distinctions between social support concepts, measures, and models. *American Journal of Community Psychology, 14*(4), 413–445. https://doi.org/10.1007/bf00922627

Bektaş, Y., Demir, A., & Bowden, R. (2009). Psychological adaptation of Turkish students at U.S. campuses. *International Journal for the Advancement of Counselling, 31*(2), 130–143. https://doi.org/10.1007/s10447-009-9073-5

Berger, R., Safdar, S., Spieß, E., Bekk, M., & Font, A. (2018). Acculturation of Erasmus students: Using the multidimensional individual difference acculturation model framework. *International Journal of Psychology, 54*(6), 739–749. https://doi.org/10.1002/ijop.12526

Berkman, L. F., Leo-Summers, L., & Horwitz, R. I. (1992). Emotional support and survival after myocardial infarction. *Annals of Internal Medicine, 117*(12), 1003–1009. https://doi.org/10.7326/0003-4819-117-12-1003

Brisset, C., Safdar, S., Lewis, J. R., & Sabatier, C. (2010). Psychological and sociocultural adaptation of university students in France: The case of Vietnamese international students. *International Journal of Intercultural Relations, 34*(4), 413–426. https://doi.org/10.1016/j.ijintrel.2010.02.009

Brummett, B. H., Barefoot, J. C., Siegler, I. C., Clapp-Channing, N. E., Lytle, B. L., Bosworth, H. B., Williams, R. B., & Mark, D. B. (2001). Characteristics of socially isolated patients with coronary artery disease who are at elevated risk for mortality. *Psychosomatic Medicine, 63*(2), 267–272. https://doi.org/10.1097/00006842-200103000-00010

Brunsting, N. C., Zachry, C., Liu, J., Bryant, R., Fang, X., Wu, S., & Luo, Z. (2019). Sources of perceived social support, social-emotional experiences, and psychological well-being of international students. *The Journal of Experimental Education,* 1–17. https://doi.org/10.1080/00220973. 2019.1639598

Cipolletta, S., & Amicucci, L. (2017). Illness trajectories in patients suffering from leg ulcers: A qualitative study. *Journal of Health Psychology, 22*(7), 932–942. https://doi.org/10.1177/13591053315619224

Cipolletta, S., Beccarello, A., & Galan, A. (2012). A psychological perspective of eye floaters. *Qualitative Health Research, 22*(11), 1547–1558. https://doi.org/10.1177/1049732312456604

Cipolletta, S., Entilli, L., Nucci, M., Feltrin, A., Germani, G., Cillo, U., & Volpe, B. (2019a). Psychosocial support in liver transplantation: A dyadic study with patients and their family caregivers. *Frontiers in Psychology, 10.* https://doi.org/10.3389/fpsyg.2019.02304

Cipolletta, S., Gammino, G. R., & Palmieri, A. (2017). Illness trajectories in patients with amyotrophic lateral sclerosis: How illness progression is related to life narratives and interpersonal relationships. *Journal of Clinical Nursing, 26*(23–24), 5033–5043. https://doi.org/10.1111/jocn.14003

Cipolletta, S., Giudici, L., Punzi, L., Galozzi, P., & Sfriso, P. (2019b) Health-related quality of life and its association with illness perception, coping strategies and the distribution of dependency in autoinflammatory diseases. *Clinical and Experimental Rheumatology, 37*(6), 156–157 https://www.ncbi.nlm.nih.gov/pubmed/31025921

Cipolletta, S., Shams, M., Tonello, F., & Pruneddu, A. (2013). Caregivers of patients with cancer: Anxiety, depression and distribution of dependency. *Psycho-Oncology, 22*(1), 133–139. https://doi.org/10.1002/pon.2081

Cohen, S. (1988). Psychosocial models of the role of social support in the etiology of physical disease. *Health Psychology, 7*(3), 269–297. https://doi.org/10.1037/0278-6133.7.3.269

Cohen, S., & Syme, S. L. (1985). Issues in the study and application of social support. In S. Cohen & S. L. Syme (Eds.), *Social support and health* (pp. 3–22). Academic Press.

Cohen, S., & Wills, T. A. (1985). Stress, social support, and the buffering hypothesis. *Psychological Bulletin, 98*(2), 310–357. https://doi.org/10.1037/0033-2909.98.2.310

Dao, T. K., Lee, D., & Chang, H. L. (2007). Acculturation level, perceived English fluency, perceived social support level, and depression among Taiwanese international students. *College Student Journal, 41*(2), 287–295.

Derogatis, L. R. (1983). *SCL-90-R: Administration, scoring & procedures manual- II.* (2nd ed.). Clinical Psychometric Research.

Faul, F., Erdfelder, E., Lang, A. G., & Buchner, A. (2007). G* Power 3: A flexible statistical power analysis program for the social, behavioral, and biomedical sciences. *Behavior Research Methods, 39*(2), 175–191. https://doi.org/10.3758/bf03193146

Fatima, S., & Jibeen, T. (2019). Interplay of self-efficacy and social support in predicting quality of life in cardiovascular patients in Pakistan. *Community Mental Health Journal, 55*(5), 855–864. https://doi.org/10.1007/s10597-018-0361-6

Fransella, F., Bell, R., & Bannister, D. (2004). *A manual for repertory grid technique* (2nd ed.). John Wiley & Sons.

Hofstede, G. (2001). *Culture's consequences: Comparing values, behaviors, institutions and organizations across nations*. Sage publications.

Horsten, M., Mittleman, M. A., Wamala, S. P., Schenck-Gustafsson, K., & Orth-Gomer, K. (2000). Depressive symptoms and lack of social integration in relation to prognosis of CHD in middle-aged women. The Stockholm female coronary risk study. *European Heart Journal, 21*(13), 1072–1080. https://doi.org/10.1053/euhj.1999.2012

Institute of International Education (2020). International students enrollment trends, 1948/49–2019/2020). Open doors report on international students educational exchange. http://www.opendoorsdata.org

Jou, Y. H., & Fukada, H. (1997). Stress and social support in mental and physical health of Chinese students in Japan. *Psychological Reports, 81*(3), 1303–1312. https://doi.org/10.2466/pr0.1997.81.3f.1303

Kelly, G. A. (1955). *The psychology of personal constructs. vol. 1. A theory of personality. vol. 2. Clinical diagnosis and psychotherapy.* Norton & Company.

Kelly, G. A. (1969). In whom confide: On whom depend for what. In B. Maher (Ed.), *Clinical psychology and personality: The selected papers of George Kelly* (pp. 189–206). John Wiley & Sons.

Kagee, A., Roomaney, R., & Knoll, N. (2018). Psychosocial predictors of distress and depression among South African breast cancer patients. *Psycho - oncology, 27*(3), 908–914. https://doi.org/10.1002/pon.4589

Kim, Y. K., Maleku, A., Lemieux, C. M., Du, X., & Chen, Z. (2019). Behavioral health risk and resilience among international students in the United States: A study of socio-demographic differences. *Journal of International Students, 9*(1), 282–305. https://doi.org/10.32674/jis.v9i1.264

Kurtović, A., & Ivančić, H. (2019). Predictors of depression and life satisfaction in visually impaired people. *Disability and Rehabilitation, 41*(9), 1012–1023. https://doi.org/10.1080/09638288.2017.1417497

Laso Ortiz, E., Hernández González, E., & Guerra Hernández, M. (2015). The dispersion of dependency grids: A method for estimating the social support. *Quadernos de Psicologia, 17*(1), 83–94. https://doi.org/10.5565/rev/qpsicologia.1293

Lee, J., Koeske, G. F., & Sales, E. (2004). Social support buffering of acculturative stress: A study of mental health symptoms among Korean international students. *International Journal of Intercultural Relations, 28*(5), 399–414. https://doi.org/10.1016/j.ijintrel.2004.08.005

Lin, Y., & Kingminghae, W. (2014). Social support and loneliness of Chinese international students in Thailand. *Journal of Population and Social Studies, 22*(2), 141–157. https://doi.org/10.14456/jpss.2014.10

Mak, A. S., Bodycott, P., & Ramburuth, P. (2015). Beyond host language proficiency: Coping Resources Predicting International Students' Satisfaction. *Journal of Studies in International Education, 19*(5), 460–475. https://doi.org/10.1177/1028315315587109

Meghani, D. T., & Harvey, E. A. (2016). Asian Indian international students' trajectories of depression, acculturation, and enculturation. *Asian American Journal of Psychology, 7*(1), 1–14. https://doi.org/10.1037/aap0000034

Mitchell, J., & Latchford, G. (2010). Prisoner perspectives on mental health problems and help-seeking. *Journal of Forensic Psychiatry & Psychology, 21*(5), 773–788. https://doi.org/10.1080/14789949.2010.488697

Mori, S. C. (2000). Addressing the mental health concerns of international students. *Journal of Counseling & Development, 78*(2), 137–144. https://doi.org/10.1002/j.1556-6676.2000.tb02571.x

Nabavi, R. T., & Bijandi, M. S. (2018). An investigation of predictors of life satisfaction among overseas Iranian undergraduate students. *Educational Process: International Journal, 7*(1), 74–93. https://doi.org/10.22521/edupij.2018.71.6

Nahidi, S., Blignault, I., Hayen, A., & Razee, H. (2018). Psychological distress in Iranian international students at an Australian university. *Journal of Immigrant and Minority Health, 20*(3), 651–657. https://doi.org/10.1007/s10903-017-0590-8

Naldi, C. (2020, January). Studenti stranieri nel Sistema di Istruzione Superiore in Italia (Anno Accademico 2018–2019). Uni-Italia. http://www.uni-italia.it/en/analysis-and-figures

O'Reilly, A., Hickey, T., & Ryan, D. (2015). The experiences of American international students in a large Irish University. *Journal of International Students, 5*(1), 86–98. https://doi.org/10.32674/jis.v5i1.445

O'Reilly, A., Ryan, D., & Hickey, T. (2010). The psychological well-being and sociocultural adaptation of short-term international students in Ireland. *Journal of College Student Development, 51*(5), 584–598. https://doi.org/10.1353/csd.2010.0011

Oxman, T. E., Berkman, L. F., Kasl, S., Freeman Jr, D., H., & Barrett, J. (1992). Social support and depressive symptoms in the elderly. *American Journal of Epidemiology, 135*(4), 356–368. https://doi.org/10.1093/oxfordjournals.aje.a116297

Powell, M. (2013). *The use of an adapted version of the dependency grid to investigate social support for young people in care* [Doctoral dissertation]. https://www.research.manchester.ac.uk/portal/en/theses/search.html

Poyrazli, S., Kavanaugh, P. R., Baker, A., & Al-Timimi, N. (2004). Social support and demographic correlates of Acculturative stress in international students. *Journal of College Counseling, 7*(1), 73–82. https://doi.org/10.1002/j.2161-1882.2004.tb00261.x

Ra, Y., & Trusty, J. (2017). Impact of social support and coping on acculturation and Acculturative stress of East Asian international students. *Journal of Multicultural Counseling and Development, 45*(4), 276–291. https://doi.org/10.1002/jmcd.12078

Rodriguez, M. S., & Cohen, S. (1998). Social support. In H. S. Friedman (Ed.), *Encyclopedia of mental health* (pp. 535–544). Academic Press.

Sarason, I. G., & Sarason, B. R. (2009). Social support: Mapping the construct. *Journal of Social and Personal Relationships, 26*(1), 113–120. https://doi.org/10.1177/0265407509105526

Sawir, E., Marginson, S., Deumert, A., Nyland, C., & Ramia, G. (2008). Loneliness and international students: An Australian study. *Journal of Studies in International Education, 12*(2), 148–180. https://doi.org/10.1177/1028315307299699

Smith, J. E., Stefan, C., Kovaleski, M., & Johnson, G. (1991). Recidivism and dependency in a psychiatric population: An investigation with Kelly's dependency grid. *International Journal of Personal Construct Psychology, 4*(2), 157–173. https://doi.org/10.1080/08936039108404770

Stevens, C. D., & Walker, B. M. (1996). How residential college students adjust socially and emotionally to first year University. *Higher Education Research & Development, 15*(2), 201–221. https://doi.org/10.1080/0729436960150206

Sümer, S., Poyrazli, S., & Grahame, K. (2008). Predictors of depression and anxiety among international students. *Journal of Counseling & Development, 86*(4), 429–437. https://doi.org/10.1002/j.1556-6678.2008.tb00531.x

Swanbrow Becker, M. A., Dong, S., Kronholz, J., & Brownson, C. (2018). Relationships between stress and psychosocial factors with sources of help-seeking among international students. *Journal of International Students, 8*(4). https://doi.org/10.32674/jis.v8i4.222

Talbot, R., Cooper, C. L., & Ellis, B. (1991). Uses of the dependency grid for investigating social support in stressful situations. *Stress Medicine, 7*(3), 171–180. https://doi.org/10.1002/smi.2460070308

Thompson, T., Pérez, M., Kreuter, M., Margenthaler, J., Colditz, G., & Jeffe, D. B. (2017). Perceived social support in African American breast cancer patients: Predictors and effects. *Social Science & Medicine, 192*, 134–142. https://doi.org/10.1016/j.socscimed.2017.09.035

Triandis, H. C. (2001). Individualism - collectivism and personality. *Journal of Personality, 69*(6), 907–924. https://doi.org/10.1111/1467-6494.696169

Uchino, B. N. (2006). Social support and health: A review of physiological processes potentially underlying links to disease outcomes. *Journal of Behavioral Medicine, 29*(4), 377–387. https://doi.org/10.1007/s10865-006-9056-5

The United Nations Educational, Scientific and Cultural Organization Institute of Statistics. (2020, February 25). *International (or internationally mobile) students.* http://uis.unesco.org/en/glossary-term/international-or-internationally-mobile-students

Walker, B. M. (1997). Shaking the kaleidoscope: Dispersion of dependency and its relationships. In G. J. Neimeyer & R. A. Neimeyer (Eds.), *Advances in personal construct psychology* (pp. 63–97). JAI Press.

Walker, B. M. (2005). Making sense of dependency. In F. Fransella (Ed.), *The essential practitioner's handbook of personal construct psychology* (pp. 78–86). John Wiley & Sons.

Wang, H. X., Mittleman, M. A., & Orth-Gomer, K. (2005). Influence of social support on progression of coronary artery disease in women. *Social Science & Medicine, 60*(3), 599–607. https://doi.org/10.1016/j.socscimed.2004.05.021

World Health Organization. (1998, February). *Wellbeing measures in primary health care. The Depcare Project.* https://www.euro. who.int/__data/assets/pdf_file/0016/130750/E60246.pdf

Yeh, C. J., & Inose, M. (2003). International students' reported English fluency, social support satisfaction, and social connectedness as predictors of acculturative stress. *Counselling Psychology Quarterly, 16*(1), 15–28. https://doi.org/10.1080/0951507031000114058

Yusoff, Y. M. (2012). Self-efficacy, perceived social support, and psychological adjustment in international undergraduate students in a public higher education institution in Malaysia. *Journal of Studies in International Education, 16*(4), 353–371. https://doi.org/10.1177/1028315311408914

Zhang, J., & Goodson, P. (2011). Predictors of international students' psychosocial adjustment to life in the United States: A systematic review. *International Journal of Intercultural Relations, 35*(2), 139–162. https://doi.org/10.1016/j.ijintrel.2010.11.011

Zimet, G. D., Dahlem, N. W., Zimet, S. G., & Farley, G. K. (1988). The multidimensional scale of perceived social support. *Journal of Personality Assessment, 52*(1), 30–41. https://doi.org/10.1207/s15327752jpa5201_2

SABRINA CIPOLLETTA, Ph.D., is an associate professor in the Department of General Psychology at the University of Padua, Italy. She is the director of PsyMed, a research laboratory of psychology in the medical field, and of a clinical service for international students. She teaches Social Psychology and Health and is the head of the International Bachelor Degree program in Psychological Science. Her research interests are in the field of health psychology and interpersonal relationships. Email: sabrina.cipolletta@unipd.it

ARIANNA MERCURIO, M.Sc., graduated in Clinical Dynamic Psychology at the University of Padua, Italy, in 2020. She is currently attending a first-level master's program in Orientation and Placement at the University of Rome 3, Italy. Her research interests are in the field of social support and personal constructs psychology. Email: arianna.mercurio@yahoo.it

RACHELE PEZZETTA, Ph.D., is a postdoctoral researcher at the San Camillo Hospital IRCCS in Venice. She obtained her PhD in Cognitive, Social and Affective Neuroscience at La Sapienza University in Rome. Her research interests are in the field of cognitive and affective psychology, and clinical neuroscience. She is currently being trained on personal constructs psychology at the School of Psychotherapy. Email: rachele.pezzetta@gmail.com

---

Research Article

© *Journal of International Students*
Volume 12, Issue 3 (2022), pp. 633-653
ISSN: 2162-3104 (Print), 2166-3750 (Online)
doi: 10.32674/jis.v12i3.3444
ojed.org/jis

International Counseling Students' Practicum Experience in a Counseling Program in the United States: A Phenomenological Study

Yiying Xiong[1]
Matthew W. Bonner
Sterling P. Travis
Feng Xing
Qingyun Zhang
*School of Education, Department of
Counseling and Educational Studies,
Johns Hopkins University, USA*

ABSTRACT

Limited attention has been given to international counseling students (ICSs) enrolled in U.S. counseling programs. This phenomenological study examines the lived experiences of six ICSs in a U.S. counseling program regarding the factors that impacted their practicum experience. The study identifies three themes: the learning and growth process, positive impacting factors, and negative impacting factors. It also provides stakeholder recommendations.

Keywords: international counseling students, practicum experience, supervision

---

[1] Correspondence regarding this article should be addressed to Yiying Xiong, Department of Counseling and Educational Studies, Johns Hopkins School of Education, 2800 N Charles Street, Baltimore, MD, 21030.

Given the declining number of college-aged American students and the institutional pressure of increasing tuition revenue, universities in the United States have increased the enrollment of international students during the recent two decades (Cantwell, 2015; Hegarty, 2014). In 2018, there were more than 1 million international students in the United States, which increased more than 60% compared with 10 years prior (Institution of International Education [IIE], 2019). Similarly, globalization trends in helping professions such as counseling and psychology and the emphasis on the diversity of student bodies have led to an increase in the number of international students in counseling-related programs (Akkurt et al., 2018; McKinley, 2019). For example, counseling programs accredited by the Council for Accreditation of Counseling and Related Educational Programs (CACREP) reported that 41% of accredited programs included international students (Ng, 2006). In 2016, CACREP reported 459 international students enrolled in CACREP accredited programs, comprising 1% of all students enrolled in those programs.

However, compared with domestic students, international counseling students (ICSs) reported unique difficulties related to their in-class learning, cross-cultural conflicts that negatively impacted their confidence, and problems in the field experience (Goh et al., 2014). Moreover, because of the differences in culture, language, and counseling systems, ICSs are concerned about transferring what they learned in the United States to their home countries (Goh et al., 2014; Lau & Ng, 2012).

Despite facing significant challenges, limited attention has been given to ICSs, including their field experience (Asempapa, 2019; Ng, 2006; Park et al., 2017). Counseling programs require students to take field experience courses to receive supervision while working with real clients (Council for Accreditation of Counseling and Related Educational Programs [CACREP], 2016). Programs that admit ICSs have the ethical and professional responsibility to respond to their unique needs (Smith & Ng, 2009). Addressing the needs of ICSs is important, as they may return to their home countries on graduation and promote the internationalization of the counseling profession (Reid & Dixon, 2012). This study, therefore, explores the lived experience of ICSs in field experience.

INTERNATIONAL COUNSELING STUDENTS' FIELD EXPERIENCES

Counseling-related programs emphasize adapting and changing to fit the needs of their students (Reid & Dixon, 2012). For example, CACREP (2016) states that programs "make continuous and systematic efforts to attract, enroll, and retain a diverse group of students and to create and support an inclusive learning community" (p. 7). However, research in counselor education and supervision about counseling students has focused on American racial/ethnic minorities but neglected ICSs' educational needs (Dao et al., 2007; Ng, 2006). With the increasing number of ICSs, counseling programs and counselor educators are faced with the challenges of perceiving a better understanding of the specialized training and unique needs of these students (Reid & Dixon, 2012).

ICSs usually come to the United States to further their education, as they may believe that counseling and psychology in the United States is at the world-leading level (QS top universities, 2020). Nevertheless, ICSs reported unique challenges related to their field experience (Liu, 2014; Park et al., 2017; Wedding et al., 2009). During field experience, they are required to counsel clients from different cultural backgrounds, and the majority of those clients may come from an American culture that is different from their own. Because of the differences, some common problems that ICSs reported were (a) language barriers, (b) a lack of understanding of the nuances of American culture and counseling systems, (c) discrimination from clients and others, and (d) cultural conflicts that negatively impacted their performance in field experience (Liu, 2014; Park et al., 2017; Wedding et al., 2009). They may experience discomfort using specific theories that conflict with their cultural practices (Wedding et al., 2009). For example, ICSs from East Asia may experience countertransference issues such as anxiety in working with emotions and being direct with clients (Liu, 2014). ICSs also reported fears related to managing relationships with coworkers, clients, and supervisors and finding appropriate interventions due to cultural differences (Park et al., 2017). In addition, ICSs have challenges adjusting to the U.S. counseling and school systems as they are vastly different from those in their home countries (Xiong et al., 2021). Moreover, some ICSs reported dissatisfaction with their programs because of perfunctory supervision, insufficient information, and difficulties in securing required field experience sites (Park et al., 2017).

To cope with the challenges, ICSs used strategies such as seeking support, communicating cultural issues with clients, improving language skills, utilizing cultural assets, restructuring cognition, avoidance, and practicing self-care (Liu, 2014). Faculty in counseling-related programs could help ICSs by enhancing their awareness of those students' experiences, such as their cultural adjustment process (Koyama, 2010). Accordingly, they can accommodate the needs of students by listening to them, respecting and recognizing their strengths and cultures, and addressing their difficulties in culturally sensitive ways (Koyama, 2010).

Despite those challenges, ICSs reported benefits of conducting cross-cultural therapy (Georgiadou, 2015; Lau & Ng, 2012). For example, Georgiadou (2015) interviewed 11 ICSs in the United Kingdom, and they reported experiences with clients that promoted clients' awareness of cultures, emotions, and thoughts; built closer relationships with clients who had similar experiences as them; enhanced anonymity with clients; and advanced the students' personal and professional development.

SUPERVISING INTERNATIONAL STUDENTS IN COUNSELING-RELATED PROGRAMS

Supervision plays a significant role in counseling-related training (Bernard & Goodyear, 2019). ICSs delineated challenges that they faced within supervision: supervisor insensitivity (supervisors did not attempt to understand their culture), interpersonal isolation (the feeling of being an outcast in various settings), and intercultural confusion and stereotyping (supervisors made culturally inaccurate or confusing comments; Sangganjanavanich & Black, 2009). Faculty and supervisors in counseling-related programs also reported the challenges of providing supervision to ICSs. In interviewing several supervisors, Attrill and colleagues (2016) reported complex teaching and learning relationships. Because of cultural differences, some supervisors described a lack of preparation to work with ICSs' complex issues and reported the challenges of aiding their professional communication skills (Attrill et al., 2016). The stereotypes held by supervisors toward ICSs' cultural backgrounds could raise tension in the supervisory relationship. Regardless of those challenges and difficulties reported by both ICSs and supervisors, both parties conveyed some positive experiences in which the mutual learning relationship was the foundation (Attrill et al., 2016; Sangganjanavanich & Black, 2009).

The impacting factors of ICSs' satisfaction with supervision included their acculturation level, multicultural discussions, personal characteristics, and the multicultural competence of supervisors (Inman, 2006; Ng & Smith, 2012; Nilsson & Anderson, 2004). A lower acculturation level of students was related to a weaker supervisory working relationship, more difficulties in supervision, more discussion of cultural issues in supervision, and less counseling self-efficacy (Nilsson & Anderson, 2004; Ng & Smith, 2012). Attrill and colleagues (2016) emphasized the importance of professional communication skills in ICSs' success in clinical practice and the relationship with their supervisors. The other factors reported were self-direction, initiating interventions with confidence, and working well with groups and others (Attrill et al., 2016). Supervisors' multicultural counseling competence and cultural discussions were also positively related to supervisory working relationships and the satisfaction of supervision (Inman, 2006; Mori et al., 2009).

In summary, with the increasing number of ICSs and the unique challenges that they face in their field experience, counseling programs, faculty, and supervisors need to develop a better understanding of their ICSs' field experience and unique needs (Behl et al.; 2017; Ng, 2006; Nilsson & Anderson, 2004). There is a lack of literature on ICSs' field experience and impacting factors (Park et al., 2017). Understanding the lived experience and impacting factors for ICSs will help stakeholders promote ICSs' success in field experience. Practicum is the first opportunity for counseling students to apply theories and counseling skills to diverse and ethnic clients in community and school settings (CACREP, 2016). Practicum can serve as a foundation to promote success in their advanced internship field experience. Therefore, the purpose of this study is to explore the practicum experience of ICSs in a counseling program. The research questions are as follows:

(1) What were the lived experiences of ICSs in the practicum?
(2) What were the positive and negative factors that impacted ICSs' success in the practicum?

METHOD

The study employed a qualitative research design from a phenomenological perspective. Phenomenological studies attempt to understand the meaning that participants derive from lived experiences or particular situations (Hays &Singh, 2012; Leedy & Ormrod, 2013). ICSs have been viewed as an underrepresented group in the literature with a lack of research and limited attention; therefore, phenomenology provides a distinct voice of ICSs' lived accounts, in contrast to quantitative methods (Branco & Bayne, 2020; Hays & Singh, 2012; Park et al., 2017). Phenomenology was an appropriate method because the researchers desired to investigate and explore ICSs' descriptions, interpretations, and experiences of counseling practicum (Moustakas, 1994; Smith et al., 2009).

Participants

We employed criterion sampling to obtain participants. Participants had to be at least 18 years old, identify as international students in the United States on a temporary visa, completed a practicum counseling course, and be enrolled in the counseling program. The counseling program was held at a large, private university in the Mid-Atlantic region of the United States, containing two tracks of school counseling and clinical mental health counseling. Researchers identified 38 ICSs who met the eligibility criteria (Leedy & Ormrod, 2013). After email invitations, six (16%) ICSs agreed to participate in the study. Since the sample is mostly homogenous with criterion sampling, a sample size of 3–10 is enough to draw conclusions for phenomenological research (Cilesiz, 2011).

All participants identified as cisgender female with a range of ages from 24 to 26 years ($M = 25.16$, $SD = 0.98$). China ($n = 4$) and India ($n = 2$) were their countries of origin. Their length of time in the United States ranged from 1.5 to 7 years ($M = 3.5$, $SD = 2.54$). Five participants were clinical mental health counseling students, and one was a school counseling student (see Table 1).

Table 1: Demographic Information of the Participants

Name	Age	Gender	Country of origin	Program	Years in the United States	Types of practicum site
JJ	26	Female	China	School counseling	7 years	Public school
RR	26	Female	India	Clinical Mental Health (CMHC)	1.5 years	Substance rehabilitation

Name	Age	Gender	Country of origin	Program	Years in the United States	Types of practicum site
MM	25	Female	China	CMHC	1.5 years	Counseling facility
CC	24	Female	China	CMHC	1.5 years	Substance rehabilitation
HH	24	Female	China	CMHC	6 years	Private practice
AA	26	Female	India	CMHC	2 years	Mental health services at hospital

Data Collection

The recruitment of participants began after approval from the institutional review board. Student researchers contacted and interviewed participants and transcribed the interviews to avoid potential dual relationship issues (American Counseling Association [ACA], 2014). Before data collection, one faculty researcher trained the two counseling student researchers on informed consent and research protocol usage. After obtaining signed informed consent from participants, the student researchers interviewed, recorded, and transcribed the interviews. For recording, the researchers employed a password-protected Skype web conference interface. Interview times ranged from approximately 10 to 40 min. Transcripts and an executive summary of the study's results were provided by the student investigators to the participants to check for accuracy. Five interviews lasted about 35 to 40 min; only the first interview lasted about 10 min, as the participant indicated having time conflicts during the interview. Researchers sent the participant the transcript afterward and solicited additional information that may not have been disclosed in the interview. The student researchers used random initials to represent the participants to maintain the confidentiality.

Instrumentation

The semi-structured interview contained four items regarding the experience of ICSs in practicum. The first item asked participants to describe their experience with practicum, including the site and the practicum course. The follow-up questions were: What has been your experience with site supervision, with university supervision, with practicum class, and at your practicum site? The questions for items two through four were: What has been helpful for you regarding your practicum experience? What were the challenges? And what are your suggestions for future ICSs in practicum? Those questions intended to probe the impacting factors about their practicum experience.

Data Analysis

Moustakas (1994) proposed a four-phase process employing content analysis in phenomenology, which includes (a) obtaining a full description, (b) reviewing the verbatim description of experience, (c) coresearchers completing a review of the verbatim process, and (d) constructing a textural–structural description of meanings and essence of the experience. First, researchers obtained a full description through transcribing and recording the interviews. Second, the first two authors reviewed the first participant's transcript separately and employed open coding to identify keywords, references, and texts. After multiple readings of the first participant's transcript, horizontalization of the data included broad categories of ICSs' experience in practicum (Creswell, 2013; Hays & Singh, 2012; Moustakas, 1994). After reviewing the transcript, the first two authors identified the themes that described the phenomenon of practicum more fully for ICSs. Third, the first two authors reached a consensus on the themes concerning the transcript. Then, they reviewed the transcript to confirm that the themes were supported by verbatim examples (Moustakas, 1994). The first two authors used the transcript as a baseline and reviewed the other five transcripts for convergence and divergence. An external auditor, the third author, reviewed all six of the transcripts and discussed the themes and verbatim examples with the first two authors until a consensus was reached. Fourth, after these steps, a codebook described the meanings of each theme, providing a universal depiction of the experience of ICSs in practicum.

Researcher Reflexivity Statement

To reduce research bias in qualitative research, Kline (2008) recommended that researchers record their roles and connections with the phenomenon of study. The research team was composed of five people. Three members of the research team were counselor educators, and two were master's level counseling students. Identifying as a cisgender, Asian female, the first author is a counselor educator whose research interests include counseling minority clients with a focus on international students. The second author is an African American, cisgender, male counselor educator with research interests in evaluation, spirituality, and diversity issues in counseling. The third author is a white, cisgender, male counselor educator whose research interests include individual psychology, evidence-based practice, and college student development. All three counselor educators had the experience of teaching numerous ICSs in their program. The first author possesses the experience of being an ICS at the doctoral level of counselor education. Both master's level counseling student researchers identified as cisgender, Chinese males who were international students.

Trustworthiness

Triangulation of data, member checking, and researcher reflexivity established trustworthiness. For member checking, the principal researcher sent participants verbatim transcripts following their interviews to verify accuracy through a password-protected email. Further, the participants received an executive summary of the study's results; they had an opportunity to provide feedback on the findings. Transferability was demonstrated by the participants meeting the criteria of being international students, speaking English, and experiencing practicum where they provided thick descriptions (Lincoln & Guba, 1985). For confirmability, the data analysis team demonstrated consensus through separately analyzing data and then coming together. Moreover, through a separate review, an outside auditor reviewed the transcripts and themes, building more consensus (Lincoln & Guba, 1985). Through journaling during the data collection, researchers reflected on ICSs and the practicum experience bracketing their assumptions.

FINDINGS

The researchers identified three themes within the practicum experience: the learning and growth process, positive impacting factors, and negative impacting factors. Subthemes emerged under the positive impacting factors, including supportive and encouraging supervision, community support, and personal strength. The subthemes under the negative impacting factors were a lack of support, students' lack of professionalism, and cultural barriers.

Theme 1: Learning and Growth Process

This theme described participants' learning and how they achieved growth during practicum. Several participants disclosed initially having self-doubts because practicum was their first experience in the field. JJ, RR, and AA reported that they were "constantly being hard on themselves," comparing themselves with their peers, and doubting whether they had "made progress" or "been beneficial to clients." However, they also revealed unexpected growth at sites. For example, CC shared her experiences of "feeling shocked" when she took over a client without preparation because her colleague had an emergency, but she calmed down and had a beneficial session with the client. She reflected that the experience was scary but rewarding, as she realized that she had the knowledge and skills to counsel a client even without full preparation. This holistic growth comprised various aspects of their personal and professional development. For example, RR described her growth regarding self-care, knowledge about licensure requirements, and job preparation.

The process of how they grew included utilizing resources, obtaining feedback from peers, and receiving training at sites. Several participants highlighted the importance of utilizing various resources at their sites and by their faculty supervisors. For example, HH reported that she learned about play therapy from the small library at her site. RR appreciated her faculty supervisor sharing information about crisis interventions and trauma-informed care. The participants also appreciated the feedback and support from their peers in their practicum class. As a part of the structure of a practicum class, students are required to share their experiences at their practicum sites and provide feedback to each other. HH, CC, JJ, and MM shared that it was beneficial to hear and learn from their peers' experiences. RR said, "I got really great feedback. They were very supportive ... [and] weren't overly critical."

The participants also valued diverse clients and training models at the sites. This helped them gain exposure to various populations in their clinical work. For example, MM reported that her site scaffolded training in which she first shadowed other counselors. Afterward, with the help of her supervisor, she counseled her own clients. RR revealed her appreciation for the thorough training system at her site, where she got exposed to "different aspects of treatment from the beginning to the end."

Theme 2: Positive Impacting Factors

This theme described the positive factors that impacted the ICSs' practicum experience. It included three subthemes: supportive and encouraging supervision, community support, and personal strength.

Supportive and Encouraging Supervision

One of the most significant factors that participants reported was the support and encouragement from their university and site supervisors. However, they expected different layers of support from the site and faculty supervisors. Moreover, ICSs identified informal supervision from other helping professionals as helpful.

Faculty Supervisors. The participants appreciated how faculty supervisors provided resources and feedback. For instance, AA stated: "I feel like I'm learning a lot from him, just that we learn techniques every week. He's able to provide a lot of feedback." RR disclosed that she was interested in trauma, and her faculty supervisor shared resources with her. Moreover, the participants reported that they found the university supervision helpful when the faculty supervisors provided them opportunities to apply counseling theories. In addition, several participants shared that the faculty supervisors had built a good rapport with them, so they felt supported during their practicum. They described their faculty supervisors as "very available," "supportive," "approachable," and "caring." For example, JJ disclosed: "I can talk with my faculty supervisor without any concerns. I know it is a safe place to talk. She is very supportive and sometimes she even reached out to me."

Site Supervisors. Several participants emphasized the availability of site supervisors. The students appreciated the weekly supervision with their site supervisors to address their concerns. They also reported feeling "supported" and "encouraged" if they could reach out to their site supervisors when needed. For example, HH stated, "I like my site supervisor a lot and each time I have questions and she [is] willing to offer me answers." Role modeling in supervision was another characteristic that the participants found beneficial. AA said, "He didn't dismiss anything I said. He was very much listening, using all his counseling skills as a supervisor. I think that was so helpful." Another helpful element was positive affirmation and validation. Besides professional knowledge and skills that students can learn in site supervision, receiving positive affirmation and validation from site supervisors promoted the participants' confidence as new professionals, leading to positive experiences.

Informal Supervision at Site. A few participants also mentioned that the interactions with other professionals at their sites were beneficial. Those interactions enabled them to get different perspectives of the helping professions. For example, HH shared her appreciation of her colleague, a social worker, who shared her own clinical experience and how she might handle difficult cases.

Community Support

Besides support from supervisors, the participants reported receiving support from friends, mental health professionals, and networking. The participants described feeling understood when they shared their practicum experiences with their peers and friends. A few participants described their appreciation to their peers in the practicum class for their support. JJ disclosed that she had a friend who was in a different practicum class but did her practicum in a similar setting. They shared their experiences and supported each other.

Only one participant mentioned receiving help from mental health professionals. JJ disclosed that she received helpful feedback and suggestions from her counselor when experiencing and managing conflicts with a site supervisor. She said, "it is helpful to know the suggestions about what I can do and what is appropriate [or not] in that situation."

Several participants brought up the importance of networking, especially when trying to find a practicum site. Participants in CMHC programs need to secure their field experience sites. AA shared her experiences of getting a site, because she knew someone who helped her connect with her supervisor. RR emphasized relying on peers and colleagues and creating a LinkedIn profile to promote networking to expedite the process.

Personal Strength

The participants reported having personal strengths, which helped them thrive in practicum. These strengths included being assertive, motivated, determined, open-minded, and confident. During interactions with their supervisors, a few students mentioned being assertive about their needs. RR also talked about constantly asking for feedback from her colleagues to promote professional growth. Moreover, the students emphasized being motivated and determined, especially when looking for a site or coming across difficulties. AA and CC disclosed that they kept reminding themselves of their professional goals that had brought them to the United States to stay motivated even when they faced difficulties. AA also shared her experiences of trying every possible way to secure a site. In addition, openness was another strength that students brought up. MM emphasized on being open-minded and curious about the practicum experiences, so she learned about various populations. Last, they highlighted the importance of being confident as ICSs and an awareness of their strengths. For example, MM said:

> … remembering that you also have something to bring to the table. Being in America, that's all they know and that's [their] whole world … [But] we have such a diverse experience that we have so much we can bring to the table.

Theme 3: Negative Impacting Factors

This theme described the negative factors that hindered ICSs' success in practicum. It included three subthemes: a lack of support, students' lack of professionalism, and cultural barriers.

Lack of Support

Even though the participants reported receiving support, several delineated how a lack of support (e.g., program, sites, supervisors, and community) made the practicum experience more challenging. The lack of support from the program was mainly around securing a site. For example, RR, MM, and JJ mentioned that the field experience orientation was helpful regarding logistics; however, they wished they could get more information regarding how to ask questions about their targeted sites. The program provided a list of qualified sites and hosted site fairs; however, the participants reported challenges securing a site, as it was their first experience of finding a job in the United States, and they did not know what questions were appropriate to ask an employer. The participants described the difficulties encountered in receiving support from sites. For example, RR reported discrimination during the search process. A site refused to take her because she was an ICS, and the site assumed she would not understand the clients and had poor language skills. When they started practicum at their sites, they experienced the challenges of feeling isolated and a lack of consistent clients. Feelings of isolation came from a lack of recognition at the sites and a lack of peer counselors-in-training. For example, AA reported feeling "consistent[ly] lonely" because she was the only counseling intern at the site and often felt "dismissed."

Several participants shared challenges because of their site and faculty supervisors. Some participants reported a lack of availability of their site supervisors. For example, MM revealed that it was hard to contact her supervisor because she and her supervisor worked at different locations. The participants reported difficulties because of the lack of professionalism of their site supervisors. JJ shared a few incidents about her supervisor's lack of cultural knowledge and sensitivity during their interactions. For instance, when her supervisor first introduced her to the other colleagues, the supervisor made an erroneous claim that there were no school counselors in China. JJ also reported her supervisor's lack of boundaries. Her supervisor texted or emailed assignments late at night or over the weekend, along with adding her on Facebook. CC also shared her frustration that her supervisor was not as professional as she expected and "did not care about the client's wellbeing sometimes." Several participants also reported a lack of validation from their faculty supervisors. For example, HH disclosed her frustration toward her faculty supervisor, who emphasized "providing tools and answers" instead of a discussion to validate their capacity.

Lack of support from the community, such as their family and friends, posed another challenge to ICSs. CC talked about her feeling of loneliness, because her family and friends in her home country did not understand her experiences, and she did not have resources to get connected with other students.

Students' Lack of Professionalism

This subtheme focused on the professional skills that students failed to demonstrate in navigating the challenges of practicum. It included the skills to secure a site and deal with conflicts with supervisors. Both MM and RR reported needing more skills to know how to choose a practicum site. MM added that she hoped to get interview tips and additional information about the site to avoid future difficulties.

JJ reported her difficulty navigating conflicts with her supervisor. As previously noted, her supervisor lacked boundaries, cultural knowledge, and sensitivity during their interactions. Moreover, she had a classmate in her practicum class who was her supervisor's friend. She was concerned that the classmate might disclose the discussion to the site supervisor, who might give her an unfavorable evaluation in practicum. Therefore, she did not report the inappropriate professional interactions to her faculty supervisor.

Cultural Barriers

Several participants shared how cultural barriers impacted their practicum experiences. Those barriers included language barriers, marginalization because of cultural differences, counseling system/structural differences, and power dynamic differences. Both CC and HH emphasized the importance of language in the counseling profession, as it requires fluent communication with clients. Specifically, CC disclosed her difficulty in understanding slang. Besides language, the participants reported feeling marginalized because of cultural differences between their home countries and the United States. For example, AA stated,

> it was not only about the language … but also how you think in this Western way and just kind of all of this comes like a commemoration thing. It's like cultural shocks for me. I think it's the most difficult thing …

The participants felt challenged to learn the differences in counseling/social system between their home countries and the United States. CC elaborated her difficulties of navigating the substance abuse intervention at her site, because it was very different from the system in her home country. HH also found it challenging to relate to her clients, as the school system was different from her home country. It took her extra effort to understand the school system in the United States.

The power dynamic differences made it difficult to navigate conflicts with their supervisors. JJ disclosed her difficulty in being assertive and holding boundaries when she had a conflict with her supervisor. She explained that obedience to authority in her culture prevented her from asserting herself. As she chose to endure the unprofessional behaviors of her supervisor, she experienced more stress and less mental well-being.

DISCUSSION

This phenomenological study described the practicum experience of ICSs at a counseling program at a large private university in the Mid-Atlantic region. The study delineated ICSs' experiences of learning and growth in practicum. It also illustrated the impacting factors that promoted ICSs' growth in practicum, such as supportive and encouraging supervision, community support, and personal strength. In addition, factors that hindered their success in practicum, including a lack of support, students' lack of professionalism, and cultural barriers, were addressed.

Regarding the ICSs' learning and growth process in practicum, the participants disclosed having self-doubts during their practicum but experiencing unexpected growth that helped build their confidence. Due to cultural differences between ICSs and their clients, ICSs faced unique challenges (Liu, 2014). However, they often found the experiences of cross-cultural counseling to be rewarding and positively impacting their clients and themselves (Georgiadou, 2015). Growth was achieved by utilizing resources, receiving support and feedback from their peers, and relying on the training process at the sites. Although some ICSs did not feel supported by their training sites, one unique finding in the study is that several participants appreciated the training process at their sites. The students who were observed to be receiving support from their training site mentioned that exposure to diverse client populations, scaffolding training models, welcoming environments, and comprehensive orientations all contributed to their feeling of being supported by their site. Previously, there was little research on how the training process at the sites may positively influence ICSs' training outcomes. This area may be worth further exploration. However, other participants disclosed negative experiences at their sites, such as discrimination and not being recognized by their coworkers. These experiences lead to feeling isolated and frustrated during their practicum experience. Therefore, it is important to help ICSs procure sites that would support their growth and educate sites about the unique needs of ICSs (Tang, 2014; Wedding et al., 2009).

The factors that promote ICSs' growth in practicum included supportive and encouraging supervision, community support, and personal strength. Similar to previous literature, participants valued supportive and encouraging supervision as one of the most important factors in their practicum experience (Liu, 2014; Park et al., 2017). However, the participants expected different layers of support or guidance from faculty supervisors, site supervisors, and informal supervision. For faculty supervisors, the participants emphasized their providing resources, emotional support, and feedback. The characteristics that they expected the site supervisors to possess were availability, role modeling of professionalism, and validation and affirmation. ICSs might hold different expectations toward faculty and site supervisors (Steadman & Brown, 2011). ICSs may regard faculty supervisors as professors but think of site supervisors as role models who directly observe and evaluate their clinical performance. The common element that the participants valued in both faculty and site supervisors was validation and affirmation, boosting their confidence, and building rapport. One factor under supervision that had not been addressed in the previous literature was informal supervision. Besides their site supervisors, participants valued the interactions with other professionals at their sites. The interdisciplinary learning from other professionals may help them learn various professionals' perspectives and prepare them for real work situations.

Another positive factor is community support, which included support from friends, professional help, and networking. International students have reported that having support from friends and family reduces stress (Xiong & Zhou, 2018). The participants shared that networking may help them secure a practicum site, which may be difficult for ICSs (Park et al., 2017). One participant mentioned the benefits of seeking professional help. Previous literature has demonstrated the benefits of counseling students utilizing counseling services (Drew et al., 2017). However, in comparison to domestic students, international students are more unwilling to seek professional help (Xiong, 2018; Xiong & Yang, 2021). More advocacy may be needed to help ICSs utilize those resources.

The participants' personal strengths to help with their practicum included assertiveness, motivation and determination, openness, and confidence. These characteristics may enable them to adopt positive coping strategies to deal with the challenges in practicum. For example, being assertive, motivated, and determined would promote advocating for themselves and insisting that the program help in difficult situations (Attrill et al., 2016; Liu, 2014; Xiong & Zhou, 2018).

The negative factors impacting ICSs' performance included a lack of support, cultural barriers, and lack of students' professionalism. Students experienced a lack of support from the program, their sites, supervisors, and the community. The participants wished they could get more information from the program to secure a site (Park et al., 2017). ICSs reported more difficulties in finding sites than domestic students did. The programs may need to assist ICSs more during the site-seeking process. Another aspect that ICSs identified was the lack of support from supervisors. As mentioned above, support from supervisors was one of the positive factors. However, the participants complained about how some supervisors were unavailable, unprofessional, and did not provide enough validation. These aspects hindered growth significantly and added stress to practicum experiences. Supervisors who work with ICSs may feel unprepared, especially regarding their multicultural competence (Attrill et al., 2016). The stigma and stereotypes that they held toward ICSs may inhibit building rapport with them and promoting their growth (Attrill et al., 2016). It is the supervisors' responsibility to maintain their professionalism and multicultural competence during their interactions with ICSs (Attrill et al., 2016; Rhinehart, 2015).

Cultural barriers negatively influenced their experiences in practicum (Ng, 2006; Park et al., 2017; Sangganjanavanich & Black, 2009). Language barriers were the most obvious difficulty that ICSs reported (Ng, 2006; Park et al., 2017). Students reported that latent cultural differences between their home countries and the United States could cause feelings of isolation. All the participants were from China and India, whose cultures are significantly different from American culture (Kim, 2001). International students may experience more difficulties in acculturation when there are more cultural differences between their original countries and the host country (Ward et al., 1998). China and India value collectivism, but America emphasizes individualism (Kim, 2001). Moreover, the cultures of emphasizing hierarchical power in China and India may prevent them from being assertive or advocating for themselves, especially with supervisors (Park et al., 2017; Xiong et al., 2021). Participants also reported difficulties in understanding the differences between the counseling systems in the United States and those in their home countries (Goh et al., 2014; Lau & Ng, 2012).

Another unique finding was the students' lack of professionalism, which served as a negative factor in their success in practicum. This factor was interwoven with being a novice in the field and cultural barriers. Lack of experience and cultural barriers resulted in students' difficulties in dealing with conflicts and challenges with supervisors. However, those skills can be obtained with experiences and more knowledge about the appropriate ways to handle cultural differences and conflicts (Park et al., 2017). More training on those topics (such as professional communication skills) may be necessary to promote ICSs' success in practicum (Attrill et al., 2016).

IMPLICATIONS

All the stakeholders who work with ICSs may need to be aware that their ethical and professional responsibility is to respond to ICSs' unique needs (Smith & Ng, 2009). Programs with ICSs need to recognize the support offered to domestic students in providing a list of potential sites or relying on students to establish their network may not be enough to provide the support needed for ICSs. They may offer information or specific training to prepare ICSs for site hunting, such as interviewing skills, questions to ask, and marketing themselves for internship positions. Programs may develop specific policies and procedures for ICSs to help with their field experience, especially when managing difficulties at their sites. A separate ICSs orientation may help prepare them to handle cultural differences, understand counseling system differences, navigate challenges, and establish coping strategies. These supports may help connect ICSs with previous students to obtain more information and feel less isolated. Finally, programs may need to be more cautious when approving a site for ICSs and train sites about ICSs' unique needs.

Counselor educators need to be aware and mindful of the unique challenges that ICSs have in field experience, such as language difficulties and cultural differences. Counselor educators may provide emotional support to ICSs by showing genuine care and building strong rapport. Counselor educators may promote inclusive teaching that addresses ICSs' unique needs to better prepare for their future careers, especially if they return to their home countries. They may also encourage international and domestic students to connect with their peers to reduce feelings of isolation.

For sites and site supervisors with ICSs, training models should be used that promote inclusive environments for trainees to be acknowledged and valued. It is critical to respect and value ICSs' unique perspectives. For the site supervisors, it is important to make themselves available to ICSs and promote their own multicultural competence. Site supervisors may show genuine curiosity and respect to ICSs and have cultural conversations with ICSs as needed. Site supervisors need to engage in continuous education regarding professionalism, multicultural competence and be role models for ICSs. When working with ICSs, site supervisors may adopt multicultural emphasized supervision models such as culturally responsive approaches (Reid & Dixon, 2012) and models that are specific to ICSs (e.g., Li & Ai, 2020).

As the limitations of the study, the findings should be carefully interpreted and generalized. The generalization of results is limited, because the purpose of the study and the participants were only females from two countries and one counseling program. Another limitation is the lack of discussion about the interactions with clients. This may be because they were at the practicum stage, and they had limited contact with clients. Further, although robust data were gathered through the interview process, the brevity of one interview may have limited the depth of their response. More research around this topic is needed to advocate for ICSs.

REFERENCES

Akkurt, M. N., Ng, K.-M., & Kolbert, J. (2018). Multicultural discussion as a moderator of counseling supervision-related constructs. *International Journal for the Advancement of Counselling, 40*(4), 455–468. https://doi.org/ 10.1007/s10447-018-9337-z

American Counseling Association. (2014). *2014 ACA code of ethics.* https:// www.counseling.org/docs/default-source/default-document-library/2014-code-of-ethics-finaladdress.pdf

Asempapa, B. (2019). Mentoring and supervising international students in School Counseling Programs. *Journal of International Students, 9*(3), 912–928. https://doi.org/10.32674/jis.v9i3.746

Attrill, S., Lincoln, M., & McAllister, S. (2016). Supervising international students in clinical placements: Perceptions of experiences and factors influencing competency development. *BMC Medical Education, 16*(1), 180. https://doi.org/10.1186/s12909-016-0702-5

Behl, M., Laux, J. M., Roseman, C. P., Tiamiyu, M., & Spann, S. (2017). Needs and acculturative stress of international students in CACREP programs. *Counselor Education and Supervision, 56*(4), 305–318.

Bernard, J. M., & Goodyear, R. K. (2019). *Fundamentals of clinical supervision* (6th ed.). Pearson.

Branco, S. F., & Bayne, H. B. (2020). Carrying the burden: Counselor's of color experiences of microaggressions in counseling. *Journal of Counseling & Development, 93*(3), 272–282.

Cantwell, B. (2015). Are international students cash cows? Examining the relationship between new international undergraduate enrollments and institutional revenue at public colleges and universities in the US. *Journal of International Students, 5*(4), 515–525.

Cilesiz, S. (2011). A phenomenological approach to experiences with technology: Current state, promise, and future directions for research. *Educational Technology Research and Development, 59*(4), 487–510. https://doi.org/10.1007/s11423-010-9173-2

Council for Accreditation of Counseling and Related Educational Programs. (2016). 2016 CACREP standards. Retrieved November 4, 2021, from http://www.cacrep.org/for-programs/2016-cacrep-standards/

Council for Accreditation of Counseling and Related Educational Programs. (2016). CACREP vital statistics 2015: Results from a national survey of accredited programs. Alexandria, VA: Author. https://issuu.com/cacrep/docs/2015_cacrep_vital_statistics_repor

Creswell, J. W. (2013). *Qualitative inquiry and research design: Choosing among five approaches* (3rd ed.). Sage Publications, Inc.

Dao, T., Donghyuck, D., & Chang, H. (2007). Acculturation level, perceived English fluency, perceived social support level and depression among Taiwanese international students. *College Student Journal, 41*(2), 287–295.

Drew, M., Stauffer, M., & Barkley, W. (2017). Personal counseling in academic programs with counselor trainees. *The Journal of Counselor Preparation and Supervision, 9*(1). http://dx.doi.org/10.7729/91.1131

Georgiadou, L. (2015). 'I was seeing more of her': International counselling trainees' perceived benefits of intercultural clinical practice. *British Journal of Guidance & Counselling, 43*(5), 584–597. https://doi.org/10.1080/03069885.2014.996735

Goh, M., Yon, K., Shimmi, Y., & Hirai, T. (2014). Experiences of Asian psychologists and counselors trained in the USA: An exploratory study. *Asia Pacific Education Review, 15*(4), 593–608.

Hays, D. G., & Singh, A. A. (2012). *Qualitative inquiry in clinical and educational settings*. The Guilford Press.

Hegarty, M. (2014). Spatial thinking in undergraduate science education. *Spatial Cognition & Computation, 14*(2), 142–167. https://doi.org/10.1080/13875868.2014.889696

Inman, A. G. (2006). Supervisor multicultural competence and its relation to supervisory process and outcome. *Journal of Marital and Family Therapy, 32*(1), 73–85. https://doi.org/10.1111/j.1752-0606.2006.tb01589.x

Institution of International Education. (2019). International scholar trends. Retrieved November 4, 2021, from https://opendoorsdata.org/data/international-scholars/international-scholars-trends/

Kim, B. S. K. (2001). Cultural value similarities and differences among Asian American ethnic groups. *Cultural Diversity and Ethnic Minority Psychology, 7*(4), 343–361. https://doi.org/10.1037/1099-9809.7.4.343

Kline, W. B. (2008). Developing and submitting credible qualitative manuscripts. *Counselor Education and Supervision, 47*(4), 210–217. https://doi.org/10.1002/j.1556-6978.2008.tb00052.x

Koyama, M. (2010). The collective voices of Asian international doctoral students in counseling psychology in the U.S.: Recommendations for faculty and training programs. [Doctoral dissertation, Western Michigan University].

Lau, J., & Ng, K.-M. (2012). Effectiveness and relevance of training for international counseling graduates: A qualitative inquiry. *International Journal for the Advancement of Counselling, 34*(1), 87–105. https://doi.org/10.1007/s10447-011-9128-2

Leedy, P. D., & Ormrod, J. E. (2013). *Practical research: Planning and design* (10th ed.). Pearson.

Li, D., & Ai, Y. (2020). Ethics acculturation of international counseling students. *Journal of International Students, 10*(4), 1103–1109. https://doi.org/10.32674/jis.v10i4.1442

Lincoln, Y. S., & Guba, E. G. (1985). *Naturalistic inquiry*. Sage.

Liu, J. (2014). East Asian international trainees experience conducting therapy in the US: A qualitative investigation. [Doctoral dissertation, University of Maryland, College Park].

McKinley, M. T. (2019). Supervising the sojourner: Multicultural supervision of international students. *Training and Education in Professional Psychology, 13*(3), 174–179. https://doi.org/10.1037/tep0000269

Mori, Y., Inman, A. G., & Caskie, G. I. L. (2009). Supervising international students: Relationship between acculturation, supervisor multicultural competence, cultural discussions, and supervision satisfaction. *Training and Education in Professional Psychology, 3*(1), 10–18. https://doi.org/10.1037/a0013072

Moustakas, C. E. (1994). *Phenomenological research methods*. Sage Publications, Inc.

Ng, K.-M. (2006). International students in CACREP-Accredited counseling programs. *Journal of Professional Counseling: Practice, Theory & Research, 34*(1–2), 20–32. https://doi.org/10.1080/15566382.2006.12033821

Ng, K.-M., & Smith, S. D. (2012). Training level, acculturation, role ambiguity, and multicultural discussions in training and supervising international counseling students in the United States. *International Journal for the Advancement of Counselling, 34*(1), 72–86. psyh. https://doi.org/10.1007/s10447-011-9130-8

Nilsson, J. E., & Anderson, M. Z. (2004). Supervising international students: The role of acculturation, role ambiguity, and multicultural discussions. *Professional Psychology: Research and Practice, 35*(3), 306–312. https://doi.org/10.1037/0735-7028.35.3.306

Park, S., Lee, J. H., & Wood, S. M. (2017). Experiences of international students in practicum and internship courses: A consensus qualitative research. *The Journal of Counselor Preparation and Supervision.* https://doi.org/10.7729/92.1137

QS top universities. (2020). Discover where to study with the QS World University Rankings by Subject 2020: Psychology. https://www.topuniversities.com/university-rankings/university-subject-rankings/2020/psychology.

Reid, L. M., & Dixon, A. L. (2012). The counseling supervision needs of international students in U.S. institutions of higher education: A culturally-sensitive supervision model for counselor educators. *Journal for International Counselor Education, 4,* 29–41. Retrieved from http://digitalcommons.library.unlv.edu/jice

Rhinehart, A. (2015). Lived experiences of beginning counselors in harmful supervision [Doctoral dissertation, University of Tennessee].

Sangganjanavanich, V. F., & Black, L. L. (2009). Clinical supervision for international counselors-in-training: Implications for supervisors. *Journal of Professional Counseling: Practice, Theory & Research, 37*(2), 52–65. https://doi.org/10.1080/15566382.2009.12033860

Smith, J. A., Flowers, P., & Larkin, M. (2009). *Interpretative phenomenological analysis.* Sage Publications, Inc.

Smith, S. D., & Ng, K.-M. (2009). International counseling trainees' experiences and perceptions of their multicultural counseling training in the United States: A mixed method inquiry. *International Journal for the Advancement of Counselling, 31*(4), 271. https://doi.org/10.1007/s10447-009-9083-3

Steadman, S. C., & Brown, S. D. (2011). Defining the job of university supervisor: A Department-wide study of university supervisor's practices. *Issues in Teacher Education, 20*(1), 51–68. http://doi.org/10.1007/s10447-009-9083-3

Tang, H.-Y. (2014). Supervisor perceptions of their multicultural training needs for working with English language learning supervisees. *Counseling & Human Services Theses & Dissertations.* https://doi.org/10.25777/xdq3-kd95

Ward, C., Okura, Y., Kennedy, A., & Kojima, T. (1998). The U-Curve on trial: a longitudinal study of psychological and sociocultural adjustment during Cross-Cultural transition. *International Journal of Intercultural Relations, 22*(3), 277–291.

Wedding, D., McCartney, J. L., & Currey, D. E. (2009). Lessons relevant to psychologists who serve as mentors for international students. *Professional*

Psychology: Research and Practice, 40(2), 189–193. https://doi.org/10.1037/a0012249

Xiong, Y. (2018). An exploration of Asian international students' mental health: Comparisons to American students and other international students in the United States [Doctoral dissertation, Ohio University].

Xiong, Y., & Yang, L. (2021). Asian international students' help-seeking intentions and behavior in American Postsecondary Institutions. *International Journal of Intercultural Relations, 80*, 170–185. https://doi.org/10.1016/j.ijintrel.2020.11.007

Xiong, Y., Young, A., Tan, H., & Wu, S., (2021). The exploration of international counseling students' experience of leadership and advocacy. *Journal of Asia Pacific Counseling, 11*(1), 35–54. https://doi.org/10.18401/2021.11.1.3

Xiong, Y., & Zhou, Y. (2018). Understanding East Asian graduate students' socio-cultural and psychological adjustment in a U.S. Midwestern university. *Journal of International Students, 8*(2), 769–794. https://doi.org/10.5281/zenodo.1250379

YIYING XIONG, Ph.D., is an assistant professor in the Department of Counseling and Educational Studies at the Johns Hopkins School of Education. Her research interests include international students' mental health, the education of international counseling students, the teaching of group counseling course, and mindfulness practice. She teaches Counseling Theories, Human Development and Counseling, and Group Counseling. Email: yxiong@jhu.edu

MATTHEW W. BONNER, Ph.D., LCPC, is a clinical assistant professor and faculty lead at the Johns Hopkins University School of Education in the Counseling Program. Currently, he is a member of various international counseling organizations. He is a licensed counselor and a certified supervisor in the state of Maryland. His research interests and published works include black men in the professoriate, assessment in counseling, grading rigor in counselor education, spirituality, and international student perspectives in counseling. Email: mbonner6@jhu.edu

STERLING P. TRAVIS, M.S., is an assistant professor in the department of counseling and educational studies at the Johns Hopkins University. He completed his Ph.D. in counselor education and supervision from the College of William and Mary, and his research focuses on individual psychology, evidence-based practices, and college student development. Email: stravis5@jhu.edu

FENG XING is a doctoral student of the Professional Psychology Program at Columbian College of Arts and Science, George Washington University. He is currently working as a clinic extern at the Center Clinic and College Living Experience. His research interests focus on group therapy, international trainees' experience in counseling/psychology programs, and multiculturalism. Email: dylanxing@gwmail.gwu.edu

QINGYUN ZHANG is a doctoral student of the Counselor Education and Supervision Program at the Pennsylvania State University. He is currently the Clinic Supervisor at the Edwin L. Herr Clinic and a Licensed Graduate Professional Counselor (LGPC) in Maryland. His research interests include training and supervision models for international counseling trainees in different cultural or linguistic settings, multicultural counseling, and collective trauma. Email: qjz5094@psu.edu

Research Article

© *Journal of International Students*
Volume 12, Issue 3 (2022), pp. 654-673
ISSN: 2162-3104 (Print), 2166-3750 (Online)
doi: 10.32674/jis.v12i3.3613
ojed.org/jis

Living Abroad During COVID-19: International Students' Personal Relationships, Uncertainty, and Management of Health and Legal Concerns During a Global Pandemic[1]

Allison R. Thorson
Eve-Anne M. Doohan
Leah Z. Clatterbuck
University of San Francisco, USA

ABSTRACT

The purpose of this study is to better understand the uncertainties that international students faced and managed throughout COVID-19 and the impact that these uncertainties had on their personal relationships. We conducted interviews with 14 international students and found that they were particularly uncertain about the health of their family members (RQ_{1a}), their own health (RQ_{1b}), and where to wait out COVID-19 (RQ_{1c}). Those uncertainties that could be navigated were managed via participants giving informational directives, providing instrumental support, making emotional appeals (RQ_{2a}), engaging in new behaviors and self-care (RQ_{2b}), and increasing communication with and withholding information from family members (RQ_{2c}). Last, we found that COVID-19 impacted international students' personal relationships in two distinct,

---

[1] A previous version of this manuscript was presented for the International/Intercultural Communication Division at the 2021 National Communication Association Convention.

positive ways: They became closer with friends and connected more with family members (RQ$_3$). Overall, the findings from our study have implications for future research and offer suggestions for supporting international students during times of future uncertainty.

Keywords: COVID-19, health, international students, uncertainty management theory

As cities and states began to "shelter in place" in response to the global 2019 coronavirus (COVID-19) pandemic, early research and media coverage centered on how communities might mitigate transmission, vaccine development, and its economic effect (Dalton et al., 2020). Less scholarship focused on how international students navigate COVID-related stressors (Wilczewski et al., 2021) and no empirical research, to date, has addressed the specific uncertainties faced by the over 1 million international students studying in the United States during this time (Institute of International Education [IIE], 2019). Thus, despite research that argues that international students experience a great deal of uncertainty when studying abroad (e.g., Bista, 2016), little is known about their experiences with uncertainty surrounding COVID-19.

Guided by the Uncertainty Management Theory (UMT; e.g., Brashers, 2001), we developed the current study to learn what, if any, uncertainties international students faced and managed in the midst of COVID-19 and the impact of these uncertainties on their personal relationships. In what follows, we explicate our rationale for the present study, provide a summary of UMT, review the literature on uncertainty among international students, and explore research on the impact of COVID-19 on personal relationships before explaining our findings, their implications, and offering suggestions for supporting international students during times of future uncertainty.

UNCERTAINTY MANAGEMENT THEORY

According to Brashers (2001), "uncertainty exists when details of situations are ambiguous, complex, unpredictable, or probabilistic; when information is unavailable or inconsistent; and when people feel insecure in their own state of knowledge or the state of knowledge in general" (p. 478). However, because uncertainties are regularly "… ubiquitous, … often reasonable and healthy, and very often, simply irreducible" (Babrow & Striley, 2015, p. 111), Brashers developed UMT in response to questions about the main premise of the Uncertainty Reduction Theory (URT; Berger & Calabrese, 1975)—namely that the main goal when faced with uncertainty is always to reduce it. The UMT is also the most dominant theory used to examine uncertainty as neither a positive nor a negative today.

As noted by Babrow and Striley (2015), some uncertainties can extend over long periods of time, whereas others can arise or dissipate as circumstances and contexts change. Relatedly, people often experience a pileup of multiple uncertainties at once—with the response to one uncertainty impacting other, related, uncertainties—requiring people to "develop responses sensitive to multiple goals and tasks" (Brashers, 2001, p. 481). Given the unprecedented, capricious, and circumstantial nature of COVID-19, and the myriad ways in which COVID-19 has simultaneously affected health, social practices, and personal relationships, UMT is an appropriate lens through which to examine international students' experiences with and their responses to this global crisis.

UNCERTAINTY, INTERNATIONAL STUDENTS, AND WELL-BEING

Research indicates that international students' experiences with studying abroad are steeped in uncertainty. Specifically, when deciding whether or not to study abroad, legal considerations (e.g., navigating legal processes, obtaining a visa, preparing appropriate documents, etc.) are among the most constraining, uncertainty inducing, structural factors that international students encounter (e.g., Bista & Dagley, 2015; Eder et al., 2010). Once abroad, although hopeful and excited, international students face additional uncertainties stemming from language deficiency/proficiency (e.g., Andrade, 2006), cultural adjustment (e.g., Smith & Khawaja, 2011), psychological stressors (i.e., anxiety and homesickness; e.g., Bista, 2016), and navigating the complex U.S. healthcare/ insurance system (Adegboyega et al., 2020). Researchers report that international students employ a variety of strategies to manage and reduce these uncertainties. For instance, international students often seek information from official sources to navigate the visa process (Bista, 2016). Mesidor and Sly (2016) found that international students engage in a variety of social strategies (e.g., connecting more with family back home, forming new connections and friendships, and expressing emotions, challenges, and needs to others) to manage their uncertainty regarding cultural adjustment.

Considering that COVID-19 affects nearly every aspect of daily life, uncertainty is likely central to many international students' experiences. Of the scant research conducted on university students' experiences with this global pandemic, Cohen et al. (2020) reported that most students were concerned about how the pandemic might impact their educational/career plans, the economy, and the health of their family members and society. However, considering that the uncertainties faced by international students throughout COVID-19 are likely distinctive, especially given that they navigated COVID-related stressors in conjunction with their unique legal status while often separated from their families, warrants further attention. Thus, we posed the following research questions:

RQ₁: What, if any, uncertainties do international students report having faced in the midst of COVID-19?

RQ₂: How, if at all, have international students managed the uncertainties they have faced in the midst of COVID-19?

INTERPERSONAL RELATIONSHIPS AND COVID-19

Brashers (2001) argued that one of the most common ways in which individuals respond to uncertainty is by way of seeking (providing) social support to/from friends and family. Relatedly, early studies suggest that COVID-19 has contributed to a number of positive and negative outcomes for personal relationships. Specifically, Luetke et al. (2020) reported that many romantic partners experience increased conflict with one another related to COVID-19 restrictions and spread. Pietromonaco and Overall (2020) suggested that couples' relational functioning, quality, and stability may be threatened by external pandemic-related stressors (e.g., loss of income, demanding jobs, etc.) and exacerbated by existing individual vulnerabilities and the broader contexts in which relationships are situated (e.g., age, social class, minority status). With regard to university students, Wilczewski et al. (2021) found that self-isolating international students experienced increased levels of loneliness after their transition to COVID-related online learning.

Contrary to these findings, Goodwin et al. (2020) reported that psychological stress and being in quarantine had mixed effects for relationships depending on the relationship type, arguing that couples in already established close relationships may benefit from navigating the challenges of COVID-19 together. Relatedly, Nitschke et al. (2021) found that social connections buffered individuals against pandemic-specific stress and worries during COVID-19-related lockdown periods.

Although these initial findings are applicable to the current examination, no empirical research has focused specifically on how COVID-19 has impacted international students' personal relationships. Although related literature suggests that highly resilient international students may be buffered from the many negative psychological/behavioral challenges that others often face when experiencing significant adversity (Kim & Cronley, 2020), it is unclear how, if at all, this resilience may function in the midst of a global pandemic. Thus, we developed the following research question to extend upon the initial findings and to address this gap in the literature:

RQ$_3$: What, if any, impact do COVID-19-related uncertainties have on international students' personal relationships?

METHOD

We used an exploratory qualitative design to answer our research questions. Specifically, we conducted interviews with international students to learn about their in-depth experiences with COVID-19.

Participants

Our participants included 14 international students (13 [92.9%] graduates and 1 [7.1%] undergraduates) enrolled in a mid-sized U.S. university on the West Coast. We recruited each participant by using snowball and network sampling and conducted all interviews between June and July 2020. All interviews were conducted in English. Among our 14 participants, 12 (85.71%) were former students of the first author. Twelve (85.71%) of our participants were female and two (14.28%) were male, ranging in age from 21 to 37 ($M = 28.85$, $SD = 4.26$). Participants were citizens of India, Kenya, Russia ($n = 2$, 14.28%, respectively), Brazil, Egypt, England, Pakistan, Singapore, and Vietnam ($n = 1$, 7.14%, respectively). Two of our interviewees had dual citizenship, Brazil/Argentina and Singapore/Saudi Arabia ($n = 1$, 7.14%, respectively). Ten (71.43%) of our participants were single. The four (28.57%) participants who were married lived with their spouses in the United States but their spouses were not current U.S. citizens (e.g., U.S. Green Card or H-1B/F1 visa holder). Only one (7.14%) participant returned home after the university's move to remote education. We provided no compensation to our interviewees for their participation.

Data Collection

After receiving approval from the Institutional Review Board, we conducted one-on-one interviews with each participant by using Zoom video conferencing (i.e., the first two authors conducted 10 and 4 interviews respectively). We used a semi-structured interview protocol (available from the first author) as a guide to ask questions related to COVID-19 and uncertainty, including "What was your family's experience with this pandemic before/after it became widespread in the U.S.?" and "What, if any, worries did you have for your family/yourself before/after this pandemic hit the U.S.?" Interviews ranged from 33 to 61 min ($M = 45.84$, $SD = 3.27$).

All interviews were transcribed verbatim by using Zoom transcription, yielding 208 pages of single-spaced data. We compared transcripts against each audio file to ensure accuracy and gave pseudonyms to each participant and their family members. We reached theoretical saturation at interview 10 (e.g., the information shared by our participants was redundant) but conducted four more interviews to ensure that no new information emerged.

Data Analysis and Validation

We employed thematic analysis by using Braun and Clarke's (2006) six-step process to answer our research questions. Specifically, each researcher first (a) individually read through the entire set of transcripts to get an overall sense of these data. Next, we each (b) individually generated initial coding categories and subcategories before (c) grouping each set of categories into themes. Although uncertainty was used as an initial lens for this analysis, we used an iterative process in which we adapted research questions and themes as we worked through

Braun and Clarke's stages and revised our results. Fourth, we met as a group to (d) collectively review and (e) label themes by using process coding (i.e., gerunds or "ing" words) to organize our results—discussing, debating, and coming to agreement as an entire group. Last, we (f) identified exemplars for each theme.

The first author had no family members living abroad, the second author's parents lived in Italy, and the third author was a dual citizen (i.e., Hong Kong and the United States) and an undergraduate student living abroad away from her family throughout the entire COVID-19 pandemic. Thus, in order to address our potential bias, we enhanced our methodological rigor by using two data validation techniques: researcher triangulation and member checks (Creswell & Miller, 2000). Specifically, all three authors completed the initial data analysis, reaching themes independently before meeting to compare themes, discuss differences, and engage in reflexivity until we reached a consensus. Last, the first author conducted member checks with three (>21%) participants to affirm that the findings rang true with their lived experience.

FINDINGS

We present our findings as three major results. First, our findings suggest that international students were particularly uncertain about the health of their family members (RQ1a), their health (RQ1b), and where to wait out COVID-19 (RQ1c). Those uncertainties that could be navigated were managed via participants giving informational directives, providing instrumental support, making emotional appeals (RQ2a), engaging in new behaviors and self-care (RQ2b), and increasing communication with and withholding information from family members (RQ2c). Last, we found that COVID-19 impacted international students' relationships in two distinct, positive, ways: They became closer with friends and connected more with family members (RQ3). The following sections highlight each set of results and provide supporting exemplars for each finding.

Worrying about Family's Health (RQ1a)

Our first finding related to RQ1 suggests that participants had ongoing concerns regarding the health of their family members as COVID-19 spread. Some interviewees shared that their worries stemmed from the cultural conditions/norms of where their family currently resided, whereas others shared that their worries were exacerbated because their family members were at a high risk for COVID-19 infection.

Concerning Cultural Conditions/Norms

A number of our interviewees explained that the worries they had concerning their family's health were compounded by the conditions/norms embedded within their home culture. For example, Prisha, whose family lives in India, shared:

> Once we [my husband and I] heard … there was a case [in India], we knew that it was going to spread. … We are overpopulated … And that

is when we actually freaked out. … [In India, to even] go to [the] grocery store, there are going to be tens of thousands of people. … It's not possible to maintain … [the needed] hygiene.

Relatedly, when explaining Brazilian culture, Gabriela said, "we like to touch. We like to, you know, stay together. … It's very different … [from] Americans in terms of personal space." These examples highlight how participants' worries with regard to the health of their family members were intensified by the cultural conditions and norms of their home country.

Concerning Threats to Specific Family Members

In addition to cultural conditions/norms, many participants shared that they worried about the health of specific family members because of their age, previous health conditions, or occupations that placed them at a greater risk of being exposed. For example, Linh, whose family resided in Vietnam, shared, "I was really worried about my grandparents. They are old and they have … one of the highest chances of getting infected." Similarly, when discussing preexisting conditions that made certain family members vulnerable, Hamza, whose family lives in Pakistan, described, "My father is … a heart patient. God forbid … [if he got] the virus, it would [be] serious."

A final set of interviewees shared that they worried about a specific family member's health because of their increased COVID-19 exposure via their occupation. For example, Nastya, whose mom and dad both worked for the Russian healthcare system, shared, "my parents are doctors. So they were working, … not with … COVID patients, but they … [are] with patients." Even though her parents shared, "'We know what we are doing. … We are grown-ups,'" Nastya was still concerned about their potential exposure. Hence, the worries that a number of participants had with regard to the health of their family members stemmed from specific risks to which the participants' family members were susceptible.

Managing Uncertainties Related to Family's Health (RQ2a)

In line with our earlier findings, participants reported engaging in three main strategies to help them manage their uncertainty about their family members' health (RQ2a): giving informational directives, providing instrumental support, and appealing to emotions.

Giving Informational Directives

The overwhelming strategy shared among participants to manage the uncertainties they experienced related to their family's health was to give informational directives. For instance, Victoria, who was particularly worried that her grandfather may be exposed to COVID-19, shared, "I would call my mom [in Russia] and I ask her not to let him … go outside." Further, Emmanual, an ordained priest, stated, "[when COVID-19 reached Kenya] I told them … don't go to church on Sunday, because … this thing moves very fast." Emmanual continued, "that's when my mother realized, whoa [this is real, because] … I've never told them to do that [stay home from church]." Combined, these statements exemplify the informational directives that our participants provided to their family members to help them manage their uncertainty about their family's health.

Providing Instrumental Support

Some participants shared that they provided instrumental support to their family even though they lived abroad. For example, Iyana explained, "My friends and my family [in Singapore] started asking me … to ship hand sanitizers and masks and stuff. … I remember [going] through different supermarkets … to look for hand sanitizers [to send to them]." Similarly, Emmanual shared, "[I have] a friend from home … buying groceries for them [my family] to drop at [their] home." Thus, for Iyana and Emmanual, providing instrumental, tangible, support to their families reduced their uncertainty about whether or not their family would have safe access to cleaning supplies and food.

Appealing to Emotions

A final way in which participants managed uncertainties related to the health of their family members was by using persuasion to appeal to their emotions. Specifically, Prisha shared, "[my family acted like] nothing will happen to us … It's not [a] big thing." She continued, describing how she finally scared them into being more careful, stating:

> One day I just got aggravated and I told them … 'if anything happens to you, like they don't allow us to travel … so I won't be able to see you, I won't be able to visit you and nobody will [be] able to … do the last rites.' … [I used] a lot of emotional blackmailing so that they [would] take me seriously.

Relatedly, Camila, who has not been able to visit her 85-year-old grandfather in Brazil for more than six years, shared how she tried everything, even guilt, to convince her grandfather to be more careful, stating, "[I would say] 'If something happens. … like, I cannot go to Brazil. … [I] cannot leave [the U.S.].'" However, Camila shared, "[even with guilt], my grandfather, he keeps going out, [he] keeps taking public transportation. He just, he doesn't listen." These examples illustrate how participants used persuasive emotional appeals, albeit at times unsuccessfully, to impress the seriousness of COVID-19 on their family members and to persuade them to mitigate health-related risks.

Worrying about Personal Health (RQ1b)

In addition to being worried about the health of their family, numerous participants shared that they also worried about their personal health as COVID-19 spread. In particular, interviewees shared that their worries were exacerbated by cultural conditions/norms in the United States and rumination about the personal behaviors in which they had engaged.

Concerning Cultural Conditions/Norms

A number of participants shared that certain U.S. cultural conditions/norms increased the concerns they had about their personal health as COVID-19 spread. In particular, Iyana shared, "[in the U.S.], I actually feel really unsafe. … You guys don't do contact tracing." She continued, explaining:

> [At home, there is] an app where you have to scan every time you enter a public place … [so] they [the Singaporean government] know who is in that space. … and if there's a positive COVID patient … they will alert those people.

Last, participants listed the costs associated with the U.S. healthcare system as a cultural concern. Specifically, even though every participant had health insurance, Mercy, who grew up in the Kenyan healthcare system, described, "In the United States, you do not have social medicine. … So that's the biggest worry … [if] you get COVID. … [it seems] health insurance does not really … help." These examples illustrate how U.S. cultural conditions/norms contributed to participants' concerns about their own health.

Ruminating about Personal Behaviors

A final element that factored into participants' concerns for their health was their rumination about whether or not their past behaviors placed them at a higher risk for contracting COVID-19. For example, after meeting face-to-face with others, Mercy commented, "different ideas come in your mind, like, 'What if the person had COVID and the person didn't know?' … So were you exposed to COVID and then boom, boom, boom?" Hence, as illustrated by Mercy, participants shared that ruminating about the everyday behaviors in which they engaged made them uncertain about their personal health.

Managing Uncertainties Related to Personal Health (RQ2b)

The main strategies used by participants to manage and reduce their concerns about personal health after the onset and spread of COVID-19 were to adopt new behaviors and engage in self-care (RQ2b).

Adopting New Behaviors

An initial strategy used by participants to manage concerns related to their personal health involved adopting new, more hygienic, behaviors to reduce their risk of COVID-19 infection. For example, Nastya, who worked as a bridal gown associate, explained, "[even] though we have much less … appointments, … you are in very close contact with people." She continued, "[I am now always using] antibacterial wipes and washing hands." Although Nastya is still at risk, adopting these new behaviors helped put her mind at ease and allowed her to manage the concerns she had about COVID-related health risks.

Engaging in Self-Care

A final strategy used by participants to manage concerns about their personal health involved engaging in self-care. For example, Mariam, a graduate student who grew up in Egypt, explained, "The first month for me, shelter in place, I was devastated. … [I] was completely alone … [and] stopped going out because I didn't want to get on Muni [the bus] or [take an] Uber." Miriam continued, stating that things did not get better until she engaged in self-care. Specifically, she shared, "when I got the bike … it just started getting better. [And now, with my roommate back] … [We] hike … as much as we can."

Like Miriam, Prisha shared how she and her husband had started taking care of themselves better, describing, "We actually started cooking together, … going to hikes together." Moreover, Ayesha, a dual citizen from Singapore and Saudi Arabia, acknowledged how beneficial it was for her to meditate during this time, explaining, "One of the gifts that COVID has given me is [that] it changed my relationship with myself … and I got really clear … about what I wanted [in life]." Combined, adopting new behaviors and engaging in self-care were key for participants as they worked to manage and reduce their health concerns.

Deciding Where to Wait Out COVID-19 (RQ1c)

Our final finding related to RQ1 suggested that participants were uncertain about where to wait out COVID-19. These uncertainties, however, were rooted in participants' understanding of existing, new, and changing legal constraints and varying emotions.

Understanding Existing, New, and Changing Legal Constraints

For many of our participants, changing visa issues, anticipated quarantine mandates, and new travel restrictions intensified their uncertainty surrounding where to wait out COVID-19.

Changing Visa Issues. With regard to where to wait out COVID-19, an overwhelming number of participants shared that a major factor contributing to their uncertainty was their fear that the laws surrounding their student visa may change or that their visa may be put in jeopardy if they left the United States. For instance, Iyana, when talking about why she had not gone home to Singapore, shared,

> There are so many uncertainties. I don't know if I can come back [to the U.S.]. I don't know if they [the U.S. government] are going to allow me to come back. … There's all these uncertainties … that are stopping me from booking a flight.

Relatedly, Gabriela, who is in the process of getting her H1B work visa, shared, "they [U.S. policies] are changing a lot in terms of the immigration, … like every month or every week. … Trump [will] tweet [and] say that he was going to … ban or freeze [student visas], … it's very concerning." She continued, explaining, "while I'm in this [H1B visa] process … I don't want to risk [it]. … [for now, staying is] the best option." Thus, fear that the rules surrounding their visa status may change served as a source of uncertainty for participants and influenced their decision to stay in the United States.

Anticipating Quarantine Mandates. In addition to being concerned about changing visa issues, many participants shared that their uncertainty related to where to wait out COVID-19 was compounded by the anticipation they had regarding differing quarantine mandates. For example, Emmanual shared, "I want to go home." However, after learning from a friend who recently returned to Kenya that he had to quarantine for more than a month, Emmanual stated, "That's my biggest fear … quarantine at my own expense … and possibly not getting to see my family." Similarly, Victoria shared, "When you travel to Moscow … you need to [quarantine] for two weeks. … I couldn't just go and visit my family. I would need to stay at least two weeks, totally isolated, in a hotel." Combined, participants' uncertainty related to where and for how long they might need to quarantine influenced their travel decisions.

Navigating Travel Restrictions. A third and final factor contributing to our participants' uncertainty related to where they should wait out COVID-19 was the ever-changing travel restrictions of the United States and their home country that they had to navigate. Specifically, Mercy shared, when COVID-19 first hit the United States, "everything was so uncertain." She continued, sharing, "[going back to Kenya] wouldn't be a wise move … [because] maybe a [travel] restriction will be imposed. … Right now there's a restriction that no one [is allowed in from the U.S.]" Thus, although the current laws reduced her uncertainty (i.e., there was no option to travel), the ever-changing nature of these restrictions exacerbated Mercy's uncertainty about booking a flight home. Mercy's comments illustrate how the changing travel restrictions added to the uncertainty she had regarding where to wait out the pandemic.

Experiencing Varying Emotions

Many participants shared that they experienced varying emotions regarding where to wait out COVID-19. Specifically, interviewees shared that their emotions were intensified by the desires of their family members with regard to returning home or staying in the United States and their feelings about the United States/U.S. policy.

Feelings about Family's Desires. A number of participants shared that they experienced ongoing emotional contradictions with regard to returning home that stemmed from their family members' desires. Specifically, Prisha, who was scared about contracting COVID-19, shared how her family motivated her and her husband to stay in the United States, explaining, "We were thinking that we might [go back], but they [my in-laws] were the ones who said that 'You don't need to come back. … [It] is temporary. It's going to go [away].'" Unlike Prisha, whose family encouraged her to stay in the United States, Lihn explained, "My dad's been pushing me. He said … 'Come home [to Vietnam]. It's safer.'" In addition, Lihn stated, "My grandma [would] call me … very emotional … [begging] 'You just need to … get a slot on that rescue flight and … go home.'" Although Lihn told her family that the reason she was staying was because it was too risky to be on an airplane, she explained, "[I'm not ready to] end my day here."

Moreover, Iyana emphasized how her emotions were ongoing, sharing, "When it [COVID-19] exploded, my mom … [said], 'Just come back.' … [Then] she kind of stopped. … [But] recently she's like, 'Oh, … [class] is online. Why don't you just come back?'" Iyana continued, explaining, "Multiple times … I thought that maybe I should … [go] home. … [but that] feeling is a bit mixed."

Combined, these examples illustrate how the conflicting desires of international students' family members influenced the varying emotions they had regarding where to wait out COVID-19.

Feelings about U.S./U.S. Policy. Despite being excited to continue their education in the United States, many participants shared that they felt frustrated and dehumanized by the messages that were put out by the U.S. government with regard to international students. For example, Camila shared, "The pandemic just made it even more clear how hard it is for internationals living away, … the obstacles, all of the challenges. … This administration makes things even harder. … It's an emotional problem." Similarly, Mercy, when responding to a subsequently overturned U.S. order stating that international students were not going to be allowed to stay in the United States if their university classes were taught online, echoed:

> [I feel like the U.S. government is telling us] 'Your health does not matter.' … The fact that [we]'ve been told 'You must go to class … to maintain your status,' … [it] makes you take a step back and wonder whether the people who are making these decisions really are thinking about humanity.

These examples illustrate how governmental messaging and U.S. policies uniquely influenced international students' experiences with COVID-19.

Managing Varying Emotions (RQ2c)

Although participants did not report engaging in specific strategies to manage their feelings about new, existing, and changing U.S. policies on international travel, two specific strategies, communicating more with and withholding information from family members, were used by participants to process the desires of their family members related to where to wait out COVID-19 (RQ2c).

Communicating More

The most common way in which participants managed the desires of their family members related to where to wait out COVID-19 was to communicate with them more often. Specifically, when sharing how she managed the pressure from her mother to come home, Iyana explained, "[we] video chat every week." Similarly, Mercy shared, "I was in constant communication with my family" and Camila stated, "[I talk to] my grandparents every day." Thus, by engaging in regular and scheduled communication with family members, participants were able to manage some of the intense emotions surrounding their family member's ongoing desires for them to either stay in the United States or return home.

Withholding Information

A final subset of participants reported that they withheld information from their family members in order to mitigate their emotions related to the ongoing pressures for them to return home. For instance, when talking to her parents, Prisha explained, "I will not share the statistics ... how many [cases] ... the death rate. ... We [my husband and I] just [say], 'We are fine, and, it's fine.'" Similarly, Kiara, who recently received an email that someone in her apartment complex tested positive for COVID-19, explained, "We didn't tell her [my mom] ... because, you know, that again [would] freak them [my parents] out." Thus, withholding information from their family members related to COVID-19 allowed the participants to manage some of the emotions surrounding their family members' ongoing desires for them to return home.

Impact on Personal Relationships (RQ3)

Although some participants shared that their relationships with family and friends did not change, many indicated that COVID-19 impacted their personal relationships in two distinct, positive, ways: (a) They became closer with friends and (b) connected more with family members (RQ3).

Becoming Closer with Friends

A number of participants indicated that their long-distance friendships thrived in the midst of COVID-19. Specifically, Victoria shared,

> At the beginning of COVID, I would call every day to my friends [in Russia] that I didn't have conversation [with] for months. ... Everyone [had] anxiety and they wanted to ... talk about that. ... So I would have like a lot of calls with my friends that I didn't have before.

Similarly, Charlotte, who returned home to England, shared that she was worried about maintaining her friendships with people in the United States, describing, "I'm actually really impressed, ... I think [I've connected with] more people than I thought I would." She continued, sharing, "I got much, much, closer with my ... friends." Hence, despite the geographical distance that

COVID-19 forced on participants, many stated that this pandemic allowed them to reengage with important friends in their life.

Connecting More with Family

In addition to becoming closer with select friends, some participants also indicated that they connected more with family members during this time. For example, Victoria explained, "[I think] fear … brings people together." In particular, she shared, "During the pandemic … [I] started calling my extended relatives [in Russia], which I did not do before. … I realized that I should talk with them and see if they're okay. … We started talking a lot." Similarly, Hamza shared: "these things do bring you a lot closer. … [when you are] that far away from where your family is … it does bring it [the family] closer." In addition, Camila explained, "[COVID-19] gives us this need to check in on each other more often. … [it] created a bigger like bond."

Thus, many participants shared that COVID-19 served as a trigger for them to foster their friendships and connect with family members in ways that they had not done earlier. Moreover, although participants did not report seeking out friends and family members as a specific uncertainty management strategy, their efforts to reengage with these individuals were often reported as resulting from their COVID-19-related anxieties.

DISCUSSION

The purpose of this study was to examine how international students experienced and managed uncertainty during the COVID-19 pandemic. Further, we aimed at understanding how, if at all, this pandemic impacted international students' personal relationships. Our findings suggest that COVID-19 was and is a significant circumstantial, episodic, uncertainty-inducing phenomenon that required international students to manage multiple, concurrent uncertainties in a diverse set of ways, which, in some cases, inadvertently and positively impacted their relationships. In what follows, we highlight how our findings connect to previous research on COVID-19 and international students, make connections between our results and theorizing on uncertainty management, and discuss the limitations and implications of this study.

First, although COVID-19 caused many individuals to be more concerned about the health of their family members (e.g., Cohen et al., 2020), our findings indicated that international students' concerns were amplified when the cultural norms of their home country facilitated the spread of this virus. Specifically, many participants expressed that their family's inability to socially distance due to population density, consumer behaviors, and regular haptic communication behaviors (e.g., touching/affection) intensified their concerns about their family members contracting COVID-19. These cultural findings add to the current body of literature on COVID-19, as they identify distinct, culturally based, health and safety uncertainties that are unique to this population. Moreover, consistent with research on uncertainty management (Brashers, 2001), support in times of crisis

(Li et al., 2020), and persuasion (Xu & Guo, 2018), we found that international students engaged in three primary strategies to manage the uncertainty they had for their family's health: They (a) provided informational directives (e.g., insisted mask wearing), (b) gave instrumental support (e.g., arranged delivery of food/goods to their family abroad), and (c) appealed to their family members' emotions (e.g., communicated their fear/sadness related to the potential illness/death of their family members). Further, these findings signal that COVID-19 may be a context in which some individuals dismissed their culture's expectations for filial piety (Dia & Diamond, 1998), such that many participants provided information, advice, and made emotional appeals to older family members because their concerns were so grave that they felt the need to provide unsolicited advice/instruction.

A second uncertainty expressed by participants was that COVID-19 gave rise to new concerns about their personal health. Specifically, participants shared that their health worries were exacerbated by cultural conditions/norms in the United States (e.g., no formal contact tracing and an expensive healthcare system) and rumination about personal behaviors in which they had engaged. Although our findings regarding participants' concerns related to health via cultural hygiene and contact tracing are new and possibly unique to COVID-19, our results regarding participants' increased uncertainty due to the U.S. healthcare system are consistent with Adegboyega et al.'s (2020) research, as they reported that understanding the U.S. healthcare system is a challenge that international students often struggle to navigate. Further, although participants were unable to change the cultural norms to which they were subjected, they adapted by adopting new behaviors and engaging in self-care to manage their uncertainty. Combined, this finding, similar to the result reported earlier, reiterates that international students' uncertainties related to their health and COVID-19 were heightened when the cultural conditions/norms of the United States deviated from those to which they were accustomed.

Third, many of the international students in our study shared that they experienced uncertainty regarding their decision about where to wait out COVID-19. This uncertainty was exacerbated by the legal constraints surrounding international travel, their family's desires for them to stay in the United States or return home, and the emotions they had about the United States/U.S. policy. Although many university students across the United States likely had to consider the desires of their family members when deciding whether or not to return home as COVID-19 spread, international students' experiences with this uncertainty were uniquely heightened, as their uncertainty was compounded by U.S. policies that they felt placed their health at risk, changing visa issues, anticipated quarantine mandates, and new travel restrictions. Specifically, our findings regarding changing visa issues and legal constraints were consistent with Eder et al. (2010), who found that, even without the additional uncertainty of a pandemic, visa concerns are a major problem faced by students when they consider studying in the United States. Moreover, this finding is further supported by Bista and Dagley (2015), as they added that the visa process and obtaining the correct documents were more difficult than actually getting accepted to a university itself.

The quarantine concerns mentioned by participants echo those of Brooks et al. (2020), who found that there were negative psychological effects associated with extended quarantine. Combined, this finding reiterates Brashers' (2001) claim that multiple uncertainties often occur simultaneously. However, considering the extent to which so many of these concerns were out of their control, the only aspects that our participants reported managing—via communicating more with their family and withholding information—were the desires of their family members related to where they should wait out COVID-19.

Last, contrary to the literature that reports that COVID-19 contributes to a number of negative outcomes for personal relationships (e.g., Pietromonaco & Overall, 2020), the international students in our study most often reported that COVID-19 gave rise to more communication and promoted feelings of closeness with their friends and family. As such, our findings are consistent with Goodwin et al. (2020), who reported that, for younger individuals, this pandemic enhanced relationships with friends, and Nitschke et al. (2021), who argued that social connections buffer individuals against pandemic-specific stress. Relatedly, our findings align with the network activation hypothesis, as it suggests that friendships and social networks are often activated and increased during times of a health crisis (e.g., Latham-Mintus, 2019). Hence, although there is a great deal of literature suggesting that COVID-19 has contributed to relationship strain, our findings suggest that international students' relationships may thrive in times of crisis, as personal connections may serve as a source of certainty for them in an otherwise chaotic situation.

Limitations/Future Research

Despite its strengths, there are limitations of this study that should be addressed in future research. First, our sample size was small, did not include a large group of individuals from one country, lacked representation from our university's Chinese international student body, and most of our participants were single. Therefore, we were unable to compare the uncertainties experienced by individuals from Eastern versus Western cultures or gauge whether or not having a spouse mitigated or exacerbated the participants' COVID-19 uncertainties.

Second, this study was cross-sectional, such that data were collected at one time during the fourth and fifth month of the COVID-19 pandemic in the United States. During this time, participants may have experienced the most acute stress, as the pandemic was a new experience. Thus, future research should explore to what extent uncertainty unfolded over time and examine whether or not the concerns felt by international students and the management techniques they reported evolved throughout the duration of the pandemic.

Implications

Our findings offer further support for examining uncertainty cross-culturally. Specifically, Hofstede (1980) reported that individuals from Western and Eastern cultures handle uncertainty differently, such that Eastern cultures are more uncertainty avoidant and Western cultures are more comfortable with uncertainty. Although our findings did not seek to uncover differences across cultures, we did find that culture and cultural circumstances/norms surrounding COVID-19 were central to participants' experiences as they served to exacerbate uncertainty and should be further explored.

Our findings also have practical implications for how universities and family members can better support international students in the midst of health crises. First, universities should work to better understand the unique circumstances of international students during a pandemic. Institutions should set up understandable mechanisms to communicate directly with international students about how to manage the concerns they have about family members, help them navigate the changing visa issues, and provide resources to help them manage their roles not only as students, but also as individuals separated from their families during a global crisis. Last, family members of international students must make time to talk to them, encourage them to express their feelings, listen, and acknowledge their concerns, as these strategies may buffer their stress during uncertain times.

In sum, our findings illustrate that international students experienced a range of uncertainties throughout the COVID-19 pandemic, many that were culturally based. In turn, participants engaged in a range of related coping mechanisms to manage their uncertainty. Despite these uncertainties, the relationships that our participants had with their family and friends often benefited from the support they offered to one another during this time. Moreover, our findings suggest that personal relationships may serve as a safeguard for international students, not only during a pandemic, but also perhaps as they face new situations, in a new country, on a day-to-day basis.

REFERENCES

Adegboyega, A., Nkwonta, C. A., & Edward, J. (2020). Health insurance literacy among international college students: A qualitative analysis. *Journal of International Students, 10*(1), 50–68. https://doi.org/10.32674/jis.v10i1.1097

Andrade, M. S. (2006). International students in English speaking universities: Adjustments factors. *Journal of Research in International Education, 5*(2), 131–154. https://doi.org/10.1177/1475240906065589

Babrow, A. S., & Striley, K. M. (2015). Problematic integration theory and uncertainty management theory: Learning how to hear and speak to different forms of uncertainty. In D. O. Braithwaite & P. Schrodt (Eds), *Engaging theories of interpersonal communication: Multiple perspectives* (2nd ed., pp. 103–114). Sage.

Berger, C. R., & Calabrese, R. J. (1975). Some explorations in initial interaction and beyond: Toward a developmental theory of interpersonal communication. *Human Communication Research, 1*, 99–112. https://doi.org/10.1111/j.1468-2958.1975.tb00258.x

Bista, K. (2016). Examining the research on international students: Where are we today? *Journal of International Students, 6*(2), I–X. https://www.ojed.org/index.php/jis/article/view/360

Bista, K., & Dagley, A. (2015). Higher education preparation and decision-making trends among international students. *College and University, 90*(3), 2–11. http://works.bepress.com/bista/45/

Brashers, D. E. (2001). Communication and uncertainty management. *Journal of Communication, 51*, 477–497. https://doi.org/10.1111/j.1460-2466.2001.tb02892.x

Braun, V., & Clarke, V. (2006). Using thematic analysis in psychology. *Qualitative Research in Psychology, 3*(2), 77–101. https://doi.org/10.1191/1478088706qp063oa

Brooks, S. K., Webster, R. K., Smith, L. E., Woodland, L., Wessely, S., Greenberg, N., & Rubin, G. J. (2020). The psychological impact of quarantine and how to reduce it: Rapid review of the evidence. *Lancet, 395*(10227), 912–920. https://doi.org/10.1016/S0140-6736(20)30460-8

Cohen, A. K., Hoyt, L. T., & Dull, B. (2020). A descriptive study of COVID-19-related experiences and perspectives of a national sample of college students in Spring 2020. *The Journal of Adolescent Health, 67*(3), 369–375. https://doi.org/10.1016/j.jadohealth.2020.06.009

Creswell, J. W., & Miller, D. L. (2000). Determining validity in qualitative inquiry. *Theory into Practice, 39*(3), 124–130. https://doi.org/10.1207/s15430421tip3903_2

Dalton, L., Rapa, E., & Stein, A. (2020). Protecting the psychological health of children through effective communication about COVID-19. *The Lancet: Child & Adolescent Health, 4*(5), 346–347. https://doi.org/10.1016/S2352-4642(20)30097-3

Dia, Y. T., & Diamond, M. R. (1998). Filial piety. A cross-cultural comparison and its implications for the well-being of older parents. *Journal of Gerontological Nursing, 24*(3), 13–18. https://doi.org/10.3928/0098-9134-19980301-05

Eder, J., Smith, W., & Pitts, R. (2010). Exploring factors influencing student study abroad destination choice. *Journal of Teaching in Travel & Tourism, 10*(3), 232–250. https://doi.org/10.1080/15313220.2010.503534

Goodwin, R., Hou, W. K., Sun, S., & Ben-Ezra, M. (2020). Quarantine, distress and interpersonal relationships during COVID-19. *General Psychiatry.* Advance online publication. https://doi.org/10.1136/gpsych-2020-100385

Hofstede, G. (1980). *Culture's consequences: International differences in work-related values.* Sage.

Institute of International Education (2019). *Open doors 2019 data online: Using data to open doors.* https://opendoorsdata.org/

Kim, Y. K., & Cronley, C. (2020) Acculturative stress and binge drinking among international students in the United States: Resilience and vulnerability approaches. *Journal of American College Health, 68*(2), 207–218. https://doi.org/10.1080/07448481.2018.1538998

Latham-Mintus, K. (2019). A friend in need? Exploring the influence of disease and disability onset on the number of close friends among older adults. *The Journals of Gerontology. Series B, Psychological Sciences and Social Sciences, 74*(8), 119–124. https://doi.org/10.1093/geronb/gbz050

Li, J., Liang, W., Yuan, B., & Zeng, G. (2020). Internalized stigmatization, social support, and individual mental health problems in the public health crisis. *International Journal of Environmental Research and Public Health, 17*(12), 4507. http://doi.org/10.3390/ijerph17124507

Luetke, M., Hensel, D., Herbenick, D., & Rosenberg, M. (2020). Romantic relationship conflict due to the COVID-19 pandemic and changes in intimate and sexual behaviors in a nationally representative sample of American adults. *Journal of Sex & Marital Therapy, 46*(8), 747–762. http://doi.org/10.1080/0092623X.2020.1810185

Mesidor, J. K., & Sly, K. F. (2016). Factors that contribute to the adjustment of international students. *Journal of International Students, 6*(1), 262–282. https://www.ojed.org/index.php/jis/article/view/569

Nitschke, J. P., Forbes, P., Ali, N., Cutler, J., Apps, M., Lockwood, P. L., & Lamm, C. (2021). Resilience during uncertainty? Greater social connectedness during COVID-19 lockdown is associated with reduced distress and fatigue. *British Journal of Health Psychology, 26*(2), 553–569. https://doi.org/10.1111/bjhp.12485

Pietromonaco, P. R., & Overall, N. C. (2020). Applying relationship science to evaluate how the COVID-19 pandemic may impact couples' relationships. *American Psychologist.* Advance online publication. http://dx.doi.org/10.1037/amp0000714

Smith, R. A., & Khawaja, N. G. (2011). A review of the acculturation experiences of international students. *International Journal of Intercultural Relations, 35*(6), 699–713. https://doi.org/10.1016/j.ijintrel.2011.08.004

Wilczewski, M., Gorbaniuk, O., & Giuri, P. (2021). The psychological and academic effects of studying from the home and host country during the COVID-19 pandemic. *Frontiers in Psychology, 12*, 644096–644107. https://doi.org/10.3389/fpsyg.2021.644096

Xu, Z., & Guo, H. (2018). A meta-analysis of the effectiveness of guilt on health-related attitudes and intentions. *Health Communication, 33*(5), 519–525. https://doi.org/10.1080/10410236.2017.1278633

ALLISON R. THORSON (Ph.D., University of Nebraska-Lincoln) is a professor in the Department of Communication Studies at the University of San Francisco. Email: athorson@usfca.edu

EVE-ANNE M. DOOHAN (Ph.D., University of Washington) is an associate professor in the Department of Communication Studies at the University of San Francisco. Email: edoohan@usfca.edu

LEAH Z. CLATTERBUCK is an undergraduate student at the University of San Francisco. Email: lzclatterbuck@dons.usfca.edu

Research Article

© *Journal of International Students*
Volume 12, Issue 3 (2022), pp. 674-693
ISSN: 2162-3104 (Print), 2166-3750 (Online)
doi: 10.32674/jis.v12i3.3667
ojed.org/jis

Resilience and Intercultural Interactions of Italian Erasmus Students: The Relation with Cultural Intelligence

Valentina Dolce[1]
Institute of Psychology, Groupe de Recherche en Psychologie Sociale (GRePS), Université Lumière Lyon 2, France

Chiara Ghislieri
Department of Psychology, University of Turin, Italy

ABSTRACT

Cultural Intelligence (CQ) is examined in the literature; nevertheless, a few studies have combined situational and personal aspects to enhance the comprehension of this construct, and none have considered resilience. Therefore, this study aims at investigating the role of international Erasmus students' resilience, the length of their experience, and the intercultural interactions of Italian Erasmus students in their relationship with CQ. Data were collected from 791 outgoing Italian Erasmus students by using a self-report questionnaire. The findings suggested the existence of a significant relationship between resilience and all dimensions of CQ, showing, with the exception of the behavioral dimension, large betas. Forming friendships with international students was positively and moderately related to motivational and metacognitive CQ. Establishing relationships with locals was only positively and weakly related to cognitive CQ. The time of sojourn was only positively and weakly associated with the metacognitive CQ. Developments in international academic mobility policies are discussed.

---

[1] Corresponding author.

Keywords: cultural intelligence, erasmus program, intercultural relations, international students, resilience

INTRODUCTION

Despite limitations related to the outbreak of the COVID-19 pandemic, international mobility has grown exponentially in the 21st century as far as education and work are concerned. In spite of the facilities introduced by the possibility of remote meetings and classes, mobility across boundaries will likely continue to be promoted in higher education through various international programs, as evidenced by the efforts of the European Commission to boost international mobility in safety. The European Region Action Scheme for the Mobility of University Students (ERASMUS) is one of the main international programs promoted in higher education in Europe. According to the Erasmus+ Annual Report 2019 more than 444,000 students, trainees and staff benefited from a learning period abroad during the 2018/2019 academic year. Erasmus Plus sustains the mobility of both students and staff for a temporary stay abroad.

A fragmented corpus of studies has been developed to monitor the expected learning outcomes of various study-abroad programs (Varela, 2017), such as global careers (e.g., Mohajeri Norris et al., 2009) and cross-cultural competencies, specifically cultural intelligence (CQ; e.g., Varela & Garlin-Watts, 2014). Our study considers the Erasmus Program and focuses on the construct of CQ (Ang et al., 2007): a set of intercultural capabilities "that determine what a person is capable of doing to be effective in culturally diverse settings" (Ang et al., 2015, p. 434).

In line with previous studies (Crowne, 2008; Moon et al., 2012; Uen et al., 2018) that found a positive relationship between international experience and CQ, this study attempts to shed more light on how situational factors of the Erasmus Program are related to CQ, focusing attention on certain quality aspects of experiences abroad. For this purpose, we explore how the length of the experience and the nature of the international network developed abroad are related to the four dimensions of CQ, namely the cognitive, metacognitive, behavioral, and motivational CQ. We also explore the role of the resilience of international students represented in our study by a sample of outgoing Italian Erasmus students. Resilience was studied in relation to the intercultural adjustment process (e.g., Mesidor & Sly, 2016), but it is still fairly unexplored in relation to all four dimensions of CQ. Resilience reflects a person's ability to adapt well in the face of stressful circumstances and to thrive despite the difficulties (Joyce et al., 2018). The investigation of its relationship with the CQ dimensions, together with other situational factors, can provide useful information for effective training or mentoring or counseling practices, for instance during the pre-departure phase. In addition to resilience, in line with the Social Learning Cognitive Theory (SLCT; Bandura, 1997), we considered both personal and situational factors in exploring the CQ. Finally, based on Ng and colleagues' theoretical recommendations (2012), which warned about the fact that very little is known about how each CQ dimension works, the present contribution pays attention separately to all four dimensions of CQ.

Research Question

This study empirically investigates the situational and personal factors related to CQ to enhance the comprehension of this construct and to provide practical implications to value the students' international mobility experience. The research question of this study is: "which are the situational and personal factors associated with the Erasmus students' CQ?". In the complexity of the abroad experience (Khanal & Gaulee, 2019), resilience has been poorly studied despite its possible role: this paper focuses on it. Beyond personal factors, by virtue of the peculiarities of Erasmus mobility programs, known for their ability to facilitate students' exchanges, the intercultural interactions with local and/or other international students were investigated. Finally, the role of the last of sojourn— which can vary from one to two semesters abroad in the case of Erasmus exchanges—was examined to better understand its role (Varela, 2017). Beyond the fact that this paper originally and simultaneously considers personal and contextual factors, it is focused on the Italian Erasmus students, a not-native English speakers' population, for which there are still a few contributions in literature, providing information and suggestions also for higher education institutions.

LITERATURE REVIEW

Theoretical Framework

Based on the Social Learning Cognitive Theory (SLCT; Bandura, 1997), we explored the link between resilience, some situational factors, and the four dimensions of CQ (Ott & Michailova, 2018). According to the Social Learning Theory (SLT, Bandura, 1977), learning stems from interactions and occurs within a social context. To provide a more comprehensive explanation, Bandura (1997) included the cognitive components, expanding SLT. In particular, Bandura (1997) deepened the role played by self-efficacy, namely the optimistic belief that a person can have in reaching a goal and performing activities. Higher levels of self-efficacy correspond to a greater tendency to consider difficulties and problems as challenges rather than as threats (Bandura, 1997); therefore, highly self-efficacious people tend to be more ambitious and look for challenging goals and demanding experiences (Schwarzer & Warner, 2013). Self-efficacy can have a positive impact on affective, motivational, and behavioral mechanisms and is closely related to resilience, namely the capability to adapt and cope with problematic situations (Schwarzer & Warner, 2013). However, self-efficacy can be present if the source of the stressor is absent, whereas resilience is strongly related to the presence of an adversity (Schwarzer & Warner, 2013). International mobility can be conceptualized as a stressful and challenging experience: when abroad, people are usually faced with intercultural misunderstandings, difficulties in communication, fatigue caused by having to manage social norms and practices, and so forth (Johnson et al., 2018; Ma & Wen, 2018; Sherry et al., 2010; Smith & Khawaja, 2011). Thus, international experiences are fertile ground for cultural competence's acquisition (Ott & Michailova, 2018), and, based on this theoretical framework (Bandura, 1997), personal and situational factors are associated with the learning process and specifically related to the four CQ dimensions.

Cultural Intelligence

CQ is a multidimensional construct defined as "an individual's capability to function and manage effectively in culturally diverse settings" (Ang et al., 2007, p. 337). This individual capability transcends cultural boundaries, and it is applicable to any culture (Ng et al., 2012). CQ comprises four dimensions that are intertwined and help people to engage in effective behaviors; to show sensibility, empathy, flexibility, and adaptation; to enjoy culturally diverse contexts; and to understand the crucial social practices, rules, and habits of other cultures (Schein, 2018). In this regard, CQ is considered a relevant requirement of today's world (Sharma & Hussain, 2017). Various studies have highlighted that CQ relates to a wide range of outcomes (Ang et al., 2015): better cultural adjustment (e.g., Leung et al., 2014), the perception of less emotional exhaustion when living or traveling abroad (Tay et al., 2008), better cultural judgment and decision making, and so forth (Ang et al., 2007). Based on the Sternberg multiple-loci conceptualization (1986), CQ consists of four components: cognitive, metacognitive, behavioral, and motivational.

More specifically, the cognitive component refers to knowledge about conventions, legal norms, economic rules, and awareness of social practices. People with a higher level of CQ are able to recognize differences and similarities among diverse countries (Ng & Earley, 2006; Ng et al., 2012). By comparison, metacognitive CQ concerns higher-order cognitive processes; it reflects mental processes that individuals use to acquire and understand cultural knowledge. People with a high level of metacognitive CQ are able to plan and monitor their own mental models, and to adjust them during and after cross-cultural interactions (Ang & Van Dyne, 2008; Earley et al., 2006; Ng et al., 2012). The motivational component reflects the ability to direct positive energy toward learning about culturally diverse systems (Ang et al., 2007, Ang & Van Dyne, 2008; Earley et al., 2006; Ng et al., 2012). Those with a high level of motivational CQ are willing to meet people from other countries, take action in another culture, travel, and interact in cross-cultural situations. Lastly, the behavioral dimension is related to all appropriate verbal and non-verbal actions such as language, tone, posture, and facial expressions, which people use differently in culturally diverse settings (Ang et al., 2007; Ang & Van Dyne, 2008; Ng et al., 2012).

Personal and Situational Factors Associated with Cultural Intelligence

CQ has recently piqued the interest of many scholars, some of whom have tried to explore the variables associated with it (Ott & Michailova, 2018). As highlighted by Ng and colleagues (2012), personality traits and international experience have been the most investigated predictors (e.g., Ang et al., 2006; Crowford-Mathis, 2009; Moon et al., 2012); however, a few studies have analyzed the quality of the experience, or other situational and environmental aspects.

In addition to personality traits, some other personal characteristics have also been investigated in relation to CQ, such as self-efficacy (e.g., MacNab & Worthley, 2012). MacNab and Worthley (2012) found that self-efficacy was a strong predictor of learning CQ as well as its three subcomponents studied metacognitive, motivation, and behavior. Despite the interest in self-efficacy, the close construct of resilience (Schwarzer & Warner, 2013) has not yet been investigated in relation to CQ; a recent contribution by Ghislieri et al. (2018), carried out on a sample of students who had participated in an exchange program during high school, showed the presence of a strong correlation between resilience and self-efficacy as well as with all four CQ dimensions. Resilience is an individual ability possessed by people who can adapt when faced with stressful situations and who manage to thrive despite hindrances, adversity, and challenges (Joyce et al., 2018). Just like self-efficacy, resilience drives people to react proactively in order to achieve their own objectives, especially in stressful situations (Schwarzer & Warner, 2013). As described by scholars since the 1960s (Ma & Wen, 2018; Oberg, 1960; Sherry et al., 2010; Smith & Khawaja, 2011), international mobility experiences can be considered a source of stress. Indeed, after an initial period of euphoria, when the feeling of satisfaction associated with the novelty of the environment declines, people abroad tend to experience a sense of personal disorientation, a culture shock (Oberg, 1960). A new cultural setting may imply for individuals a change in one's values, behaviors, and beliefs, generating a certain amount of acculturative stress (Berry, 1997, 2005). In line with the challenge model (O'Leary, 1998) according to which if a risk factor is not too extreme, it can enhance a person's adaptation (Ledesma, 2014) and in line with SLCT (Bandura, 1997), resilience can be identified as a key individual ability related to the intercultural adjustment and cultural learning (Mesidor & Sly, 2016; Van der Zee & Van Oudenhoven, 2013) and, more generally, in assisting students to overcome challenges in higher education (Brewer et al., 2019). Indeed, similar to self-efficacy (MacNab & Worthley, 2012), resilience can be strongly associated with motivational, behavioral, cognitive, and metacognitive mechanisms; thus, we assumed:

Hypothesis 1. Resilience is positively and strongly related to all components of CQ.

In addition to personal characteristics, some scholars have also studied the roles played by certain situational factors as predictors of CQ (e.g., Crowne, 2008, Moon et al., 2012; Uen et al. 2018). More specifically, some scholars found that the number of countries visited for employment and for education is positively related to the total CQ (Crowne, 2008), as well as to the length of the experience abroad (Crowford-Mathis, 2009; Li et al., 2013). In particular, Crowford-Mathis (2009) conducted a longitudinal study on a sample of Belizean volunteers involved in service-learning activities and found that the participants who spent the most time abroad and interacted more with the locals benefited the most in terms of CQ. In a more recent work, involving a sample of international managers from China, Li et al. (2013) found that the length of overseas work was positively associated with CQ although the betas were relatively low, and this relationship was stronger for those with a divergent-style learning.

In the light of these findings and Varela's (2017) meta-analysis, which not only invited us to explore the role of time spent abroad but also indicated that short programs (< 8 weeks) seem to play a role in attitudinal and behavioral learning, we hypothesized:

> *Hypothesis 2.* The length of the stay abroad is positively but weakly related to all components of CQ.

Finally, also intercultural contact is a core element of international experience, and people abroad usually develop three types of friendship networks, namely monocultural (interaction with compatriots), bicultural (interaction with locals), and multicultural (interaction with non-compatriot foreigners) (Bochner et al., 1977; McFaul, 2016; Ward et al., 2001); each social network serves specific psychological functions. Since the 1990s, some scholars have pointed out the benefits of intercultural contact (Smith & Khawaja, 2011; Ward et al., 2001), underlining, for instance, the reduced perception of loneliness, as found by Sawir and colleagues (2008), who conducted a study with international students in Australia, or the positive relationship with the sojourn satisfaction (Rohrlich & Martin, 1991). Further, according to SLT (Bandura, 1977), the interaction with individuals is the core component of learning. Some empirical studies (e.g., Moon et al., 2012; Ng & Earley, 2006) have suggested that social contacts enhance opportunities for enhancing cross-cultural competencies. More specifically, Moon et al. (2012), who conducted a study involving a sample of expatriates from Korean companies, found that the relation between the number of local employees and metacognitive and behavioral CQ is moderated by expatriates' portion of interaction with local employees; in addition, Ng and Earley (2006) suggested that intercultural contact in working environments may have an impact on CQ. Therefore, paying attention to a student population, we hypothesized that:

> *Hypothesis 3a:* Friendships with local students are positively and strongly related to all components of CQ.

> *Hypothesis 3b:* Friendships with international students are positively and strongly related to all components of CQ.

CQ and the variable related to it have been examined in the literature; however, a few studies have combined situational and personal aspects, and none have considered resilience.

METHOD

Participants and Procedure

The sample consisted of 791 outgoing Italian Erasmus students; their average age was around 22 years ($M = 22.42$, $SD = 1.69$). The students were enrolled at a university in northwest Italy and hailed from different fields of study: 30% from law, political and economic sciences; 26% from the humanities; 19% from life sciences; 16% from psychological, educational, and anthropological sciences; 3% from math and physics; 3% from earth science; and 3% from other study courses. Regarding the country of sojourn, Spain was the destination chosen by the highest proportion of the participants (33%), followed by France (21%), Germany (9%), Scandinavian countries (8%), Portugal (8%), Poland (4%), the United Kingdom and Ireland (5%), Balkan States (3%), Baltic States (2%), Belgium (2%), and other countries (5%). Students spent on average almost 7 months abroad ($M = 6.74$, $SD = 2.32$).

A total of 75% females took part in this study; this rate is in line with female participation in Erasmus programs at the university where the study was conducted, which stands at 68%. Further, at this university, males outnumber females in the fields of study of Computer Science, Math, Physics, and Earth Sciences,[2] which were underrepresented in the present sample.

The students completed a self-report questionnaire online on the LimeSurvey platform. Participants in the study completed the questionnaire about one month after the end of their Erasmus experience, a time interval far enough from the experience to avoid the disturbing effect of emotional charge due to the return, but relatively close to avoid the other experiences that would interfere with the results. Data were collected from three cohorts of Erasmus students, between 2016 and 2018; this sample represents 21% of the outgoing Erasmus student population of the Italian university in which the research was conducted. The voluntary and unpaid nature of participation in the research as well as the confidentiality of data were emphasized. We obtained each participant's informed consent. The study was conducted in accordance with the Helsinki Declaration (World Medical Association [WMA], 2001); since it did not involve medical treatment or other procedures capable of causing any psychological or social discomfort to participants, no further ethical approval was required.

Measures

The first section of the questionnaire collected sociodemographic data and information about international mobility (e.g., destination, length of experience). In particular, the time of sojourn was measured in months. Age, gender, and cultural distance were used as control variables.

---

[2] University internal sources.

Cultural distance: In order to calculate cultural distance, we used the formula by Kogut and Singh's (1988), taking into consideration the differences in cultural dimensions between Italy and the other countries. We considered the six dimensions of the updated Hofstede model (2011): power distance, individualism, masculinity, uncertainty, indulgence, and long-term orientation. All countries' indices were obtained, starting from Hofstede's (2015) site. The countries identified as culturally distant from Italy were as follows: the Scandinavian countries, certain Balkan States, Portugal, the United Kingdom, and Austria.

Cultural Intelligence: This was measured by 20 items from the Ghislieri et al.'s Italian adaptation (2018) of the CQS (Ang et al., 2007), using a 7-point Likert scale with scores ranging from 1 (strongly disagree) to 7 (strongly agree). Four dimensions define the factor-structure of this scale: cognitive, metacognitive, motivational, and behavioral. The *cognitive dimension* was measured by six items; an example item is "I know the legal and economic systems of other cultures." Cronbach's alpha was .79. The *metacognitive dimension* was evaluated by using four items; an example item is "I am conscious of the cultural knowledge I use when interacting with people with different cultural backgrounds." Cronbach's alpha was .82. The *motivational dimension* was measured by five items; an example item is "I enjoy interacting with people from different cultures." Cronbach's alpha was .83. Finally, the *behavioral dimension* was evaluated by using five items; an example item is "I change my verbal behavior (e.g., accent, tone) when a cross-cultural interaction requires it." Cronbach's alpha was .85.

Resilience: This was measured by 10 items from the Italian adaptation by Di Fabio and Palazzeschi (2012) (Connor & Davidson, 2003), with a 5-point Likert scale with scores ranging from 1 (strongly disagree) to 5 (strongly agree); an example item is "I tend to bounce back after illness, injury, or other hardships." Cronbach's alpha was .83.

Intercultural contacts: Students were asked whether they had established relationships and made friends first with local students (1 item) and second with foreign students (1 item) by using a 5-point Likert scale, with scores ranging from 1 (not at all) to 5 (completely).

Data Analysis

SPSS 25 statistics software was used to perform descriptive data analysis. Pearson correlations were tested to detect relationships between variables, and Cronbach's alpha coefficient was calculated to verify scale reliability. A full structural equation model (SEM) was tested by using Mplus7 in order to estimate the hypothesized regressions. The method of estimation was Maximum Likelihood (ML). According to the literature (Bollen & Long, 1993), the model was assessed by using several goodness-of-fit criteria: the $\chi2$ goodness-of-fit statistic; the Root Mean Square Error of Approximation (RMSEA); the Comparative Fit Index (CFI); the Tucker Lewis Index (TLI); and the Standardized Root Mean Square Residual (SRMR).

RESULTS

Correlations and Descriptive Statistics

The four dimensions of CQ, as illustrated in the correlation matrix (Table 1), were significantly positively related one with another. The control variables did not correlate with resilience and the dimensions of CQ, except for gender, which was positively related to the motivational dimension ($r = .07$, $p < .05$). Internal consistency of measures was good, since all α values met the criterion of .70 (Nunnally & Bernstein, 1994), as they ranged between .79 and .83.

Table 1: Correlation Analysis and Descriptive Statistics

	M	SD	1.	2.	3.	4.	5.	6.	7.	8.	9.	10.	11.
1. Cognitive CQ	4.07	.88	(.79)										
2. Metacognitive CQ	5.04	.93	.63**	(.82)									
3. Motivational CQ	5.55	.96	.35**	.52**	(.83)								
4. Behavioral CQ	4.66	1.18	.40**	.50**	.45**	(.85)							
5. Resilience	3.82	.55	.32**	.32**	.39**	.19**	(.83)						
6. Friendship with locals	3.46	1.22	.15**	.09*	.15**	.09*	.20**	-					
7. Friendship with international students	4.29	.97	.10**	.18**	.30**	.09*	.19**	.08*	-				
8. Length of experience	6.74	2.37	.08*	.08*	.05	.05	.04	.09**	.02	-			
9. Gender (1 = F)	-	-	−.05	−.02	.07*	.03	−.07*	−.05	.01	−.01	-		
10. Age	22.42	1.69	−.01	−.01	−.01	−.04	−.03	.02	−.01	−.11**	−.11**	-	
11. Cultural distance	-	-	.01	.01	.02	−.01	.04	−.05	.05	−.13**	−.10**	.01	-

Note: means, standard deviations, Cronbach's alpha, correlations,
**$p < .01$, * < .05

Confirmatory Factor Analysis

The confirmatory factor analysis was performed by using Mplus7 on the whole sample ($N = 791$). The solution fit adequately to the data, confirming the four-factor structure of CQS: $\chi^2(160) = 617.025$; $p = .00$; RMSEA = .06 (.05; .06); CFI = .93; TLI =.92; SRMR = .05. The factor loadings for cognitive CQ ranged from .44 to .68; the factor loadings for metacognitive CQ ranged from .69 to .78; the factor loadings for motivational CQ ranged from .64 to .80; and the factor loadings for behavioral CQ ranged from .59 to .81. Moreover, this solution fit better to the data than the one-factor solution model: $\chi^2(166) = 1978.554$; $p = .00$; RMSEA = .12 (.11; .12); CFI = .74; TLI = .70; SRMR = .09. The final four-factor solution showed the covariance between residuals of two items of cognitive CQ, two items of motivational CQ, and two pairs of items of behavioral CQ (Table 2).

Table 2: Results of CFA, Alternative Models ($N = 791$)

	χ^2	**Df**	**p**	CFI	TLI	RMSEA	SRMR	Comparison	$\Delta\chi^2$	**p**
M_1	617.025	160	(.79)	.93	.92	.06 (05, .06)	.05			
M_2	1978.554	166	.00.	.74	.70	.12 (11, .12)	.09	$M_2 - M_1$	1361.529	<.001

Note: M_1 4-factor model; M_2 1-factor model.

Legenda. CFI = Comparative Fit Index; TLI = Tucker Lewis Index; RMSEA = Root Mean Square Error of Approximation; SRMR = Standardized Root Mean Square Residual.

Full Structural Equation Model

The full SEM of the hypothesized model fit well to the data: $\chi^2(230) = 749.468$; $p = .00$; RMSEA = .05 (.05; .06); CFI = .92; TLI = .91; SRMR = .05. As shown in Figure 1, the model presented a significant positive relationship between resilience and the CQ dimensions, strong for the cognitive [$\beta = .38, p < .001$], the motivational [$\beta = .46, p < .001$], and the metacognitive [$\beta = .37, p < .001$] dimension, and slightly weaker for the behavioral dimension [$\beta = .23, p < .001$]. These results fully confirmed our first hypothesis, except for the behavioral dimension, which was significant but not strongly associated with resilience. On the contrary, the second hypothesis was only partially confirmed: Indeed, the length of experience [$\beta = .08, p < .05$] was weakly and positively related only to the metacognitive dimension.

Finally, also our third hypotheses were partially confirmed. Indeed, forming friendships with local students (Hypothesis 3a) showed a significant but weak positive relation with the cognitive dimension [$\beta = .09, p < .05$]; whereas no significant association was found with the other three dimensions. Further, the association between friendships with international students (Hypothesis 3b) was significant and positive with the metacognitive [$\beta = .14, p < .001$] and the motivational dimensions [$\beta = .25, p < .001$], showing relatively low-medium betas; the cognitive and the behavioral dimensions were not significantly related to friendships with international students. As regards the control variables, the cultural distance was not associated with the four dimensions of CQ. Age did not show any relationships with the four endogenous variables. On the contrary, the model presented a significant and positive relationship between the female gender [$\beta = .12, p < .001$] and the motivational CQ.

The model explains 29% of the variation in the motivational CQ, 16% of the variation in both the cognitive and the metacognitive CQ, and only 7% of the variation in the behavioral CQ.

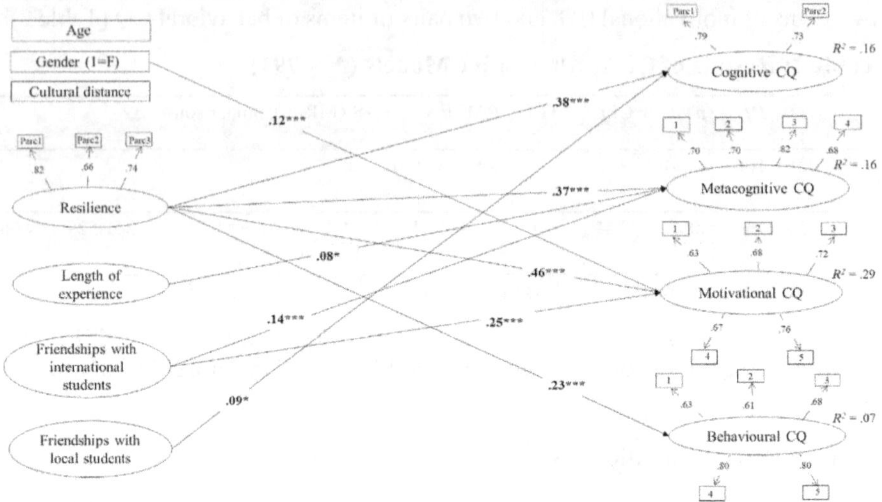

Figure 1: Full Structural Equation Model (*N* = 791).

Notes: Only significant relationships were reported.
*** $p < 0.001$; ** $p < 0.01$; * $p < 0.05$.

DISCUSSION

In line with the reflections of Ng et al. (2012), the results of our study showed that the four components of CQ are associated with different variables, confirming the complexity of a construct in its definition and development. In particular, the most interesting findings are those related to resilience and intercultural interactions.

More specifically, the confidence of socializing with people from other cultures and the enjoyment of living in a different country—namely what synthesizes the motivational component of CQ—are positively associated, although with different effect sizes, with an interesting set of factors. Indeed, resilience seems to be strongly related to motivational CQ; however, intercultural interactions with other international students show medium betas, and the female gender is also significantly but weakly related to it.

Although resilience shows a stronger beta than the intercultural interactions with local students, both are significantly associated with the capacity to acquire knowledge about the values, religious beliefs, social practices, legal and economic systems, and linguistic rules of other cultures. The capability to be conscious and adjust the cultural knowledge to better interact in a different culture—namely the metacognitive CQ dimension—appears to be positively associated with the following set of variables: resilience, friendships with international students, and length of experience; however, in line with the other CQ dimensions, their effect sizes differ and are particularly strong only for resilience. On the contrary, the capability to change the verbal and non-verbal behaviors when a cross-cultural interaction requires was not so well explained by this set of variables, and only resilience appeared to be largely positively related to it. On the basis of previous research (Crowford-Mathis, 2009; Engle & Nerht, 2012; Tay et al., 2008), the SLCT theoretical framework (Bandura, 1997), and Bandura's triadic model, some other personal characteristics, behaviors, and environmental factors might contribute toward further explaining the dimensions of CQ and, in particular, the behavioral component. For stays that exceed a year, such as in the case of international assignments for work, the duration of the stay abroad might contribute to behavioral CQ.

More specifically, in line with SLCT (Bandura, 1997) and consistent with previous findings on the cultural adjustment process (Mesidor & Sly, 2016; Van der Zee & Van Oudenhoven, 2013), our first assumption was confirmed: Resilience seems to be associated with all dimensions of CQ *(Hyphotesis1)*, with large betas except for the behavioral component, which shows a lower beta. Findings confirmed that, similar to highly self-efficacious people (Schwarzer & Warner, 2013), highly resilient people tend to interpret difficulties as learning opportunities (Mesidor & Sly, 2016; Tugade & Fredrokson, 2004) rather than exclusively as stressful situations and threats. Resilience is elicited in culturally diverse situations on the grounds that these are often stressful. Indeed, students abroad often have to deal with problems related to language barriers, differences in values and ideals, discrepancies in learning methods and views of the teacher–student relationship, initial transition issues, discrimination, and so forth (Sherry et al., 2010; Smith & Khawaja, 2011). How well international students adapt depends on how they manage these aspects (Smith & Khawaja, 2011). Resilient people should be able to overcome intercultural barriers, be confident to socialize in an unfamiliar cultural context, to deal with the stresses of adjusting to a culture, and to change verbal and non-verbal behaviors when a cross-cultural interaction requires it. Thus, linguistic barriers could be a source of motivation for improving language proficiency; discrepancies in view of the teacher–student relationship could be read as an opportunity to gain a better understanding of certain social aspects and values; and, finally, financial or bureaucratic problems could help students learn more about the law, economic issues, and administrative rules.

As regards situational factors, contrary to expectations, the length of the experience was not a significant factor for the components of CQ, except to a slight extent for the metacognitive dimension (*Hypothesis 2*); therefore, compared with resilience, the role of the length of the experience seems to be more marginal. The duration of the stay in the Erasmus Program is, in any case, limited to between a minimum of 3 months and a maximum of 12; therefore, it could be argued that for relatively brief periods of time abroad, such as in the case of the Erasmus Program, time does not play a significant role. In any case, as suggested by Varela (2017), who pointed to the need for further exploration of this topic, time plays a discontinuous role. Future studies could investigate this variable in more detail, reconsidering the moderation effect of divergent learning style as shown by Li and colleagues (2013).

Social relationships with international students were positively related to the desire to learn and to be in culturally diverse environments, to a feeling of confidence in social situations, in cultural adaptation and adjustment to cross-cultural conditions (Ang & Van Dyne, 2008; Ng et al., 2012). Building a multicultural network was also related to the ability to modify one's own mental model and manage interactions effectively by using the cultural knowledge developed (*Hypothesis 3a*). Although the intercultural interactions with international students show betas not large as those of resilience, their relationship with two out of four CQ dimensions is anyway significant and moderately strong.

Contact with local students during the Erasmus Program was related, although only weakly, to the cognitive component of CQ, namely a wide range of knowledge about social practices, economic rules, habits, customs, and so forth (*Hypothesis 3b*). All results, which partially confirmed the relation between intercultural contacts and competence development, can be explained by SLT (Bandura, 1977), according to which learning comes from interactions with other people.

In addition to what was deduced from Smith and Khawaya's review (2011) about the acculturation experiences and in detail about the positive role played by social support networks in decreasing acculturative distress of international students, these findings allow us to shed light on the peculiarities of the various types of intercultural networks with both international and local students, which are differently associated with the CQ dimensions.

As regards the control variables, age was not found to be related to any components of CQ. In line with the results of Varela's meta-analysis (2017), no association was found between cultural distance and the four dimensions of CQ. Prior to assuming the non-existent role of cultural distance in learning, future research is needed to take into consideration countries that are more culturally distant from Italy than those considered in the present study, such as the Asian countries. Indeed, one limit of this research is to have considered only European countries due to the Erasmus Program exchange criteria.

Beyond the scope of our assumptions, the female gender was found to be significantly but also weakly related to motivational CQ. These results were in line with those reported by Maeland and Wattenberg (2017), who carried out a study on a sample of university students in Norway, according to which the female gender is positively related to motivational CQ. One of the elements of the motivational dimension is the pleasure derived from interacting with people from other countries (Ang et al., 2007); therefore, the social component appears to be relevant. As reported by Groves (2005), who conducted a study on female leadership with a sample of senior leaders and their direct followers, levels of social and emotional skills were higher among women than among men. Moreover, higher levels of emotional intelligence, which at least partially overlaps with CQ (Crowne, 2009), were also observed, more so among women than among men, as shown by Naghavi and Redzun's review (2011) of empirical studies conducted on a sample of students (2011). Further research is needed to explore these differences between men and women in greater detail and to better explain this aspect.

CONCLUSION

In light of the findings of our study, training sessions could be implemented in order to encourage international students to develop self-awareness about their emotions, strengths, and weaknesses before embarking on their Erasmus Program (Mesidor & Sly, 2016). Further, through online delivery, specific interventions could be implemented to sustain students during their stay abroad, using approaches as mindfulness-based stress reduction strategies (Brewer et al., 2019).

Beyond the interventions focused on emotions, linguistic training may be reinforced or implemented where absent in both the pre-departure phase and during the stay in the country. For the non-native English populations, such as the Italian one, the improvement of English can enable students to be more easily involved in exchange with the other international students, with their teachers, and with academic institutions and mobility services. Beyond the English proficiency, in particular for those countries such as France, Spain, or Portugal where the lessons are often taught in the local language, specific linguistic training should be implemented. Therefore, the calls may be planned in time to ensure that students have the necessary time for language preparation. Further, the host university should provide opportunities for meeting both local and international peers. For instance, specific orientation programs for Erasmus students could be implemented and improved at the beginning of the experience and could involve local students for coordinating activities. Regarding accommodation, this could be managed, where possible, so that international students have roommates from different countries. Even teachers can play a key role in promoting intercultural interactions (Ma & Wen, 2018), paying attention to curriculum content, instructional approaches, and giving space to specific moments of dialogue to favorite intercultural exchanges (Schein, 2018). Evaluations (such as group assignments) can also be useful to promote interactions and to prepare students for future multicultural working collaborations.

In addition to the mobility services offered by universities, it seems important to emphasize the reinforcement and maintenance of Erasmus Students Network (ESN),[3] whose mission is to work in the interest of international students, improving their social and practical integration often through a tradition of mutual acceptance among students. Students who have returned from their mobility experience can be valued: Students can become, on a voluntary basis, experts of the country where they studied and resided; they can be invited to participate in seminars to prepare other future outgoing Erasmus students or to help the incoming students.

---

[3] https://esn.org/.

Apart from having practical implications for fostering the development of intercultural networks and building resilience, this study also presents some limitations and some suggestions for future studies. First, the cross-sectional design did not allow us to establish the existence of causality relationships between variables (Podsakoff et al., 2012). Despite the difficulties due to the COVID-19 pandemic, further longitudinal studies are currently ongoing. In addition to longitudinal research, which monitors the changes and causality relationships between the variables before and after the mobility experience, future research could use the diary study method, asking international students to complete self-administered forms at specified times or at time intervals. Second, the use of self-reported data may have potentially inflated the results (Conway, 2002). In future studies, it would be interesting to consider other-reported and objective ratings as well and by integrating quantitative and qualitative methods. Third, the sampling procedure limited the data collection only to a single university in Northwest Italy for reasons such as time and resources; in future, data will be collected in other Italian or abroad universities. Finally, in future research, cross-cultural studies should be conducted in order to monitor cultural differences.

ACKNOWLEDGMENT

The authors are grateful to the international relations office of the University of Turin for its collaboration in data collection.

REFERENCES

Ang, S., Rockstuhl, T., & Tan, M. L. (2015). Cultural intelligence and competencies. *International Encyclopedia of Social and Behavioural Sciences, 2*, 433–439. https://doi.org/10.1016/B978-0-08-097086-8.25050-2

Ang, S., & Van Dyne, L. (Eds.). (2008). *Handbook on cultural intelligence: Theory, measurement and applications*. M.E. Sharpe.

Ang, S., Van Dyne, L., & Koh, C. (2006). Personality correlates of the four-factor model of cultural intelligence. *Group and Organization Management, 3*, 100–123. https://doi.org/10.1177/1059601105275267

Ang, S., Van Dyne, L., Koh, C., Ng, K. J., Tay, C., & Chandrasekar, N. A. (2007). Cultural intelligence: Its measurement and effects on cultural judgment and decision making, cultural adaptation and task performance. *Management and Organization Review, 3*, 335–337. https://doi.org/10.1111/j.1740-8784.2007.00082.x

Bandura, A. (Ed.). (1977). *Social learning theory*. Prentice-Hall.

Bandura, A. (1997). *Self-efficacy: The exercise of control*. W. H. Freeman.

Berry (1997). Immigration, acculturation and adaptation. *Applied Psychology: An International Review, 46*(1), 5–34.

Berry, J. W. (2005). Conceptual approaches to acculturation. In K. M. Chun, P. Balls Organista, & G. Marìn (Eds.), *Acculturation: Advances in theory, measurement, and applied research* (pp. 17–37). American Psychological Association. https://doi.org/10.1037/10472-004

Bochner, S., McLeod, B. M., & Lin, A. (1977). Friendship patterns of overseas students: A functional model. *International Journal of Psychology, 12*, 277–297. https://doi.org/10.1080/00207597708247396

Bollen, K. A., & Long, J. S. (1993). *Testing Structural Equation Models*. Sage.

Brewer, M. L., van Kessel, G., Sanderson, B., Naumann, F., Lane, M., Reubenson, A., & Carter, A. (2019). Resilience in higher education students: A scoping review. *Higher Education Research & Development, 38*(6), 1105–1120. https://doi.org/10.1080/07294360.2019.1626810

Connor, K.M., & Davidson, J.R.T. (2003). Development of a new resilience scale: The Connor-Davidson resilience scale (CD-RISC). *Depression and Anxiety, 18*, 76–82. https://doi.org/10.1002/da.10113

Conway, J. (2002). Method variance and method bias in I/O psychology. In S. G. Rogelberg (Ed.), *Handbook of research methods in industrial and organizational psychology* (pp. 344–365). Blackwell Publishers.

Crowford-Mathis, K. J. (2009). The relationship between cultural intelligence and self -monitoring personality: A longitudinal study of U.S.-based service learners in Belize. Doctoral Dissertation. Ann Arbor: USA.

Crowne, K. A. (2008). What leads to cultural intelligence? *Business Horizons, 51*, 391–399. https://doi.org/10.1016/j.bushor.2008.03.010

Crowne, K. A. (2009). The relationships among social intelligence, emotional intelligence and cultural intelligence. *Organization Management Journal, 6*, 148–163. https://doi.org/10.1057/omj.2009.20

Di Fabio, A., & Palazzeschi, I. (2012). Connor-Davidson Resilience Scale: Proprietà psicometriche della versione italiana Connor-Davidson Resilience Scale: Psychometric properties of the Italian version. *Counseling Giornale Italiano Ricerca Applcata, 5*, 101–110.

Earley, P. C., Ang, S., & Tan, J. S. (Eds.). (2006). *CQ: Developing cultural intelligence at work*. Stanford Business Books.

Engle, R. L., & Nehrt, C. C. (2012). Antecedents of cultural intelligence: The role of risk, control, and openness in France and the United States. *Journal of Management Policy and Practice, 13*(5), 35–47.

European Commission (2019). Erasmus+ Annual Report 2019 - Questions and Answers. https://ec.europa.eu/commission/presscorner/detail/en/QANDA_20_2447

Ghislieri, C., Molino, M., Dolce, V., Mercogliano, C., & Mosso, C. O. (2018). Cultural Intelligence scale: Italian validation preliminary study. *Applied Psychology Bullettin [Bollettino di Psicologia Applicata], 66*(282), 45–53. https://doi.org/10.26387/bpa.282.4

Groves, K. S. (2005). Gender differences in social and emotional skills and charismatic leadership. *Journal of Leadership and Organizational Studies, 11*, 30–46. https://doi.org/10.1177/107179190501100303

Hofstede, G. (2011). Dimensionalizing cultures: The Hofstede Model in context. *Online Readings in Psychology and Culture, 2*(1), 1–26. Retrieved from http://scholarworks.gvsu.edu/orpc/vol2/iss1/8.

Hofstede, G. (2015). Hofstede center site. http://geert-hofstede.com/index.php.

Johnson, L. R., Seifen-Adkins, T., Sandhu, D. S., Arbles, N., & Makino, H. (2018). Developing culturally responsive programs to promote international student adjustment: A participatory approach. *Journal of International Students, 8*(4), 1865–1878. https://doi.org/10.5281/zenodo.1468100

Joyce, S., Shand, F., Tighe, J., Laurent, S. J., Bryant, R. A., & Harvey, S. B. (2018). Road to resilience: A systematic review and meta-analysis of resilience training programmes and interventions. *BMJ Open, 8*(6). https://doi.org/10.1136/ bmjopen-2017–017858

Khanal, J., & Gaulee, U. (2019). Challenges of international students from pre-departure to post-study: A literature review. *Journal of International Students, 9*(2), 560–581. https://doi.org/10.32674/jis.v9i2.673

Kogut, B., & Singh, H. (1988). The effect of national culture on the choice of entry mode. *Journal of International Business Studies, 19*, 411–432. https://doi.org/10.1057/palgrave.jibs.8490394

Ledesma, J. (2014). Conceptual frameworks and research models on resilience in leadership. *Sage Open, 4*(3), 1–8. https://doi.org/10.1177/2158244014545464

Leung, K., Ang, S., & Tan, M.L. (2014). Intercultural competence. *Annual Review of Organizational Psychology and Organizational Behavior, 1*, 489–519. https://doi.org/10.1146/annurev-orgpsych-031413–091229

Li, M., Mobley, W. H., & Kelly, A. (2013). When do global leaders learn best to develop cultural intelligence? An investigation of the moderating role of experiential learning style. *Academy of Management Learning & Education, 12*(1), 32–50. https://doi.org/10.5466/amle.2011.0014

Ma, J., & Wen, Q. (2018). Understanding international students' in-class learning experiences in Chinese higher education institutions. *Higher Education Research & Development, 37*, 1186–1200. https://doi.org/10.1080/ 07294360.2018.1477740

MacNab, B. R., & Worthley, R. (2012). Individual characteristics as predictors of cultural intelligence development: The relevance of self-efficacy. *International Journal of Intercultural Relations, 36*(1), 62–71. https://doi.org/ 10.1016/j.ijintrel.2010.12.001

Maeland, A., & Wattemberg, P. (2017). *The role of education and gender in Cultural Intelligence.* Master's thesis in business administration, University of Adger. https://uia.brage.unit.no/uiaxmlui/bitstream/handle/11250/ 2452976/M%C3%A6land%2C%20Arnfinn%20og%20Wattenberg%2C%20 Pia.pdf?sequence=1&isAllowed=y.

McFaul, S. (2016). International students' social network: Network mapping to gage friendship formation and student engagement on campus. *Journal of International Students, 6*(1), 1–13. https://doi.org/10.32674/jis.v6i1.393

Mesidor, J. K., & Sly, K. (2016). Factors that contribute to the adjustment of international students. *Journal of International Students, 6*(1), 262–282. https://doi.org/10.32674/jis.v6i1.569

Mohajeri Norris, E., & Gillespie, J. (2009). How study abroad shapes global careers. *Journal of Studies in International Education, 13*, 382–397. https://doi.org/10.1177/1028315308319740

Moon, H. K, Choi, B. K., & Jung, J. S. (2012). Comprehensive examination on antecedents of cultural intelligence: Case of South Korea. *Personnel Review, 42*, 440–465. https://doi.org/10.18843/ijms/v5i3(7)/09

Naghavi, F., & Redzuan, M. (2011). The relationship between gender and emotional intelligence. *World Applied Sciences Journal, 15*(4), 555–561.

Ng, K. Y., & Earley, C. P. (2006). Culture and intelligence: Old constructs, new frontiers. *Group and Organization Management, 31*, 4–9. https://doi.org/10.1177/1059601105275251

Ng, K-Y., Van Dyne, L., & Ang, S. (2012). Cultural intelligence: A review, reflections, and recommendations for future research. In A. M. Ryan, F. T. L. Leong, & F. L. Oswald (Eds.), *Conducting multinational research: Applying organizational psychology in the workplace* (pp. 29–58). American Psychological Association.

Nunnally, J. C., & Bernstein, I. H. (Eds.). (1994). *Psychometric theory (McGraw-Hill Series in Psychology) (Vol. 3)*. McGraw-Hill.

O'Leary, V. E. (1998). Strength in the face of adversity: Individual and social thriving. *Journal of Social Issues, 54*(2), 425–446. http://doi.org/10.1111/j.1540-4560.1998.tb01228.x

Oberg, K. (1960). Cultural shock: Adjustment to new cultural environments. *Practical Anthropology, 7*(4), 177–182. https://doi.org/10.1177/009182966000700405

Ott, D. L., & Michailova, S. (2018). Cultural intelligence: A review and new research avenues. *International Journal of Management Reviews, 20*(1), 99–119. https://doi.org/10.1111/ijmr.12118

Podsakoff, P. M., Mackenzie, S. B., & Podsakoff, N. P. (2012). Sources of method bias in social science research and recommendations on how to control it. *Annual Review of Psychology, 63*, 539–569. https://doi.org/10.1146/annurev-psych-120710-100452

Rohrlich, B. F., & Martin, J. N. (1991). Host country and re-entry adjustment of student sojourners. *International Journal of Intercultural Relations, 15*(2), 163–182. https://doi.org/10.1016/0147–1767(91)90027-E

Sawir, E., Marginson, S., Deumert, A., Nyland, C., & Ramia, G. (2008). Loneliness and international students: An Australian study. *Journal of Studies in International Education, 12*(2), 148–180. https://doi.org/10.1177/1028315307299699

Schein, E. (2018). *Cultura d'azienda e leadership*, Raffaello Cortina Editori, Milan, Italy.

Schwarzer, R., & Warner, L. M. (2013). Perceived self-efficacy and its relationship to resilience. In S. Prince-Embury & D. H. Saklofske (Eds.), *Resilience in children, adolescents, and adults* (pp. 139–150). Springer.

Sharma, N., & Hussain, D. (2017). Current status and future directions for cultural intelligence. *Journal of Intercultural Communication Research, 46*, 96–110. https://doi.org/10.1080/17475759.2016.1264444

Sherry, M., Thomas, P., & Chui, W. H. (2010). International students: A vulnerable student population. *Higher Education, 60*, 33–46. https://doi.org/10.1007%2Fs10734-009-9284-z

Smith, R. A., & Khawaya, N. G. (2011). A review of the acculturation experiences of international students. *International Journal of Intercultural Relations, 35*(6), 699–713. https://doi.org/10.1016/j.ijintrel.2011.08.004

Sternberg, R. J. (1986). A framework for understanding conceptions of intelligence. In R. J. Sternberg & D. K. Detterman (Eds.), *What is intelligence? Contemporary view points on its nature and definition* (pp. 3–15). Ablex.

Tay, C., Westman, M., & Chia, A., 2008. Antecedents and consequences of cultural intelligence among short-term business travelers. In S. Ang & L. Van Dyne (Eds.), *Handbook of cultural intelligence* (pp. 126–144). M.E. Sharpe,

Tugade, M. M., & Fredrickson, B. L. (2004). Resilient individuals use positive emotions to bounce back from negative emotional experiences. *Journal of Personality and Social Psychology, 86*(2), 320–333. https://doi.org/10.1037/0022-3514.86.2.320

Uen, J-F, Teng, S-K., Wu, L-C., & Tsao, S-A. (2018). *The antecedents and consequences of cultural intelligence: An exploratory study of Taiwanese.* Expatriates 5th International Conference on Business and Industrial Research (ICBIR), Bangkok, Thailand.

Van Der Zee, K., & Van Oudenhoven, J. P. (2013). Culture shock or challenge? The role of Personality as a determinant of intercultural competence. *Journal of Cross-Cultural Psychology, 44*, 928–940. https://doi.org/10.1177/0022022113493138

Varela, O. E. (2017). Learning outcomes of Study-Abroad Programs: A meta-analysis. A*cademy of Management Learning & Education, 16*(4), 531–561. https://doi.org/10.5465/amle.2015.0250

Varela, O. E., & Gatlin-Watts, R. (2014). The development of the global manager: An empirical study on the role of academic international sojourns. *Academy of Management Learning & Education, 13*(2), 187–207. https://doi.org/10.5465/amle.2012.0289

Ward, C., Bochner, S., & Furnham, A. (2001). *The psychology of culture shock* (2nd ed.). Routledge.

World Medical Association (2001). Declaration of Helsinki. Ethical principles for medical research involving human subjects. *Bulletin World Health Organization, 79*(4), 373–374. https://apps.who.int/iris/handle/10665/268312

VALENTINA DOLCE (Ph.D.) is associate professor at the Institute of Psychology (GRePS) of University Lumière Lyon 2 (France). Her research focuses on contemporary changes and their consequences on individuals' well-being and on professional, family, and social domains. She is particularly interested in two phenomena: globalization and the advent of new technologies. Dr. Dolce's research includes international mobility, transversal competences, intercultural competences, international career paths, well-being at work, work–family interface, technology use, leadership, followership, and entrepreneurship. Email: valentina.dolce@univ-lyon2.fr

CHIARA GHISLIERI (Ph.D.) is associate professor in Work and Organizational Psychology at the Department of Psychology of the University of Turin (Italy). Her research interests particularly include: gender perspective in work and organizational psychology, work–family conflict and enrichment, job insecurity, well-being in organizations, vocational guidance and international careers, leadership, followership, and entrepreneurship. Email: chiara.ghislieri@unito.it

Research Article

© *Journal of International Students*
Volume 12, Issue 3 (2022), pp. 694-715
ISSN: 2162-3104 (Print), 2166-3750 (Online)
doi: 10.32674/jis.v12i3.3930
ojed.org/jis

The Effects of Online Learning Experience During the COVID-19 Pandemic on Students' Satisfaction, Adjustment, Performance, and Loyalty

Michał Wilczewski[1]
Faculty of Applied Linguistics,
University of Warsaw, Warsaw, Poland

Oleg Gorbaniuk
Institute of Psychology, The John Paul II Catholic University of Lublin, Poland

Terence Mughan
School of Business, Portland State University, Oregon USA

Ewelina Wilczewska
SWPS University of Social Sciences and Humanities, Warsaw, Poland

---

ABSTRACT

This research investigates the student online learning experience (SOLE) during the 2020 spring COVID-19 pandemic. We collected quantitative data through an online survey from 362 international students and 488 domestic students at a large Polish University. Correlation and path analysis within a conceptual model of SOLE and its academic outcomes established that (1) SOLE explained adjustment, performance, satisfaction, and loyalty; (2) academic adjustment predicted performance, satisfaction, and loyalty; (3) academic performance and

---

[1] Corresponding author.

satisfaction predicted student loyalty; and (4) academic performance predicted satisfaction. Interestingly, time spent in quarantine/self-isolation did not exert any effect on academic outcomes in SOLE. Moreover, qualitative data collected via narrative interviews with 13 students (11 international and 2 domestic) developed our understanding of SOLE and its outcomes. We propose some research and practice implications for universities to enhance SOLE.

Keywords: academic adjustment, academic performance, Covid-19, international students, online learning, student satisfaction, university support

INTRODUCTION

The COVID-19 outbreak pushed governments toward introducing lockdown restrictions, such as social distancing and self-isolation, aimed at tackling the spread of the virus (Bretas & Alon, 2020). Studies point out the negative outcomes of the lockdown, social distancing measures, and concentrated self-isolation, such as not only devastating economic, political, and social disruption (Bretas & Alon, 2020; Nicola et al., 2020), but also educational (Fischer, 2020) disruption. More than one year into the pandemic, almost half of the world's students at primary, secondary, and tertiary levels have been affected by full or partial closures of educational institutions (The United Nations Educational, Scientific and Cultural Organization [UNESCO], 2020) whose activities have been forced into a remote learning mode. Unlike prior experiences of remote learning, which were generally planned and designed as a deliberate feature of certain programs of study, pandemic-era students were obliged to switch from the face-to-face learning mode to the online learning mode suddenly and with little preparation.

Research has suggested that the effectiveness of online learning and face-to-face traditional courses may be measured equally (Sitzmann et al., 2006; Verduin & Clark, 1991) provided that the course design and methods are appropriately adapted to the technology (Rovai, 2003) and instructional tasks, and that courses ensure student–student and teacher–student interactions in online learning (Verduin & Clark, 1991). Nevertheless, students generally exhibit significant dissatisfaction with remote education during the COVID-19 pandemic (de Haas et al., 2020), as they miss the interactional and social aspects of their academic experience. The adverse effects of the missing interactions are confirmed in teachers' perception of their students' emotional and academic difficulties experienced in the online learning during the pandemic (Jelińska & Paradowski, 2021). Further, some students face problems with a poor Internet connection in some locations and an unfavorable study environment in the household (Kapasiaa et al., 2020).

Recent studies call for exploratory research into the effects of university closures on students (Fischer, 2020; Nicola et al., 2020). Besides the social and emotional disruptions caused by the social isolation, switching to the remote learning mode entails a challenging experience of studying and interacting with peers and teachers (Jelińska & Paradowski, 2021). The quality of this experience and satisfaction with university services may determine students' loyalty, that is, the intention to persist with the program of study (van Rooij et al., 2018), and decision making about future options. Such options include returning to the home country in case of international students (Cao & Chieu, 2021; Fischer, 2020), that is, students who have crossed national borders for the purpose of study (Organisation for Economic Co-operation and Development [OECD], 2013). Indeed, reports have shown a pandemic-related decline in persistence and retention among international and domestic students (National Student Clearinghouse Research Center [NSCRC], 2021). Thus, it is relevant to explore the student online learning experience (henceforth SOLE) during the pandemic to better support students in the process.

This article investigates SOLE and its academic outcomes during the 2020 spring coronavirus pandemic among domestic and international students at a large Polish university (henceforth Polish University); most teaching activities were switched to online mode in mid-March, 2020. We will seek to answer the following research questions (RQs):

RQ1: What were the relationships between various aspects of the pandemic SOLE and students' academic adjustment, satisfaction, performance, and loyalty?

RQ2: What sense did the students make of their experience?

The paper will continue with a theoretical framework that will develop the hypothesized relationships between the variables, which are then tested by two empirical studies. To answer RQ1, Study A will test a hypothetical model of the effects of SOLE on academic outcomes by using data collected from students through an online questionnaire survey. To answer RQ2, Study B will explore how students understood their experience by using narrative interview data. After a discussion of the results, conclusions, limitations, and implications will be drawn.

LITERATURE REVIEW

SOLE

The pandemic-imposed abrupt transition to online learning has been psychologically and educationally challenging for students due to a radical change of the learning environment and the means of class attendance and interactions with other students and faculty. *Student online learning experience* (SOLE) is defined as a student's personal experience of various aspects of online learning that impacts their achievement and psychological/emotional comfort (i.e., satisfaction) with online learning as a method of education.

Research on student academic experience and online learning models recognizes the importance of student–student, student–content (including technologies and pedagogical tools), student–teacher (Marks et al., 2016), and student–university interactions (Pascarella & Terenzini, 1980, 2005) in shaping academic experience, persistence, and dropout decisions. Based on those theoretical considerations and our informal talks with teachers and students during the first two months (March and April 2020) of the transition to online learning at Polish University, followed by our pilot online survey in May 2020 aiming at exploring SOLE of 120 Polish University international and domestic students, we have established four major aspects of SOLE in the pandemic-related context:

1. *Interactions with students*—which contribute to students' academic achievement (Broadbent & Poon, 2015), perceived learning, and satisfaction (Marks et al., 2016), where *student satisfaction* is defined as their assessment of services provided by the university (Wiers-Jenssen et al., 2002). Such interactions may also be perceived as a support structure compensating for socialization deficits during the pandemic (Commodari & La Rosa, 2020).

2. *Students' technical capacity to participate in online learning*—which conditions the degree to which students will enjoy the benefits of the university's educational offer (Gibson, 1998; Johnson et al., 2009) and how fast and effectively they will adjust to online learning, especially during the pandemic-induced transition to online learning. Students with prior technical experience with online learning feel more comfortable with online courses (Jones & Wolf, 2001), which should increase their satisfaction, although some research has found no empirical support for this impact (Marks et al., 2016).

3. *Organization of online learning*—this includes online programs, courses, cultural initiatives, and support offered by the university, which contribute to students' success (Harms et al., 2006). Empirical research has confirmed the positive impact of certain elements of student-content interaction (e.g., online group projects) on students' satisfaction (Marks et al., 2016).

4. *Interactions with teachers*—which determine students' academic development (Al-Harthi, 2005) and influence students' perceived learning and satisfaction (Marks et al., 2016). Interactions with teachers serve as a support structure in pre-pandemic (MacDonald & Thompson, 2005) and pandemic learning (Jelińska & Paradowski, 2021).

The conceptualization of SOLE cited earlier and its impact on students' academic success leads to formulating the following hypotheses:

Hypotheses 1a-d: SOLE predicts (1a) academic performance, (1b) adjustment, (1c) student satisfaction, and (1d) loyalty.

Academic Outcomes of the Pandemic SOLE

Academic Adjustment as Predictor of Academic Success

Lowe and Cook (2003) have found that about a third of first-year university students drop out of the university due to difficulty transitioning into university life. A student's success exceeds their scholarly potential and is considerably dependent on their adjustment to the challenges of their student life (Gerdes & Mallinckrodt, 1994). *Adjustment* refers to an individual's affective psychological response to a new context, which is defined by how much they fit in and how comfortable they feel in that context (Black et al., 1991). In a similar vein, *academic adjustment* will be defined as the degree to which a student fits in the academic context of studying in the university and how comfortable they feel in that context. It is the result of a student's interaction with academic expectations and the university's demands (Poyrazli et al., 2001; van Rooij et al., 2018).

Prior research has linked academic adjustment with student performance, satisfaction (Rienties et al., 2012; van Rooij et al., 2018), and loyalty, although loyalty is best explained by satisfaction (van Rooij et al., 2018). Academic adjustment is, thus, hypothesized to affect students' academic success in the pandemic SOLE.

Hypotheses 2a-c: Academic adjustment predicts (2a) academic performance, (2b) student satisfaction, and (2c) loyalty.

Student Satisfaction, Performance, and Loyalty

Student satisfaction models link various antecedents and factors; among others are the image of the university, meeting students' expectations (to academic and non-academic services), the perceived value (of service quality relative to the price paid), and loyalty (Dib & Alnazer, 2013; Turkyilmaz et al., 2018). As student satisfaction has been linked with academic performance (Suhre et al., 2006; van Rooij et al., 2018), these variables are hypothesized to be also related in the pandemic SOLE:

Hypothesis 3: Academic performance predicts student satisfaction.

Moreover, satisfaction has been linked with achievement and loyalty (Chandra et al., 2018; Suhre et al., 2006; Turkyilmaz et al., 2018; van Rooij et al., 2018), which leads to:

Hypotheses 4a-b: (4a) Academic performance and (4b) student satisfaction predict student loyalty.

Because of the different nature of the academic experience of international and domestic students (language and cultural challenges, different forms of support or levels of understanding of the educational model in the host country), it was relevant to test the conceptual model (Figure 1) in those two groups of students.

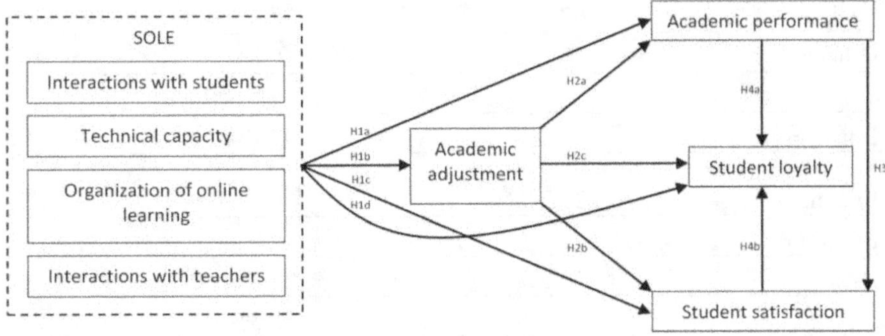

Figure 1: Conceptual Model and Hypotheses.

RESEARCH DESIGN

We used a sequential mixed-method approach to answer RQ1 and RQ2 through, respectively, a quantitative Study A and qualitative Study B. Study A aimed at establishing relationships between SOLE and academic outcomes by testing the conceptual model (see Figure 1). Study B aimed at understanding those relationships through an analysis of students' experiential narratives.

STUDY A

Method

Participants

The sample includes 362 international students and 488 domestic students from Polish University. International students originated from 62 countries, with the majority coming from Ukraine (21.8%), Belarus (18.7%), China (5.5%), Spain (5.5%), Italy (5%), Turkey (4.2%), Russia (2.9%), and France (2.4%). Both international and domestic samples are heterogenous as they involve students of different types and programs, and those who stayed in quarantine/self-isolation and participated in online learning from Poland and abroad (see Table 1). This allowed for the collection of data from students with a broad range of academic experience.

Table 1: Background of the Sub-samples ($N = 850$)

Background variables	International students	Domestic students
Age	$M = 22.88$ ($SD = 4.95$)	$M = 23.34$ ($SD = 4.93$)
Gender		

Background variables	International students	Domestic students
Male	31.8%	20.5%
Female	67.7%	78.7%
Other	0.5%	0.8%
Type of student		
Long-term	78.7%	99.2%
Short-term (e.g., Erasmus)	21.3%	0.8%
Program[a]		
BA	60.8%	72.5%
MA	32.3%	22.3%
Doctoral	5.5%	6.1%
Other	2.2%	0.4%
Quarantine/self-isolation		
Yes	61.0%	44.5%
No	39.0%	55.5%
Country of current residence		
Poland	66.3%	97.1%
Outside of Poland	33.7%	2.9%

[a] Percentage totals for program are higher than 100%, as some students attended different programs at the same time.

Measures

SOLE   Participants completed a Student Online Learning Experience (SOLE-S) scale, developed for the purpose of this research due to the lack of relevant instruments measuring SOLE. It includes 12 items rated on a 7-point scale (1 = strongly disagree, 7 = strongly agree), which measures four aspects (three items per subscale) of SOLE: (1) *interactions with students* (e.g., "My communication with other students has had a positive effect on my online learning experience"); (2) *technical capacity* to participate in online learning (e.g., "I have enough technical ability to participate in online classes/lectures"); (3) perceived *organization of online learning* (e.g., "My university organizes online learning well"); and (4) *interactions with teachers* (e.g., "I find my teachers supportive in my online learning").

For all the 12 items, the correlation matrix determinant was .01; Kaiser-Meyer-Olkin index: .846; Bartlett's significance test of sphericity: $\chi^2(66) = 1194.47$, $p < .001$. The statistics cited earlier justify searching for common factors. To validate SOLE-S, we conducted confirmatory factor analysis (CFA) on a sample of 256 international students from Polish University. The estimated model fits were satisfactory: $\chi^2(48) = 77.59$, $p = .004$; CFI = .974, RMSEA = .048 (CI90 [.027;.067]), SRMR = .036. All factor loadings of items in a measurement model were statistically significant. Next, we measured discriminant validity by comparing the average variance extracted (AVE) values with the squared correlations between paired constructs. The AVE values did not exceed the squared correlations between Factor 3 (organization of online learning) and Factor 4 (interactions with teachers). The correlation between these two factors was .92, which indicates that they measure the same phenomenon and, hence, potentially constitute a common factor. To test this hypothesis, we examined the validity of the three-factor model in which items from Factors 3 and 4 comprise one factor labeled "organization of online learning/interactions with teachers." CFA showed that the three-factor model fits the data well: $\chi^2(51) = 93.24$, $p < .001$; CFI = .963, RMSEA = .056 (CI90 [.038;.074]), SRMR = .041. All AVE values exceeded the squared correlations for each pair of factors. Overall, these values indicate that discriminant validity was achieved. Absolute values of factor loadings for Factor 1 ranged between .58 and .83, for Factor 2 between $-.56$ and .78, and for Factor 3 (comprising six items) between $-.64$ and .78. The inter-item correlation ranged between .28 and .52.

In view of what has been stated earlier, instead of measuring the conceptualized four factors of SOLE, we decided to merge the overlapping factors and measure SOLE composed of three distinct factors: (1) interactions with students ($\alpha = .74/.72$ for English/Polish version); (2) capacity to participate in online learning ($\alpha = .72/.65$ for English/Polish version); and (3) organization of online learning/interactions with teachers ($\alpha = .81/.75$ for English/Polish version).

SOLE Outcomes SOLE outcomes included student satisfaction, adjustment, performance, and loyalty measured by using scales from Wilczewski et al. (2021). Their content, face, and response process validity were assessed by two researchers who verified, through interviews, whether students understood the questions in line with their expected content; selected questions covering various aspects of the construct measured; as well as selected questions that best expressed the constructs measured through a pilot online survey.

Student Satisfaction. Participants rated six items expressing satisfaction with (1) general academic experience, (2) studying at the university during the pandemic, (3) studying conditions, (4) online learning, (5) self-perceived scholarly development, and (6) achievement in online learning, by using a 7-point scale (1 = strongly disagree, 7 = strongly agree). An exemplary item was: "I am satisfied with my academic experience in this university." Those components constituted a one-factor scale ($\alpha = .83/.82$ for English/Polish version).

Academic Adjustment. Participants rated adjustment to five aspects of the university: (1) teaching methods, (2) student assessment methods, (3) expectations that the university teachers have of [them], (4) studying conditions, and (5) online learning, by using a 7-point scale (1 = very unadjusted, 7 = very adjusted). The scale yielded a one-factor structure ($\alpha = .83$ for English/Polish version).

Academic Performance. Self-perceived academic performance in online learning as compared with the pre-pandemic experience in stationary learning was measured with one direct item: "My academic performance is better in online learning than before the COVID-19 pandemic." It was assessed on a 7-point scale (1 = disagree strongly, 7 = agree strongly).

Student loyalty. Similar to prior studies that used one-item scales for measuring students' intention to persist (van Rooij et al., 2018), student loyalty was measured with one direct item: "I would not recommend online learning experience in this university to other students." It was assessed on a 7-point scale (1 = disagree strongly, 7 = agree strongly), which was reverse coded.

Control Variables

The study controlled for the *time in quarantine/self-isolation* (in weeks) to determine the effect of this variable on SOLE and academic outcomes.

Procedure

We collected self-report data from international and domestic students from Polish University through an anonymous online questionnaire survey approved by Rector's Committee for Ethics of Research with Human Participants at Polish University (no. 60/2020). We recruited international students through an e-mail invitation sent out from the university's office for international students, whereas offices for student affairs distributed the invitation among domestic students. Participation was voluntary with no remuneration. After giving written consent, participants completed the survey over the span of 10 days at the turn of May and June 2020 during the lockdown period in Poland. The survey lasted approximately 15 min.

Data Analysis

We calculated Pearson's correlation coefficients to establish correlations between variables for samples of international and domestic students. We used CFA to determine the fit of the measurement model and path analysis to test the relationships between the variables within the conceptual model. We evaluated the fit of models to data by using: the goodness-of-fit test χ^2 (maximum likelihood estimation); the Root Mean Square Error of Approximation (RMSEA); the Standardized Root Mean Residual (SRMR); and the Confirmatory Fit Index (CFI). The CFI values of >.90 were acceptable. Hu and Bentler (1999) suggest that the probability of accepting an invalid model is very small when RMSEA is lower than .08 and SRMR is lower than .08. We used Amos 27.0 to test the hypotheses.

Results

We calculated descriptive statistics and correlations between variables separately for international and domestic students (see Table 2). The obtained coefficients were statistically significant among all three aspects of online experience and academic outcomes, thereby supporting all hypotheses. Time spent in isolation did not determine academic outcomes, but it was only related to the student's technical capacity, in that the longer the time spent in self-isolation, the higher the capacity that both groups of students showed to participate in online learning.

Table 2: Pearson's *r* Correlations and Descriptive Statistics

		1	2	3	4	5	6	7	*M*	*SD*
1	Satisfaction IS	–							4.44	1.22
	Satisfaction DS	–							4.20	1.19
2	Adjustment IS	.62**	–						5.01	1.17
	Adjustment DS	.73**	–						4.71	1.22
3	Performance IS	.51**	.39**	–					3.12	1.66
	Performance DS	.45**	.33**	–					3.24	1.71
4	Loyalty IS	.56**	.44**	.37**	–				4.36	1.90
	Loyalty DS	.69**	.57**	.43**	–				4.15	1.81
5	Interactions with students' IS	.37**	.29**	.33**	.30**	–			4.62	1.32
	Interactions with students' DS	.27**	.25**	.26**	.22**	–			4.29	1.13
6	Technical capacity IS	.28**	.32**	.14**	.22**	.17**	–		4.04	1.45
	Technical capacity DS	.29**	.27**	.20**	.30**	.20**	–		4.51	1.40
7	Organization of online learning/Interactions with teachers' IS	.79**	.65**	.47**	.59**	.39**	.33**	–	5.76	1.15
	Organization of online learning/Interactions with teachers' DS	.76**	.69**	.34**	.68**	.27**	.31**	–	5.57	1.12
8	Time in isolation IS	.06	.05	.03	.06	−.05	.16*	.02	9.31	3.20
	Time in isolation DS	.04	.01	.04	.07	−.05	.20**	.02	9.89	2.58

Note: IS = international students (*N* = 362); DS = domestic students (*N* = 488).
*p < .05 level (2-tailed). **p < .01 level (2-tailed).

Due to the potential correlations between explanatory variables, we tested the hypotheses within the conceptual model (see Figure 1), by using path analysis individually for international and domestic students. RMSEA indicated an unsatisfactory fit to the model for both international ($\chi^2(2) = 16.86$, $p < .001$; CFI = .984, RMSEA = .143 (CI90 [.086;.210]), SRMR = .021) and domestic students ($\chi^2(2) = 20.09$, $p < .001$; CFI = .973, RMSEA = .198 (CI90 [.147;.254]), SRMR = .030). To obtain a better model fit, we deleted statistically insignificant paths, which resulted in a satisfactory fit of the model to input data for international ($\chi^2(9) = 17.682$, $p = .039$; CFI = .991, RMSEA = .052 (CI90 [.011;.087]), SRMR = .048; see Figure 2) and domestic students ($\chi^2(7) = 10.694$, $p = .153$; CFI = .997, RMSEA = .033 (CI90 [.001;.070]), SRMR = .024; see Figure 2).

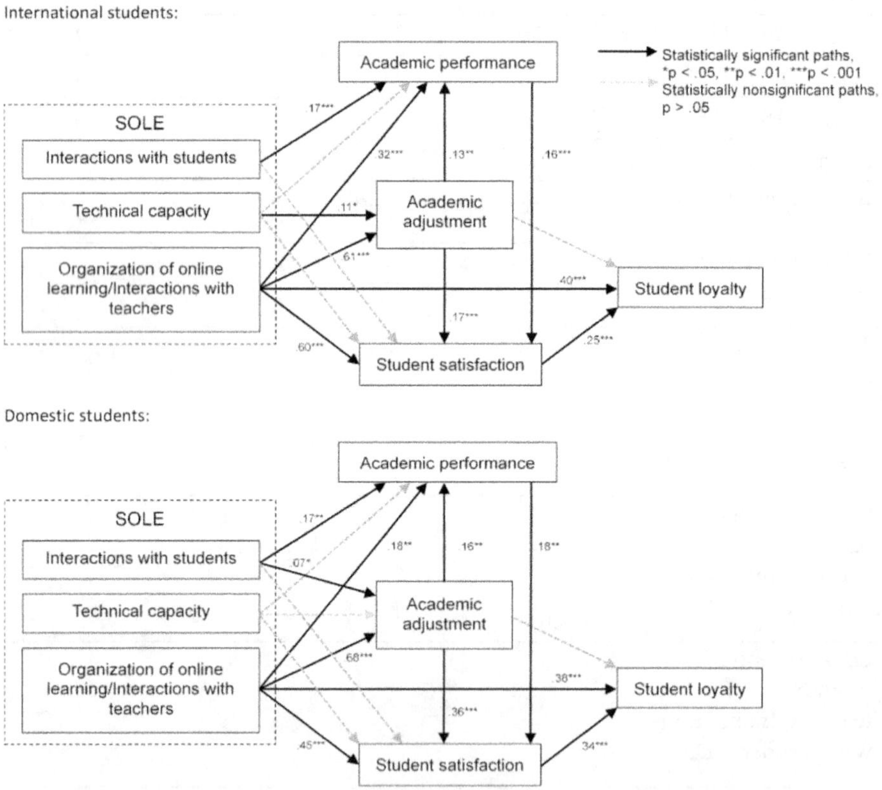

Figure 2: Path Analysis for International and Domestic Students (Standardized Coefficients).

STUDY B

Method

Interviewees

Out of the 850 students who had completed the online survey, 291 students (137 international and 154 domestic) agreed to participate in further research by leaving their e-mail address. Thirteen students accepted an email invitation to participate in an online interview. The sample is diverse and gender-balanced (eight females, five males). It includes 11 international students and two domestic students, 10 long-term (foreign) and three short-term (Erasmus) students from different faculties and programs (five in B.A., six in M.A., and two in Ph.D.) and of different years of study. They came from 10 countries (two from Poland; three from Ukraine; and one from Belarus, China, Hungary, Italy, Israel, Norway, Russia, and South Korea). Ten students studied from their home situated in Poland, and three studied in their home country. Their experience in Poland ranged between 6 months and 16 years.

Procedure

The first author conducted semi-structured narrative interviews in Polish and English via Google Meet between July 6 and 11, 2020 during the second semester or exam session, depending on the program. The interviews lasted between 37 and 95 min (60 min on average). Following the recommendations given by S. Jovchelovitch and M. W. Bauer (2000), we asked interviewees a general experiential question: "Please, tell me (a story) about your online learning experience at Polish University during the coronavirus pandemic." After delivering a story, we asked detailed questions regarding their experience. Finally, we asked "why" questions to deepen our understanding of a particular experience related in the story.

We audio-recorded interviewees with the interviewee's consent and transcribed them verbatim. Being guided by RQ2, two authors coded the material to extract narratives in which interviewees reflected on SOLE.

Analysis of Interview Material

Two authors analyzed the coded data thematically (Charmaz, 2014) to establish major themes meaningful to SOLE, whereas all four authors discussed and resolved divergent opinions through online meetings. The analysis established one overarching theme: SOLE during the COVID-19 pandemic; six subthemes: advantages of online learning, disadvantages of online learning, interactions with students, interactions with teachers, organization of online learning, and capacity to participate in online learning. The themes served to structure the findings section, which presents the results of the narrative analysis aimed at showing the sense that interviewees made of their experience (Polkinghorne, 1988).

Findings

Advantages of Online Learning

Students stressed that online learning was comfortable and time-saving. For example, David (M/31/Israel/PhD)[2] was satisfied with online communication tools as he could continue teaching activities from Israel: "I can give a guest lecture online for my university next week." Monika (F/25/Poland/MA), in turn, found remote communication with lecturers convenient and online exams less stressful:

> Online oral exams save our time. You don't wait for your turn for three hours in the university corridor. (…) We've reached a completely new level of communication due to this [pandemic] situation. Before, I had to arrange consultations with some lecturers via e-mail and received dates when they were available. Now, we can meet online.

Students allocated the time previously spent on commuting to the university to online assignments, reviewing the literature, and writing dissertations. The possibility of recording an online lecture allowed them to improve their understanding of the lecture's content. This helped them review the material for exams or better understand the parts misunderstood due to a language barrier, which facilitated their performance: "I feel positive about my study efficiency. My English is not that good and sometimes I couldn't catch the professor. But now, we can play the recording of a class and see what professors said, so it is easier" (Ling/F/21/China/BA).

Finally, students appreciated the opportunity to develop Internet and online communication skills, as well as to garner confidence to speak and share their opinions in public: "[The online class] helped me improve my confidence. When we meet online, I can ask anything I want, so it's good for me" (Ling/F/21/China/BA); "Before, I felt intimidated by other students, but now I don't find it difficult to share my opinion" (Monika/F/25/Poland/MA).

Disadvantages of Online Learning

Online learning was less favorably assessed by students who needed access to labs or face-to-face interaction (e.g., to practice foreign language skills). For Marina (F/26/Belarus/MA), an archeology student, pandemic restrictions prevented excavations, which considerably decreased her satisfaction with the program: "We need to practice and some of the things that are supposed to go on in the lab are not possible now. I wouldn't like it [online learning] to extend into the next semester."

---

[2] We marked the authorship of the narratives by name/gender/age/country of origin/pursued degree. Interviewees' names are fictitious to protect their anonymity.

Some students emphasized that online learning deprived their experience of the unique academic atmosphere, which prevented their adjustment and decreased satisfaction:

> My classmates and I felt we are not part of this online learning mode. When in a classroom, we think together, solve problems, and here … the class is somewhat beyond us. It is difficult to concentrate. An online lecture lacks eye contact with the lecturer, so the whole university atmosphere is gone (Pavlo/M/20/Ukraine/MA).

Interactions with Students

Some international students were able to develop relationships with other students in online learning: "I've made friends with a couple of students thanks to group assignments, so we communicate more now than before" (Nadya/F/35/Russia/BA). For others, remote communication opened up out-of-class interaction opportunities with domestic students: "I have a [Polish] friend with whom I'm going on Erasmus next autumn. She is from another program, but we started to talk [online] about Erasmus" (Andriy/M/28/Ukraine/MA).

Nonetheless, most students emphasized that they missed in-class interactions, which caused dissatisfaction, hampered adjustment, and decreased studying efficiency as students could not hold debates or discussions: "I missed debates and contact with other students, which is one of the things I enjoy the most … " (Anne/F/26/Norway/MA).

Finally, students used online groups to support each other: "Facebook is the most used means of communication among international students. We talk about any problems: 'Have you managed to connect to this class?,' 'What is going on and why everyone is having technical problems?'" (Marina/F/26/Belarus/MA).

Interactions with Teachers

Students interpreted limited interactions with teachers in terms of teachers' transferring work to students: "We had one lecture in the first two months [of the pandemic], so our academic life has simply died. Instead of giving classes, one lecturer sent us books to read, which was exhausting" (Nadya/F/35/Russia/BA). The lack of interaction with teachers was detrimental to the overall academic experience: "In some classes, we needed to learn most of the stuff by ourselves, which was bad for the academic outcome generally, because we could not ask the teachers" (Anne/F/26/Norway/MA). In general, online teacher–student interactions did not measure up to the pre-pandemic academic context:

> [Before], I'd go to the university, attend a lecture, and the next day I'd practice in class what I'd learned in the lecture. Then I'd return home and do my homework, and everything would be fine. But online, I need to read the lecture and go through the slides, read the book and materials sent by the teacher, and then try to figure out how she's solved the problem in the lecture. This takes much more time … (Anastasia/F/18/Ukraine/BA).

Importantly, Marco (M/25/Italy/PhD) remarked that a flipped class format fostered students' understanding of the material, because students could read the material before the lecture and ask questions during the lecture. Moreover, students viewed constant contact with teachers and their timely responses to emails as a source of support and consolation in the difficult pandemic situation, which increased their satisfaction with the general study experience.

Organization of Online Learning

Students viewed the transition to online learning as disorganized, chaotic, and stressful, although some of them ascribed the organizational issues to the extraordinary pandemic situation: "The March and half of April were hell to me. Some classes didn't take place, and others were rescheduled. But, overall, considering how extraordinary the situation was, I think the university passed the test" (Marta/F/23/Poland/BA).

In terms of conducting classes, students raised a problem of using numerous online platforms, which hampered adjustment to online learning and caused dissatisfaction: "Our classes spread around four platforms. And you need to check several emails trying to get to what is going on" (Marina/F/26/Belarus/MA); "I had to make a list about what teacher wanted what and what kind of assignments to complete. It took me some time to get the hang of it" (Anne/F/26/Norway/MA).

Numerous changes to class schedules disoriented students and caused delays and stress. Monika (F/25/Poland/MA) related that her practical foreign language classes were stacked up, which was physically overwhelming and affected her study performance: "We lost the first month, so our classes were multiplied and we had to attend some classes three times a week. To catch up with the material, some classes lasted 2.5 hours, which was exhausting."

Students viewed email communication with university administration as an important support structure that relieved their stress regarding the pandemic: "The Dean's Office informed us about everything … they cared about us. They provided all the necessary information to prevent us from coronavirus" (Anastasia/F/18/Ukraine/BA). By contrast, insufficient information on the organization of online learning caused ambiguity and dissatisfaction: "The lack of phone contact with the Dean's Office was disruptive. I had problems figuring which classes I should attend, which stressed me out as I didn't want to take extra courses next year" (Monika/F/25/Poland/MA). Also, some international students appreciated the university's support in dealing with visa extension: "My faculty offered help with extending our visas and sent me an e-mail with the details of prolonging our stay here" (Ling/F/21/China/BA). Those who did not receive such help felt abandoned by the university, which, in turn, affected their loyalty to the university:

> I have to go back to my country to get a visa where I have to go on a 14-day quarantine. I've been trying to apply for a visa online, but the system is not working. And the university is not helping so I have to deal with it

by myself. (…) Maybe I could recommend studying here if some administrative things changed (Hae/F/29/South Korea/MA).

In terms of university support, most students expressed satisfaction with free access to psychological help at Polish University, although those who had used it stressed that three counseling sessions per semester did not suffice to deal with the pandemic stress.

Finally, students appreciated the extracurricular activities offered by the university, which helped them reduce academic stress: "[The International Student Office] invited us to attend different social gatherings and programs: from how to deal with the exam pressure, into learning Chinese, Polish, and to attending virtual museum tours. They did a very good job" (Anne/F/26/Norway/MA). Through online discussion groups, students could start relationships with other students and share their experiences with them: "There's an online foreign languages group. You can register online and the admin will give you partners to talk to. And I've known someone thanks to that" (Ling/F/21/China/BA).

Capacity to Participate in Online Learning

Essentially, students did not lack technical skills or access to Internet infrastructure. Prior online learning experience facilitated adjustment to new studying conditions during the pandemic. However, students' capacity to participate in online classes was determined by external studying conditions. For some students, learning from home was motivating and fostered concentration, but others found it distracting due to other household members or noises heard from other students' homes. Nevertheless, overall, domestic students who resided with their families during the pandemic implied that they experienced support from their family during their academic experience and their home relieved their stress: "When we had oral exams, everybody went out to the garden, so I had perfect conditions for the exam, maybe even support … " (Monika/F/25/Poland/MA); "We tried to be together in the pandemic, having a laugh at a glass of wine, barbecuing, or simply watching TV" (Marta/F/23/Poland/BA).

DISCUSSION

This research aimed at exploring the academic outcomes of SOLE for international and domestic students studying at Polish University during the coronavirus pandemic. To determine the relationships between SOLE and academic adjustment, performance, student satisfaction, and loyalty, and understand how those relationships were shaped, we conducted Study A and Study B based on, respectively, online survey and interview data.

Study A supported all hypotheses (H1a-d) predicting the relationships between SOLE and students' academic performance, adjustment, satisfaction, and loyalty. This finding contributes to the literature by establishing the relationships between the pandemic SOLE and academic outcomes. The perceived organization of online learning/interactions with teachers has the most predictive power in the model due to strong relationships with all academic outcomes, which suggests that it plays a crucial role in both international and domestic students' experience.

We found that interactions with students are related to academic performance in both groups. Study B explained this relationship by the important role of in-class debates and discussions in students' understanding of the material. Interactions with students are also related to domestic students' academic adjustment, although this relationship is weak (.07, $p < .05$).

Finally, students' technical capacity is significantly but weakly (.11, $p < .05$) associated only with academic adjustment for international students, which suggests that this aspect has a marginal effect on the academic outcomes. Moreover, although some research suggests that prior experience in online learning translates to students' higher comfort with online learning (Jones & Wolf, 2001), our research established no link between students' technical capacity and their satisfaction, which confirms relatively recent empirical results (Marks et al., 2016). Study B revealed that students felt comfortable participating in online classes. Although they encountered minor problems using microphones and cameras during online class, they could overcome them over time. Moreover, despite the external distractors (e.g., inconvenient household conditions), their adverse impact seemed to be counterbalanced by the advantages of online learning, such as the time-saving remote access to the class, an opportunity to replay online lectures or stay with the family at home, which relieved the pandemic stress of domestic students.

We found that academic adjustment directly predicted performance and satisfaction, and it indirectly predicted loyalty through satisfaction (H2a-c supported). This result not only corresponds with conventional learning models (van Rooij et al., 2018), which show that motivational and behavioral variables affect academic success via adjustment, but also extends them to online learning. Next, satisfaction was explained by performance (H3 supported), whereas loyalty was explained by satisfaction (H4b supported) and indirectly by performance via satisfaction (H4a supported). These results extend research on student experience in conventional learning that has linked satisfaction with loyalty (Chandra et al., 2018; Turkyilmaz et al., 2018; van Rooij et al., 2018) to online learning.

This research extends the validity of prior results on students' experiences in conventional and online learning to, first, the pandemic SOLE and, second, to both international and domestic students. Interestingly, the time spent in self-isolation did not affect the SOLE outcomes, although students could develop their technical capacity to participate in online learning over time. This suggests that the results may be extrapolated to online learning in general, regardless of disruptive events such as pandemics.

Another important contribution is establishing a significant relationship between the perceived organization of online learning/interactions with teachers and loyalty to university for both international (.40, $p < .001$) and domestic (.38, $p < .001$) students. Study B revealed that students found the transition to online learning stressful due to using numerous learning platforms, frequent schedule changes, and too much workload; in addition, their loyalty was dependent on the perceived supported from the university (e.g., with visa extension, psychological help). For domestic students, the relationship between the organization of online learning and loyalty is direct. For international students, academic adjustment mediates the relationship between the organization of online learning and satisfaction (e.g., with information on the organization of online learning received from the Dean's Office, which mitigated uncertainty and ambiguity regarding online class attendance). This finding extends prior research linking student satisfaction with loyalty (e.g., Turkyilmaz et al., 2018) by pointing to the mediating role of adjustment in the satisfaction–loyalty relationship in the group of international students. Adjustment is critical to international students' academic experience, especially during the pandemic (Forbes-Mewett, 2020), and is the main predictor of academic performance and success (Rienties et al., 2012).

CONCLUSIONS, LIMITATIONS, AND IMPLICATIONS

In sum, this research contributes to the emerging literature on SOLE during a pandemic and its academic outcomes. It established, based on online survey data, relationships between SOLE and academic adjustment, performance, and student satisfaction and loyalty. Further, interview data contextualized SOLE at a Polish University during the pandemic, deepening our understanding of the phenomena captured by the structural models.

This research has certain limitations, which, nonetheless, warrant future investigations. First, the data were collected through self-reports to capture the pandemic SOLE. Further triangulation of data sources, for example, including teachers and university staff, could introduce more plurivocality of perspective. Second, SOLE was investigated in one national and academic context. Although data were collected from students from 63 countries, comparative research across various national and educational contexts, for example, considering SOLE in the hybrid learning mode, could shed more light on the effects of particular aspects of SOLE. Third, because the SOLE-S primarily captured student engagement at the institutional level, future research could consider some non-institutional factors. These could include pandemic-related hardships (e.g., loss of income), students' mental health, social support structures, and others. Finally, although we investigated SOLE in two groups of students, future research could consider the within-group variation in that experience. For example, exploring the impact of students' economic status, cultural background, and the COVID-19 pandemic-related challenges (e.g., visa concerns, social exclusion, culture-based discrimination in case of international students) that contribute to students' vulnerability (Forbes-Mewett, 2020) could further our understanding of SOLE.

The established three-factor structure of SOLE-S successfully captured relationships between distinctive realities of SOLE and academic outcomes among culturally diverse students. Thus, using SOLE-S in cross-cultural research could serve to validate the universality of the model established.

In terms of practical implications, given the mediating role of adjustment between students' satisfaction and loyalty, universities should support students' coping with university demands. For example, our findings point to the relevance of up-to-date information on the pandemic and the organization of online learning for fostering students' awareness of university demands and decreasing ambiguity (e.g., regarding class attendance or teachers' expectations), uncertainty, and stress. Further, compensatory support structures should be developed to mitigate stress caused by limited socialization in SOLE. Our interviewees' positive experience with psychological counseling, extracurricular events, and student online groups organized and administered by the university suggests that the development of those support structures could improve students' psychological well-being and generate a feeling of being cared for (Forbes-Mewett, 2020). Moreover, this research established that students' perceptions of the organization of online learning and their interactions with teachers determine their loyalty. Therefore, universities should raise student–teacher online interactions by training teachers on up-to-date online teaching methods and tools that allow teachers to monitor and better satisfy students' needs, facilitate teacher–student communication, and promote creative in-class collaboration.

ACKNOWLEDGMENTS

This research was supported by the Polish National Agency for Academic Exchange within the Bekker Programme (PPN/BEK/2019/1/00448/U/00001) to Michał Wilczewski. The authors wish to thank all international students who participated in the survey and interviews.

DECLARATIONS OF INTEREST

None

REFERENCES

Al-Harthi, A. S. (2005). Distance higher education experiences of Arab Gulf students in the United States: A cultural perspective. *International Review of Research in Open and Distance Learning, 6*(3). https://doi.org/10.19173/irrodl.v6i3.263

Black, J. S., Mendenhall, M. E., & Oddou, G. (1991). Toward a comprehensive model of international adjustment: An integration of multiple theoretical perspectives. *Academy of Management Review, 16*(2), 291–317. https://doi.org/10.5465/AMR.1991.4278938

Bretas, V. P. G., & Alon, I. (2020). The impact of COVID-19 on franchising in emerging markets: An example from Brazil. *Global Business and Organizational Excellence, 39*(6), 6–16. https://doi.org/10.1002/joe.22053

Broadbent, J., & Poon, W. L. (2015). Self-regulated learning strategies & academic achievement in online higher education learning environments: A systematic review. *Internet and Higher Education, 27*, 1–13. https://doi.org/10.1016/j.iheduc.2015.04.007

Cao, T. Q., & Chieu, Q. K. (2021). To return or not to return. *Journal of International nStudents, 11*(2), 2166–3750. https://doi.org/10.32674/jis.v11i2.2115

Chandra, T., Ng, M., Chandra, S., & Priyono. (2018). The effect of service quality on student satisfaction and student loyalty: An empirical study. *Journal of Social Studies Education Research, 9*(3), 109–131. https://doi.org/10.17499/jsser.12590

Charmaz, K. (2014). *Constructing grounded theory: A practical guide through qualitative analysis* (2nd ed.). Sage Publications.

Commodari, E., & La Rosa, V. L. (2020). Adolescents in quarantine during COVID-19 pandemic in Italy: Perceived health risk, beliefs, psychological experiences and expectations for thefuture. *Frontiers in Psychology, 11,* 559951. https://doi.org/10.3389/fpsyg.2020.559951

de Haas, M., Faber, R., & Hamersma, M. (2020). How COVID-19 and the Dutch 'intelligent lockdown' change activities, work and travel behaviour: Evidence from longitudinal data in the Netherlands. *Transportation Research Interdisciplinary Perspectives, 6,* 100150. https://doi.org/10.1016/j.trip.2020.100150

Dib, H., & Alnazer, M. (2013). The impact of service quality on student satisfaction and behavioral consequences in higher education services. *International Journal of Economy, Management and Social Sciences, 6*(2), 285–290. https://doi.org/10.5296/jmr.v2i2.418

Fischer, K. (2020). Confronting the seismic impact of Covid-19: The need for research. *Journal of International Students, 10*(2), i–ii. https://doi.org/10.32674/jis.v10i2.2134

Forbes-Mewett, H. (2020). Vulnerability and resilience in a mobile world: The case of international students. *Journal of International Students, 10*(3), ix–xi. https://doi.org/10.32674/jis.v10i3.2002

Gerdes, H., & Mallinckrodt, B. (1994). Emotional, social, and academic adjustment of college students: A longitudinal study of retention. *Journal of Counseling & Development, 72*(3), 281–288. https://doi.org/10.1002/j.1556-6676.1994.tb00935.x

Gibson, C. C. (Ed.). (1998). *Distance learners in higher education.* Atwood.

Harms, C. M., Niederhauser, D. S., Davis, N. E., Roblyer, M. D., & Gilbert, S. B. (2006). Educating educators for virtual schooling: Communicating roles and responsibilities. *Electronic Journal of Communication/La Revue Electronique de Communication, 16*(1–2), 1–16. https://dr.lib.iastate.edu/handle/20.500.12876/Qr9m4j5r

Hu, L. T., & Bentler, P. M. (1999). Cutoff criteria for fit indexes in covariance structure analysis: Conventional criteria versus new alternatives. *Structural Equation Modeling, 6*(1), 1–55. https://doi.org/10.1080/10705519909540118

Jelińska, M., & Paradowski, M. B. (2021). Teachers' perception of student coping with emergency remote instruction during the COVID-19 pandemic: The relative impact of educator demographics and professional adaptation and adjustment. *Frontiers in Psychology, 12,* 648443. https://doi.org/10.3389/fpsyg.2021.648443

Johnson, R. D., Gueutal, H., & Falbe, C. M. (2009). Technology, trainees, metacognitive activity and e-learning effectiveness. *Journal of Managerial Psychology, 24*(6), 545–566. https://doi.org/10.1108/02683940910974125

Jones, H. J., & Wolf, P. J. (2001). Teaching a graduate content area reading course via the Internet: Confessions of an experienced neophyte. *Reading Improvement, 38*(1), 2–9. https://link.gale.com/apps/doc/A74437616/AONE?u=anon~7cc9e978&sid=googleScholar&xid=04b37f85

Jovchelovitch, S., & Bauer, M. W. (2000). Narrative interviewing. In M. W. Bauer & G. D. Gaskell (Eds.), *Qualitative researching with text, image and sound* (pp. 58–75). Sage. https://doi.org/10.4135/9781849209731.n4

Kapasiaa, N., Paulb, P., Royc, A., Sahac, J., Zaveric, A., Mallickc, R., Barmanc, B., Dasc, P., & Chouhanc, P. (2020). Impact of lockdown on learning status of undergraduate and postgraduate students during COVID-19 pandemic in West Bengal, India. *Children and Youth Services Review, 116*, 1–5. https://doi.org/10.1016/j.childyouth.2020.105194

Lowe, H., & Cook, A. (2003). Mind the Gap: Are students prepared for higher education? *Journal of Further and Higher Education, 27*(1), 53–76. https://doi.org/10.1080/03098770305629

MacDonald, C. J., & Thompson, T. L. (2005). Structure, content, delivery, service, and outcomes: Quality e-Learning in higher education. *International Review of Research in Open and Distance Learning, 6*(2). Athabasca University Press. https://doi.org/10.19173/irrodl.v6i2.237

Marks, R. B., Sibley, S. D., & Arbaugh, J. B. (2016). A structural equation model of predictors for effective online learning. *Journal of Management Education, 29*(4), 531–563. https://doi.org/10.1177/1052562904271199

National Student Clearinghouse Research Center. (2021). *Persistence & retention*. https://nscresearchcenter.org/persistence-retention/

Nicola, M., Alsafi, Z., Sohrabi, C., Kerwan, A., Al-Jabir, A., Iosifidis, C., Agha, M., & Agha, R. (2020). The socio-economic implications of the coronavirus pandemic (COVID-19): A review. *International Journal of Surgery, 78*, 185–193. https://doi.org/10.1016/j.ijsu.2020.04.018

Organisation for Economic Co-operation and Development. (2013). *Education Indicators in Focus*. https://www.oecd.org/education/skills-beyond-school/EDIF 2013--N°14 (eng)-Final.pdf

Pascarella, E. T., & Terenzini, P. T. (1980). Predicting freshman persistence and voluntary dropout decisions from a theoretical model. *The Journal of Higher Education, 51*(1), 60. https://doi.org/10.2307/1981125

Pascarella, E. T., & Terenzini, P. T. (2005). *How college affects students: A third decade of research* (2nd ed.). Jossey-Bass.

Polkinghorne, D. E. (1988). *Narrative knowing and the human sciences*. Suny Press.

Poyrazli, S., Arbona, C., Bullington, R., & Pisecco, S. (2001). Adjustment issues of Turkish college students studying in the United States. *College Student Journal, 35*(1), 52. https://link.gale.com/apps/doc/A74221507/AONE?u=anon~66b98a44&sid=googleSc holar&xid=dabbfba5

Rienties, B., Beausaert, S., Grohnert, T., Niemantsverdriet, S., & Kommers, P. (2012). Understanding academic performance of international students: The role of ethnicity, academic and social integration. *Higher Education, 63*(6), 685–700. https://doi.org/10.1007/s10734-011-9468-1

Rovai, A. P. (2003). A practical framework for evaluating online distance education programs. *Internet and Higher Education, 6*(2), 109–124. https://doi.org/10.1016/S1096-7516(03)00019-8

Sitzmann, T., Kraiger, K., Stewart, D., & Wisher, R. (2006). The comparative effectiveness of web-based and classroom instruction: A meta-analysis. *Personnel Psychology, 59*(3), 623–664. https://doi.org/10.1111/j.1744-6570.2006.00049.x

Suhre, C. J. M., Jansen, E. P. W. A., & Harskamp, E. G. (2006). Impact of degree program satisfaction on the persistence of college students. *Higher Education, 54*(2), 207–226. https://doi.org/10.1007/S10734-005-2376-5

Turkyilmaz, A., Temizer, L., & Oztekin, A. (2018). A causal analytic approach to student satisfaction index modeling. *Annals of Operations Research, 263*(1–2), 565–585. https://doi.org/10.1007/s10479-016-2245-x

The United Nations Educational, Scientific and Cultural Organization. (2020). *Education: From disruption to recovery.* https://en.unesco.org/covid19/educationresponse

van Rooij, E. C. M., Jansen, E. P. W. A., & van de Grift, W. J. C. M. (2018). First-year university students' academic success: The importance of academic adjustment. *European Journal of Psychology of Education, 33*(4), 749–767. https://doi.org/10.1007/s10212-017-0347-8

Verduin, J. R., & Clark, T. A. (1991). *Distance education: The foundations of effective practice.* Jossey-Bass.

Wiers-Jenssen, J., Stensaker, B., & Grøgaard, J. B. (2002). Student satisfaction: Towards an empirical deconstruction of the concept. *International Journal of Phytoremediation, 21*(1), 183–195. https://doi.org/10.1080/1353832022000004377

Wilczewski, M., Gorbaniuk, O., & Giuri, P. (2021). The psychological and academic effects of studying from the home and host country during the Covid-19 pandemic. *Frontiers in Psychology, 12*, 644096. https://doi.org/10.3389/fpsyg.2021.644096

MICHAŁ WILCZEWSKI, PhD, is associate professor of the Faculty of Applied Linguistics at the University of Warsaw, Warsaw, Poland. He maintains an active research agenda with a particular focus on intercultural communication in international business and intercultural experiences of international students, business expats, and missionaries. Email: m.wilczewski@uw.edu.pl

OLEG GORBANIUK, PhD, is associate professor of the Institute of Psychology at the John Paul II Catholic University of Lublin, Poland. His research focuses on social perception, psycholexical studies, methodology, and consumer behavior. Email: oleg.gorbaniuk@gmail.com

TERENCE MUGHAN, PhD, is adjunct faculty at the School of Business, Portland State University, Oregon, USA. His major research interests lie in the area of languages in international business, intercultural communication, and international management. Email: tmughan@pdx.edu, terrymughan@me.com

EWELINA WILCZEWSKA, MA, is an MA Psychology student at the SWPS University of Social Sciences and Humanities, Warsaw, Poland. Her interests center around psychological aspects of intercultural experiences and studying foreign languages. Email: e.wi@op.pl

Research Article

© *Journal of International Students*
Volume 12, Issue 3 (2022), pp. 716-735
ISSN: 2162-3104 (Print), 2166-3750 (Online)
doi: 10.32674/jis.v12i3.3776
ojed.org/jis

"I Am Not an Immigrant. I Am an International Student:" A Qualitative Study of Adaptation Experiences of Turkish International Students in Germany

Seda Erturk
Kemal Oker
Lan Anh Nguyen Luu
Institute of Psychology, Eötvös Loránd University, Hungary

ABSTRACT

This study uses the consensual qualitative research method and examines the adaptation process of 15 Turkish international students at different German universities. The results of this study yielded four primary domains of adaptation experiences: the perceptions of Germany, adaptation challenges, the contributing factors in adaptation experiences, and attitudes toward counseling services. Implications for counseling practice and future directions are discussed in light of the results of this study.

Keywords: adaptation, college counseling, consensual qualitative method, sojourner, Turkish international students

According to the United Nations Educational, Scientific and Cultural Organization Institute of Statistics [UNESCOIS] (2020), Germany was one of the most popular countries with more than 311,000 international students in 2018. Turkey ranks within the top 10 countries that send students to Germany for education, and the number of Turkish international students (TIS) at German universities has increased consistently over the past 10 years (Statistisches Bundesamt, 2018). Germany's physical proximity to Turkey and possible job opportunities, as well as the high reputation of German universities, are factors that attract TIS (Suoglu, 2012). Further, Germany's public higher education institutions have been providing greater diversity in fields of study and have waived tuition fees since 2014 (Hüther & Krucken, 2018). Thus, the free education offered in various fields by the highly reputable universities of a country geographically close to Turkey plays a key role in making German higher education more attractive to TIS.

Despite the growing number of TIS sojourning to Germany for educational purposes, no research was found about how they experience the cross-cultural adaptation. Therefore, this research study focuses on the adaptation experiences of TIS in Germany while considering their cultural and educational backgrounds. The knowledge gained has the potential to contribute to the existing literature on the culture-specific experiences of international students to better address their needs and enrich their cross-cultural experiences. One contribution involves the findings regarding the impact on one country's international students, of disparaging stereotypes and discrimination aimed at a large community of immigrants from the same country. The study also contributes to the extant literature by calling attention to the sharply different experiences of TIS regarding the safe, supportive, and enabling institutional, on-campus context on the one hand, and the much more challenging, discriminative off-campus, larger host society context on the other hand. It also makes recommendations regarding the role of the universities in helping TIS' adaptation in this under-investigated circumstance. Knowledge about the TIS' experiences in Germany may provide important implications and inform college counselors working with them at German universities, in the delivery of culturally relevant and effective counseling services.

Specifically, the purpose of this research study was to investigate the adaptation experiences of TIS in Germany and fill a crucial gap in the literature by shifting the focus to TIS sojourning in Germany as a growing segment of German international higher education students. Accordingly, in the light of culture-specific issues, there is a need for an in-depth exploration to better understand the adaptation experiences of TIS. A review of the existing literature on the adaptation of international students led us to addressing the following research questions:

1) What are TIS' perceptions regarding Germany?

2) What are the challenges in the adaptation process of TIS in Germany?

3) What are the contributing factors to the adaptation process of TIS in Germany?

4) What are the attitudes of TIS toward the college counseling services as a contributing factor in the adaptation process?

LITERATURE REVIEW

This study was informed by the literature that focuses on the adaptation of Turkish international students, Turks in Germany, and a theoretical framework developed by Ward and colleagues that describes the cross-cultural adaptation as a dynamic process (Ward et al., 2001). Each of these is described as follows:

Adaptation of Turkish International Students

Most of the existing literature concerns studies conducted in the United States, and they provide insights about important components of TIS' adaptation. Among such studies, Duru and Poyrazli (2007) demonstrated that higher levels of social connectedness, good English language competency, and being open to new experiences are associated with a lower level of acculturative stress. In another study, Duru and Poyrazli (2011) showed that, in the United States, TIS studying for more years reported lower levels of adjustment difficulties, and Turkish students with higher levels of perceived discrimination had a harder time in their new social environment, experiencing additional adjustment difficulties. Also, Burkholder (2014) indicated that Americans' misperceptions about Turks as Arabs and their prejudices toward Islam affected the TIS' overall experience in the United States. Besides, Bektas and colleagues (2009) studied the psychological adaptation of TIS on U.S. university campuses and explained that perceived social support from co-nationals significantly contributed to their adaptation. In addition, Kilinc and Granello (2003), in researching the life satisfaction and help-seeking attitudes of TIS in the United States, found that experiencing discrimination possibly caused their homesickness, and TIS' friends were their primary source of psychological support in the U.S. experience. Despite this profusion of U.S.-based literature, the adaptation of TIS sojourning in Germany for education is yet to be studied.

Turks in Germany

The Turkish-West German labor recruitment agreement was signed in 1961 and has led to the largest population of Turks outside of Turkey (İçduygu, 2012). Since then, their number has continued to grow and now, at more than 7 million individuals, Turkish immigrants constitute the largest minority group in Germany (Zestos & Cooke, 2020). Turks in Germany are often exposed to negative attitudes and are targeted for discrimination (Greitemeyer & Schwab, 2014). In addition, they are stereotyped in Germany as being uneducated and religious (Horrocks & Kolinsky, 1996). Issues around Turkish immigration are frequently discussed in German media and on academic platforms. Therefore, besides an examination of their adaptation experiences and the culture-specific (i.e., cultural values and affiliation to the Turkish minority group) as well as sojourner-specific (i.e., motivation for adaptation) conditions of TIS in Germany, the impact of the generally negative stereotypes of Turkish immigrants in this country should also be considered.

Theoretical Framework

To explore the adaptation experiences of TIS in Germany, this study is informed by Ward et al.'s (2001) conceptual framework that describes sojourning as a dynamic process for students and local individuals. This framework argues that there are two distinct types of adaptation: (a) psychological adaptation and (b) sociocultural adaptation (Ward et al., 2001). Psychological adaptation signifies emotional satisfaction with life and feelings of psychological well-being during the cross-cultural transition (Ward et al., 2001). Sociocultural adaptation describes an individual's competency and ability to fit in or to negotiate the new cultural milieu (Ward et al., 2001). This approach considers different dimensions of cross-cultural travelers, such as status (e.g., immigrant, international student, refugee) and situation (e.g., purpose, timespan, type of involvement) (Ward et al., 2001). Therefore, this model provides a comprehensive framework to explore and analyze the adaptation process of TIS who sojourned in Germany voluntarily and temporarily for education.

METHOD

To explore the adaptation experiences of TIS in Germany, we chose to use consensual qualitative research (CQR), which is a descriptive, inductive method (Hill, 2015). Hill (2015) emphasized that "this method is particularly good for investigating inner experiences that are not easily observable to outsiders" (p. 486). Essential to its use is the need to stay close to the participants' narratives and stories in order to fully understand the data (Hill, 2015). It is, therefore, well suited to the in-depth and rich descriptions of the psychological processes involved in this study and helps us to explore the phenomenon.

Sample

To reach the target sample, recruitment flyers including detailed information about the study were disseminated through social media groups consisting of Turkish people living in Germany. The sample size recommended by the CQR method is 8 to 15 individuals (Hill, 2015). This study was carried out with 15 volunteer TIS from different German universities, consisting of five individuals with a bachelor's degree, six with a master's degree, and four with a Ph.D. The individuals who participated in this study had been studying in Germany for a minimum of one year and a maximum of four years at the time of data collection. The participants' age (seven males and eight females) ranged from 20 to 30 years. All the participants had spent their lives in Turkey until they moved to Germany for education. In addition, four of the participants defined their German language proficiency as intermediate level and 11 defined it as upper-intermediate level.

Researchers

The research team for this study consisted of two social psychologists and two clinical psychologists. Consistent with the CQR method, one of the researchers participated in the study as an auditor and the other three researchers formed the primary team. All of us had experienced counseling with international students and were also familiar with the literature in the area of acculturation, adjustment, and adaptation. Prior the study, we were trained on the CQR method. Although bias in the CQR method is minimized due to teamwork, each study takes place in a certain cultural context, and each member develops a particular way of thinking about the data (Hill, 2015). As a whole team, we discussed and reported our biases and expectations regarding the potential findings of the study prior to data collection.

Data Collection Tool

Ethical approval to conduct this study was received from the university's Institutional Review Board (IRB). We created a data collection form to record information for each TIS, including their arrival time in the host country, age, gender, educational background, family background, language competence, etc. Based on adaptation literature related to international students (e.g., Smith & Khawaja, 2011; Ward et al., 2001), a semi-structured interview protocol involving open-ended questions was prepared as is typical of the CQR method. Then, we applied a pilot study to two TIS in Germany who were not involved in the study; based on their feedback, some of the interview questions were revised to make them more understandable. After that, we reorganized the order of some questions and finalized the protocol, which included four question groups that focused on the following subjects: (a) perceptions and feelings; (b) challenges, problems, or stressors faced initially, later, and presently; (c) Turkish versus German culture; and (d) relationship networks, resources, and coping strategies.

Data Collection Process

Prior to the Skype interviews held at the volunteers' convenience, information and a consent form were sent to them via email, and, for consistency, all interviews were conducted by the same researcher. Depending on the participants' preference, the researcher, a native Turkish speaker, conducted the interviews in Turkish. The interviews were audio-recorded with the consent of the participants. Each interview lasted about 60 to 90 min, after which the researcher wrote notes about the interviewee's impressions to provide further details and help interpret the results based on the data analysis. In addition, although the interviewer referred to participants by their name during interviews, neither their names nor any identifying features were subsequently used. The participants' names were replaced by codes, that is, 01, 02... to 15 with the prefix "G" for Germany. Therefore, cases are referred to by the codes G01, G02 etc. While transcribing, expressions such as "ahh" "hmm" were deleted. We translated all data into English, individually, and we then met to reach a consensus on the translations. Afterward, a professional transcription service checked for clarity and error in them.

Analysis

Each step of the intensive and long data analysis process of CQR requires continuously examining the raw data to obtain multiple perspectives and reach a consensus on these multiple perspectives, and intra-team trust is essential in this process (Hill, 2015). Accordingly, we conducted a qualitative analysis that employed the procedure recommended by Hill (2015). First, the primary team examined the data independently and formed the domains, which are meaningful topics that arise from the content of the interviews (Hill, 2015). Second, the primary team came together to prepare an agreed list of domains. Third, the primary team determined the core ideas for each domain that were abstracted from the participants' responses in each case. Thus, we were able to reflect the essence of the participants' utterances and, working independently, demonstrate their meanings. The primary team then met again and continued discussion until a consensus was reached. During objective elimination of the excess data, we paid thorough attention to the language usage of the participants to be able to convey their meanings precisely.

Audit

Several times, the auditor carefully read the domains and core ideas and provided feedback related to the sufficiency of the information. The team then made any consequent changes that were necessary within the domains and core ideas.

Cross-Analysis

The next step, following the work on individual cases, involved the primary team meeting to determine any similarities in the core ideas of each domain across all the cases and to examine any patterns. These patterns were labeled as categories (Hill, 2015), and the team placed each core idea in its relevant category (or categories). The same individual who audited the domains and core ideas audited the cross-analysis and presented her feedback to the primary team a few times, resulting in the primary team reviewing the raw materials and making any necessary changes through several rounds of feedback. Then, we all came together again to establish an agreed and final version of all categories and, lastly, the categories were labeled as "general," "typical," or "variant," depending on how often they had been noted.

RESULTS

This section is organized based on the results regarding each research question. First, an overview of the cross-analysis of the interviews with TIS is provided in

Table 1 with the summary of domains, categories, and subcategories. Following Hill's (2015) criteria, case frequencies are nominated "general," "typical," or "variant," as stated earlier. In the cross-analysis, "general" means applicable to 13 to 15 cases, "typical" means applicable to 8 to 12 cases, and "variant" means applicable to three to seven cases in our study. Cases applicable to only two were ignored because they did not represent the sample, as suggested by Hill (2015). As shown in Table 1, the analysis was conducted in four domains based on these results; as Hill et al. (2005) recommends, at least one example for each category was chosen to be illustrated in the text. Accordingly, each research question is presented with a major theme capturing these domains.

Table 1: Summary of Domains, Categories, and Subcategories from the Cross-Analysis of the Interviews with Turkish International Students ($N = 15$)

Domain, category, and subcategory	Frequency
Perceptions of Germany	
Cheapest but the best education system	General
Better job opportunities	Variant
Germany is a multicultural country	General
A safe and free country	General
Two different lives, on- and off-campus	Typical
Challenges	
Cold and cloudy weather	General
Language proficiency	General
Negative stereotypes	Typical
Germans consider all foreigners as immigrants	Typical
Germans stigmatize Turks as uneducated	Typical
Germans stigmatize Turks as conservative	Typical
Discrimination	Typical
Academic stress	Typical
Homesickness	Variant
Cultural distance	Typical
The contributing factors in the adaptation process	
Coping strategies	
Acceptance	Typical
Focusing on the academic setting and avoidance of generalization	General
Problem-focused coping strategy	Typical
Seeking social support from family and friends	Typical

Domain, category, and subcategory	Frequency
Support system	
Supportive family	General
Supportive heterogenous peer network	General
Supportive school structure	General
Attitudes toward counseling services	
Negative attitudes toward counseling services	Variant
Having misperception about counseling services	Variant
Lack of information about counseling services	Typical

Note: General = applicable to all cases or all but two of the cases are considered; Typical = applicable to more than half of the cases; Variant = applicable to at least three (Hill, 2015).

Perceptions of Germany Domain

According to data analysis, participants' general perception of Germany was largely positive at the levels of country and academic institution. Initially, participants generally believed that they received the cheapest but the best education in Europe, which is their main motivation in Germany. For example, G01 reported, "My university is the best in Europe for my subject. There is no other country which offers free [no tuition fee] and such high-quality education with top-ranking universities."

A variant category emerged from the data in this domain. According to the participants' perceptions, Germany is a very developed country and it offers job opportunities as well as a very prestigious degree that provides high-level job opportunities worldwide. G05 explained,

> After graduation, I can find a top job anywhere in the world through having a highly prestigious German degree. My dream is to gain experience in a famous German company such as BMW or Mercedes and then return to Turkey.

The participants noted that this perception led to the idea of continuing their lives in Germany or another developed country for a while after graduating from university.

Further, participants typically acknowledged the intercultural opportunities to be gained from involvement with the various peoples, religions, and cultures of Germany and its multicultural environment is potentially as important for their personal development as their formal education. In the words of G06:

> People of all cultures, religions and races live here together. So, studying here is more than only having a degree, and it is an opportunity for intercultural experiences and getting to know the world better. I have

improved my language, intercultural, interpersonal and communication skills that are necessary for my self-development and future business life.

Besides, all of the participants stated that they thought that Germany was a safe and free country, especially when compared with Turkey. In the words of G10:

I feel more secure and also free here. While expressing my opinions openly in Germany, I would hesitate to do so in Turkey due to social and political pressure. Also, I can walk the streets late at night, whereas this would not be possible in Turkey.

Moreover, participants typically defined their experiences in academic settings differently to their experiences in societal settings. Therefore, they stated that their interpersonal relationships and reactions differed on- and off-campus. As G13 noted:

Campus culture is different to, and easier than the one outside. Some locals, especially older Germans, are not as flexible and open-minded as local students and university staff. Consequently, our relationships and communications with others may differ on- and off-campus. We spend most of our lives on-campus and while off campus, it is possible to be exposed to prejudice and discrimination.

Accordingly, despite some negative experiences, especially off-campus, students developed a positive perception of Germany and did not report a negative perception that would demotivate them in the adaptation process.

Challenges Domain

According to data analysis, all participants reported more than one source of stress in their adaptation process. First, participants generally defined cold and cloudy weather as an important challenge that caused them to feel depressed. G02 reported, "There is no sunshine even in summer. It is so depressing and affects me so much. I feel like a zombie that is living in the dark." Also, all participants stated that the lack of language proficiency caused interpersonal problems, with the language barrier affecting their social life more than their academic life. As participants reported, they could not express themselves sufficiently, which caused superficiality or misunderstanding in their relationships. For example, in the words of G10, "Sometimes, I cannot correctly express exactly what I wanted to say due to my limited vocabulary. This makes my claims less significant. Also, I sometimes feel anxious as using the wrong words can cause problems."

Moreover, participants typically reported that negative stereotyping about being Turks, Muslims, and immigrants is a major source of stress in their daily life and therefore they are at a disadvantage compared with many other international students. Three subcategories emerged from this category: First, participants typically mentioned that Germans considered all foreigners as immigrants. They emphasized that they were exposed to some negative stereotyping, not because of being Turkish but due to being foreign. For example, G07 said:

> Germans do not think of foreigners as international students, that is the problem. I am not an immigrant; I am an international student and have come here for education. They get benefits from my being here but still prefer to be rude.

Second, participants typically mentioned that Germans stigmatized Turks as uneducated, and the main reason is the first- and second-generation Turkish immigrants who live in Germany as workers. G05 noted:

> Due to the first- and second-generation immigrants, Turks' reputation is not good here, even though there are some successful Turkish immigrants. All Turks are not as they are perceived to be. I am Turkish, but I am certainly not an uneducated migrant worker, as some of them have labelled me, but I still need to put more effort into building relations, because of existing prejudgments. Since I come from there, I try to introduce the modern side of Turkey. It is crucial to break down their biases by representing Turkey well.

Third, participants typically stated that Germans stigmatized Turks as conservative. According to the participants, there are two reasons for this stigma: The existing conservative Muslim-Turks living in Germany and some Germans do not differentiate Turkish culture from Arabic culture, because of their having the same religious background. G08 reported:

> While chatting with someone, he learned that I am Turkish. Then, his face changed, and he ask me some strange questions, such as 'Do you wear a burka in Turkey? How many wives does your father have? … ' I tried to answer that not every Turk are Muslin or wears a scarf, and also Islam and Arab culture are different things, but he did not believe me.

In addition, although emphasizing that they did not experience any discriminative attitude on-campus, participants typically mentioned that, due to being a foreigner or a Turk, they were exposed to discrimination off-campus, which was a challenge in their life in Germany. G07 reported, "Once, an old guy asked me something and I could not answer. He yelled at me in German, like, 'if you cannot speak German do not come here, do not live here!' This humiliation made me feel horrible." Also, G15 stated:

> I went to the dentist. She said that I needed a tooth filling. Instead of starting treatment, she made an appointment for a future date. When I went back for the appointment, she told me to get my treatment in Turkey.

Besides, participants typically indicated having academic stress due to the challenging education system that affected their life negatively. For example, G03 explained, "The German education system is very challenging. According to the rules, students who fail the same exam three times are expelled from the school. So, I have to study every day. Otherwise, I cannot pass." Further, a variant category emerged from the data in this domain. Participants explained that sometimes they felt homesick, especially in difficult times such as exam periods. G06 noted, "Occasionally, I am homesick. It is like a wave that comes and goes. I feel it when I am stressed, especially in the exam term, and have a problem." However, most of the participants specified that they did not feel homesick due to the geographical proximity between Germany and Turkey because they could easily go to Turkey whenever they wanted.

Last, participants typically expressed that they perceived large differences between Turkish and German cultures that cause challenges in interpersonal relationships with locals and make their adaptation harder. Accordingly, participants considered Germans as distant in relationships, superficial, and polite, as a result of German culture. For example, G04 noted, "Germans are cold but nice. You need to pay attention to their personal space and avoid touching them, and do not talk about your private lives. Compared to Turks, they prefer such superficial relationships that are far from sincere" Also, G12 reported, "We are too different from Germans. They are so individualistic, and hospitality is completely different. For example, they do not offer any food or drink when you visit them."

The Contributing Factors in the Adaptation Process Domain

Participants mentioned the coping strategies and resources they applied in dealing with problems relating to their adaptation process in Germany. The first category under this domain is coping strategies as representative of participants' responses and the strategies they used in managing difficulties, as well as enhancing intercultural interactions and reducing the stress associated with such contact. Four subcategories stemmed from this category: First, participants typically defined acceptance as a "means of coping" strategy. They respected and accepted the German culture and values. Acceptance facilitated their cultural learning and, consequently, their adaptation. G09 noted, "I accept that Germany is my home for as long as I stay here and that makes everything easier. After accepting, I improved my language and got involved with the locals." Also, G12 said, "I kept pace with the Germans and their culture. I accept people as they are. The world does not just consist of Turks. This makes everything easier." Second, participants generally considered negative experiences to be an exception, avoided generalizing as a coping strategy, and focused on the academic setting instead. As G01 reported:

> Some individual things can happen off-campus such as at the supermarket. They see your name on the credit card and they do not behave very nicely. I cannot generalize because I never experienced such things in an academic setting and it is not always the case, but it does happen.

Third, participants typically stated that they tried to overcome problems by dealing with stressors directly. As G10 explained,

> At first, I lived in a suburb. This part of the city was not good and was far from the campus. It was a disappointment for me. So, I said, 'whenever you turn from loss, there is gain' and I relocated.

Further, all interviewees either participated in a German language school or attended extracurricular German language classes in order to quickly solve the language barrier problem. Namely, most of the participants indicated that when they identified the source of their problems, they took action directly without any delay to solve them. Fourth, the participants typically noted that they sought social support from friends and family to cope with their adaptation problems in Germany. G09 reported, "I call my parents when I miss home or feel lonely."

The second category under this domain is the support system. It describes relations with others and opportunities for reducing stress and for facilitating the adaptation process of participants on- and off-campus. In this context, three subcategories were examined separately:

First, results showed that the participants generally had strong family bonds and their family supported them financially and emotionally in the adaptation process. G11 stated, "Apart from my financial needs, my family also supports me emotionally. They understand me best. Sometimes just hearing their voices is enough to improve my mood." Second, the participants mentioned that they had a supportive heterogeneous peer network, including co-nationals, other internationals, and locals. Depending on the nature of the stress, they get support from different groups to cope with different types of challenges they face during their adaptation process. Also, most of them indicated that their best friend was Turkish. In the words of G13:

> I have a relationship with everyone but sharing emotional issues with my best Turkish friend is easier due to the common culture and language. Local friends, however, know everything and support me in both academic and daily life, especially in improving my German language proficiency. Therefore, I try to chat with them as much as possible. Also, as we face similar challenges in Germany, we are in strong solidarity with other internationals and, through them, I learn about different cultures.

Third, the results showed that participants generally considered themselves as having a supportive school structure that contributed to their adaptation and motivated participants' integration by means of a friendly atmosphere and social facilities. For example, G08 explained, "I can say that the staffs at university are well-organized. They are very sensitive and feel an obligation to help international students in their integration. In the classroom, professors are helpful and motivate you to be interactive." Also, participants described supportive school facilities that increased interaction among students during the adaptation process. G14 noted:

Library is real life here. Sometimes, I only go to the library to socialize and avoid feeling alone. Also, there is a lunch culture here. We always have lunch, all of us together. Besides, the school organizes free events, and everyone is invited.

Attitudes toward the Counseling Services Domain

This domain defines the participants' perceptions and attitudes toward getting professional counseling support or use of mental health services to cope with stress and problems in the adaptation process. A variant category showed that half of the participants were not completely open to the counseling services for getting psychological support to deal with stressors. For example, G07 indicated, "When I need it, my family or friends, who know and understand me best, immediately support me. The counselor is only a last resort." Another variant category stemming from this domain indicated that participants had inaccurate information about using professional counseling services for psychological support associated with adaptation. For example, G04 reported, "I have not experienced a problem serious enough to go to the counselor." In addition, the participants typically did not have enough information about school counseling services. G08 noted, "I remember when I started university, I received an email about the counseling service. But I cannot remember anything about it." Also, G15 stated, "I have no idea about it. Maybe there is not a counseling service at the university. Because I have not heard about one from others, either." Overall, the results showed that counseling services or any other mental health intervention services were not a part of the adaptation process of the TIS who participated in this study. In addition, participants did not have any awareness about the possible consequences of adaptation challenges.

DISCUSSION

The study aimed at investigating the adaptation experiences of TIS sojourners in Germany. It also contributed to adaptation literature as it focused on defining themes related to TIS, a particular nationality-cultural group that has not been studied in the context of Germany. According to the study's findings, various issues affected the adaptation of TIS, including their perceptions of Germany, the unique challenges they faced, the contributing factors to the adaptation process (social support networks, strategies for coping with adaptation problems), and the attitudes of TIS toward counseling services in the process.

The findings of this study showed that TIS' perceptions of German universities differ from their perceptions of Germany itself. According to Ward and Geeraert (2016), different contexts, including institutional and societal, affect the adaptation process, and a supportive school environment can be important and effective in motivating students to have a positive attitude toward the host country. The participants' motives for adaptation focused foremost on the academic context, depending on their sojourner status and migration goals. They defined Germany as a country that contributes to their self-development with its multicultural structure, and its attitudes to safety and freedom. The participants also believed that Germany offers them not only free and high-quality education but also high-level job opportunities. These positive perceptions increased TIS' motivation for their stay in Germany (e.g., Suoglu, 2012). Similarly, Burkholder (2014) mentioned that a prestigious American degree and possible job opportunities are essential motivational factors for TIS in the United States.

In addition, the challenges experienced by TIS in Germany during the adaptation process are in line with previous studies on the adaptation difficulties of Turkish international students in the United States (e.g., Burkholder, 2014; Duru & Poyrazli, 2011; Kilinc & Granello, 2003) as well as other international student groups in Germany (e.g., Yu & Wang, 2011). In this study, however, findings showed that TIS were exposed to many negative stereotypes owing to being Turkish, Muslim, and foreigner; accordingly, they reported themselves as being more disadvantaged than many other international student groups in Germany. Due to longstanding social and political turmoil, Turks have been stereotyped as being in a lower class, conditioned by Islam, monochrome (Horrocks & Kolinsky, 1996), oppressive, inferior, and backward (Erensü & Adanli, 2004). Participants, aware of the out-group homogeneity perception of Germans, do not accept to be stigmatized or to be generalized with a low reputation. TIS, culturally belonging to the Turkish minority group in Germany, perceive negative stigmas as a threat to their social identity and consider themselves to be representatives of a modern aspect of Turkey. Consequently, they make more effort when dealing with German friends and try to break their prejudices. Also, TIS consider themselves as having a higher status than immigrants; the study's findings suggest that they believe that being an international student (sojourner) is a sign, in itself, that they are well educated and have a financially stable background.

Moreover, TIS in Germany experienced discrimination, but only off-campus. This finding supports the results of a study conducted by Hanassab (2006), who reported that international students in the United States were exposed to discrimination more frequently off-campus, spanning from covert interactions to overt acts. This kind of experience demotivates international students from establishing friendships with locals (Mori, 2000). Similarly, Yu and Wang (2011) stated that Chinese international students were rejected by the Germans due to prejudice and discrimination, causing them to separate from the locals. This study, however, shows that TIS perceptions differentiate between host culture members on- and off-campus. Increased off-campus negative experiences, particularly stereotyping and discrimination, contributed to TIS' motivation to focus more on the academic context and the young locals whom TIS identified as open-minded. According to our findings, TIS perceived that the border between themselves and their German peers was not impermeable (e.g., Tajfel, 1978). Through the positive campus atmosphere and sojourn motivation, TIS continued to maintain and leverage relationships with locals to develop their language and intercultural communication skills as well as to provide practical information. However, acculturative stressors such as prejudice, discrimination, and academic challenges, especially in exam terms, caused TIS to continue to experience adaptation problems such as homesickness. Similarly, Duru and Poyrazli (2011) and Kilinc and Granello (2003) mentioned that perceived discrimination brings about additional adjustment challenges for TIS in the United States.

The findings of this study indicated that TIS in Germany used several coping strategies to deal with the challenges and also to facilitate their adaptation process. Ward et al. (2001) claimed that problem-focused coping during adaptation is the best strategy for international students, and TIS in Germany preferred coping directly with their challenges and stressors such as by learning the German language. The effort toward language learning is a key factor that increases their motivation to communicate with locals in the adaptation process (e.g., Burkholder, 2014; Duru & Poyrazli, 2011). In addition, Nakamura and Orth (2005) stated that active acceptance was an adaptive response when an individual was challenged by unchanging situations, which is consistent with the results of this study. Also, the purpose of TIS' moving to Germany and their experiences, mostly off-campus, has led students to highlight their international student identity and focus more on the academic context, self-development, and motivation. Thus, they avoided generalizing their negative experiences, which contributed to the reduction of cultural stress, the perception of out-group heterogeneity, and their gaining of a positive perception of Germany.

Besides coping strategies, social support contributed to the reduction of TIS' stress during adaptation to their new environment. Bender et al. (2019) showed that having multiple sources of social support is associated with getting the most positive outcomes from the adaptation. Consistently, participants in this study reported having positive and supportive networks within their family and heterogenous peer groups, including locals, co-nationals, and other internationals. In line with their academic, social, and practical needs, TIS established multiple sources of social support and they sought help from these sources as and when necessary. However, the main source of emotional support for TIS in Germany is their family members and co-national friends, due to language, familiarity, and cultural background. The literature highlights that family support increases cultural integration and decreases stress (Bertram et al., 2014). The findings of this study support previous results of TIS-related research (e.g., Bektas et al., 2009; Duru & Poyrazli, 2007, 2011), where the importance of co-national support in the adjustment of TIS is mentioned.

In addition, Gloria et al. (2005) noted that students' perceptions of university affect their social integration. For the TIS in this study, university was not only the place where they received their education, but also an interactive environment for socializing. They also stated that the staff as a whole enabled a supportive and organized school system for them, but the results of this study showed that TIS remain unaware of the existence or functioning of the counseling services at their universities. The underutilization of counseling services in the adaptation process of international students has been widely mentioned in the literature (Mori, 2000). Consistently, participants did not seek professional support when addressing their adaptation challenges. Participants had the perception that counseling services were only for serious mental problems (e.g., Smith & Khawaja, 2011). However, those who report a negative attitude toward counseling services, considering them to be a last resort, are not completely closed to the idea of using them. In addition, the literature highlights that concern about negative stigma is an important reason for international students' underutilization of counseling services (e.g., Mori, 2000). Throughout the interviews in this study however, participants did not report any concerns about stigma regarding the use of counseling services. Our findings are in line with previous studies on the utilization of counseling services of Turkish students in Turkey (e.g., Topkaya et al., 2017) and international students, including TIS (e.g., Kilinc & Granello, 2003; Mori, 2000).

IMPLICATIONS

This study reveals several implications about TIS for advisors, administrators, professors, and other employees at German universities; it also highlights the importance of systematic programs for TIS' adaptation. The results of this study suggest that the universities need to develop different strategies for counseling services. Moreover, during and after the pre-term orientation week, workshops and training sessions that introduce German culture may be useful for improving well-being and enabling the behavioral adaptation of TIS.

In addition, universities can consider intercultural competence training for students and university personnel in order to enlighten them on the harmful effects of stereotyping and discrimination. Thus, social boundaries between host and TIS would collapse and the degree of perceived social acceptance of TIS could be enhanced. For example, under the control of counselors, culturally sensitive posters and social clubs that include local students may be helpful to both local and international students in improving cultural sensitivity, the ability to make friends and in increasing interaction between students. Thus, TIS are encouraged to become actively involved in their adaptation. Also, counselors may contribute to the development and strengthening of TIS' ability to cope with stress through participating in group activities. Therefore, psychologists may help TIS find their most effective coping strategy.

Moreover, counselors ought to take into account TIS' cultural background when providing professional services, and they must remember that personal and cultural limitations may prevent many TIS from seeking counseling services to address their extreme experiences (e.g., discrimination). Thus, counselors play a vital role in helping TIS recognize their stress levels and in recognizing when mental health intervention is needed. Pedersen (1991) emphasized that counselors must go beyond their personal background and biases in a multicultural environment to better serve their international clients. They should be sensitive and positive toward TIS, as their well-being depends on it. Although TIS have useful support networks and some beneficial coping strategies to overcome harmful discrimination and stigma, they still feel threatened and have negative emotions and perceptions about themselves, and about in-group/out-group distinctions. Besides, the future of the currently positive atmosphere on German campuses is uncertain, and TIS could experience discriminatory threats at any time. When these risks are taken into consideration, counselors should attempt to reach international students by using various channels and keep them informed about the available therapeutic, preventive, and guidance services.

LIMITATIONS AND FUTURE RESEARCH DIRECTIONS

This study has three limitations to be considered due to its context and the nature of the methodology chosen. First, the findings of the study are limited to the experiences of the 15 participants. Second, because there was no earlier study regarding the adaptation of TIS in Germany, the interpretations of the results of this study may not be integrated with the relevant literature to provide convergence or divergence. Lastly, although "Skype" interviews helped with increasing participant honesty, it is possible that some nonverbal behaviors of the participants were missed. Nevertheless, this study provided insights about the adaptation process of TIS. Since this was the first study to investigate the adaptation experiences of TIS in Germany by using qualitative analyses, further studies are needed to explore the phenomenon by using different lenses and to compare and contrast the findings of this study.

ACKNOWLEDGMENT

The authors have reported no potential conflict of interest.

Lan Anh Nguyen Luu was supported by a grant from the Hungarian National Research, Development and Innovation Office, NKFIH, Budapest, Hungary (K-120433).

All correspondence concerning this article should be addressed to Seda Erturk, Eötvös Loránd University, PPK, Doctoral School of Psychology, Kazinczy u. 23–27, 1075 Budapest/Hungary. Email: erturk.seda@ppk.elte.hu

REFERENCES

Bektas, Y., Demir, A., & Bowden, R. (2009). Psychological adaptation of Turkish students at US campuses. *International Journal for the Advancement of Counselling, 31*(2), 130–143. https://doi.org/10.1007/s10447-009-9073-5

Bender, M., van Osch, Y., Sleegers, W., & Ye, M. (2019). Social support benefits psychological adjustment of international students: Evidence from a meta-analysis. *Journal of Cross-Cultural Psychology, 50*(7), 827–847. https://doi.org/10.1177/0022022119861151

Bertram, D. M., Poulakis, M., Elsasser, B. S., & Kumar, E. (2014). Social support and acculturation in Chinese international students. *Journal of Multicultural Counseling and Development, 42*(2), 107–124. https://doi.org/10.1002/j.2161-1912.2014.00048.x

Burkholder, J. R. (2014). Reflections of Turkish international graduate students: Studies on life at a US Midwestern university. *International Journal for the Advancement of Counselling, 36*(1), 43–57. https://doi.org/10.1007/s10447-013-9189-5

Duru, E., & Poyrazli, S. (2007). Personality dimensions, psychosocial-demographic variables, and English language competency in predicting level of acculturative stress among Turkish international students. *International Journal of Stress Management, 14*(1), 99–110. https://doi.org/10.1037/1072–5245.14.1.99

Duru, E., & Poyrazli, S. (2011). Perceived discrimination, social connectedness, and other predictors of adjustment difficulties among Turkish international students. *International Journal of Psychology, 46*(6), 446–454. https://doi.org/10.1080/00207594.2011.585158

Erensü, S., & Adanlı, Y. (2004). Turkey in the eye of the beholder: Tracking perceptions on Turkey through political cartoons. *Kontur, 10*, 58–71. https://kontur.au.dk/fileadmin/www.kontur.au.dk/OLD_ISSUES/pdf/kontur_10/sinan.yasar.pdf

Gloria, A. M., Castellanos, J., Lopez, A. G., & Rosales, R. (2005). An examination of academic nonpersistence decisions of Latino undergraduates. *Hispanic Journal of Behavioral Sciences, 27*(2), 202–223. https://doi.org/10.1177/0739986305275098

Greitemeyer, T., & Schwab, A. (2014). Employing music exposure to reduce prejudice and discrimination. *Aggressive Behavior, 40*(6), 542–551. https://doi.org/10.1002/ab.21531

Hanassab, S. (2006). Diversity, international students, and perceived discrimination: Implications for educators and counselors. *Journal of Studies in International Education, 10*(2), 157–172. https://doi.org/10.1177/1028315305283051

Hill, C. E. (2015). Consensual qualitative research (CQR): Methods for conducting psychotherapy research. In O. Gelo, A. Pritz, & B. Rieken (Eds.), *Psychotherapy research* (pp. 485–499). Springer. https://doi.org/10.1080/10503300802702113

Hill, C. E., Knox, S., Thompson, B. J., Williams, E. N., Hess, S. A., & Ladany, N. (2005). Consensual qualitative research: An update. *Journal of Counseling Psychology, 52*(2), 196–205. https://doi.org/10.1037/0022–0167.52.2.196

Horrocks, D., & Kolinsky, E. (Eds.). (1996). *Turkish culture in German society today* (Vol. 1). Berghahn Books.

Hüther, O., & Krücken, G. (2018). *Higher Education in Germany--Recent Developments in an International Perspective.* Springer International Publishing.

İçduygu, A. (2012). 50 years after the labour recruitment agreement with Germany: The consequences of emigration for Turkey. *Perceptions: Journal of International Affairs, 17*(2), 11–36. https://dergipark.org.tr/en/download/article-file/816403

Kilinc, A., & Granello, P. F. (2003). Overall life satisfaction and help-seeking attitudes of Turkish college students in the United States: Implications for college counselors. *Journal of College Counseling, 6*(1), 56–68. https://doi.org/10.1002/j.2161-1882.2003.tb00227.x

Mori, S. C. (2000). Addressing the mental health concerns of international students. *Journal of Counseling & Development, 78*(2), 137–144. https://doi.org/10.1002/j.1556–6676.2000.tb02571.x

Nakamura, Y. M., & Orth, U. (2005). Acceptance as a coping reaction: Adaptive or not? *Swiss Journal of Psychology/Schweizerische Zeitschrift für Psychologie/Revue Suisse de Psychologie, 64*(4), 281–292. https://doi.org/10.1024/1421-0185.64.4.281

Pedersen, P. B. (1991). Multiculturalism as a generic approach to counseling. *Journal of Counseling & Development, 70*(1), 6–12. https://doi.org/10.1002/j.1556–6676.1991.tb01555.x

Smith, R. A., & Khawaja, N. G. (2011). A review of the acculturation experiences of international students. *International Journal of Intercultural Relations, 35*(6), 699–713. https://doi.org/10.1016/j.ijintrel.2011.08.004

Statistisches Bundesamt. (2018). Bildung: Auszug aus dem Datenreport 2018 [Education: Excerpt from the 2018 Data Report]. https://www.destatis.de/DE/Service/Statistik-Campus/Datenreport/Downloads/datenreport-2018-kap-3.pdf?__blob=publicationFile

Suoglu, B. B. (2012). Trends in student mobility from Turkey to Germany. *Perceptions: Journal of International Affairs, 17*(2), 61–84. https://dergipark.org.tr/en/download/article-file/816409

Tajfel, H. E. (1978). *Differentiation between social groups: Studies in the social psychology of intergroup relations*. Academic Press.

Topkaya, N., Vogel, D. L., & Brenner, R. E. (2017). Examination of the stigmas toward help seeking among Turkish college students. *Journal of Counseling & Development, 95*(2), 213–225. https://doi.org/10.1002/jcad.12133

United Nations Educational, Scientific and Cultural Organization Institute of Statistics (2020, September). *Education: Outbound internationally mobile students by host region* [data set]. http://data.uis.unesco.org/index.aspx

Ward, C., Bochner, S., & Furnham, A. (2001). *The psychology of culture shock*. Routledge.

Ward, C., & Geeraert, N. (2016). Advancing acculturation theory and research: The acculturation process in its ecological context. *Current Opinion in Psychology, 8*, 98–104. https://doi.org/10.1016/j.copsyc.2015.09.021

Yu, W., & Wang, S. (2011). An investigation into the acculturation strategies of Chinese students in Germany. *Intercultural Communication Studies, 20*(2), 190–210. https://web.uri.edu/iaics/files/15WeihuaYuShuWang.pdf

Zestos, G. K., & Cooke, R. N. (2020). *Challenges for the EU as Germany approaches recession*. Levy Economics Institute. https://www.researchgate.net/profile/George-Zestos/publication/339241779_Challenges_for_the_EU_as_Germany_Approaches_Recession/links/5e45e533299bf1cdb9284ba6/Challenges-for-the-EU-as-Germany-Approaches-Recession.pdf

SEDA ERTURK is currently a Ph.D. candidate at the Faculty of Education and Psychology, University of Eotvos Lorand, Budapest/Hungary. She holds a BA in Psychological Counseling and guidance from Ondokuz Mayis University, Samsun/Turkey, and an MA in Intercultural Psychology and Education from the University of Eotvos Lorand, Budapest/Hungary. Her research interests include intercultural adaptation, acculturation, multiculturalism, and cross-cultural studies. Email: erturk.seda@ppk.elte.hu

KEMAL OKER is currently a Ph.D. candidate at the Faculty of Education and Psychology, University of Eotvos Lorand, Budapest/Hungary. He holds a BA in Psychology from Middle East Technical University, Ankara/Turkey, and an MA in Clinical Psychology from the University of Eotvos Lorand, Budapest/Hungary. His primary research interests lie in the area of clinical and health psychology. Email: kemal.oker@ppk.elte.hu

LAN ANH NGUYEN LUU is an associate professor and director of the Institute of Intercultural Psychology and Education and the Socialization Process Ph.D. Program at the Doctoral School of Psychology at the University of Eotvos Lorand, Budapest/Hungary. Her primary research interests lie in the area of acculturation, ethnic/national identity, and gender beliefs. Email: lananh@ppk.elte.hu

Research Article

© *Journal of International Students*
Volume 12, Issue 3 (2022), pp. 736-755
ISSN: 2162-3104 (Print), 2166-3750 (Online)
doi: 10.32674/jis.v12i3.3603
ojed.org/jis

Socialization towards Internationalization: Survey Research on University Students in China

Zheng Ren
Institute of Higher Education, Beihang University, China

Fei Wang
Faculty of Education, University of British Columbia, Canada

ABSTRACT

Although students are the main recipients of internationalization in higher education (IHE), research on IHE mainly focuses on particular nations or educational institutions rather than on the individual. The perceptions of university students toward internationalization, particularly what may impact their preparedness for and critical awareness of internationalization, are largely lacking. This study explores the ways in which students' diverse socialization or experiences of socializing with different stakeholders impact their preparedness for and awareness of increasing internationalization in higher education institutions. The study utilizes data from a survey conducted with 511 students at two Chinese universities. The study found that students with diverse socialization backgrounds are more likely to develop a critical awareness of the social impact of internationalization, and that they believe that internationalization enables them to learn from others, to develop capacities to analyze global issues, to develop skills to work with cultural others, and to make ethical decisions on social issues.

Keywords: Chinese University students, cognitive differences, diverse socialization, internationalization in higher education

INTRODUCTION

Over the years, the internationalization of higher education (IHE) has been and continues to be the central focus of research and academy (Mertkan et al., 2016). A plethora of research has been conducted on IHE that involves stakeholders at multiple levels on issues concerning educational policies, practices, and transnational collaborations, including programs, services, and curriculum delivery. One major focus of such research is the international mobility of students, which has contributed to a substantial and growing population flow globally (Gu & Schweisfurth, 2015). Along with such global trends, Chinese students continue to be the primary contributing force to the international mobility and economic prosperity of many destination countries. Although the existing pandemic has interrupted education programs and disrupted the international mobility of students, recent research shows that the demand for overseas study is still strong (Quacquarelli Symonds, 2021).

To date, IHE research on student mobility tends to emphasize its "benefits" for students, such as opportunities for transnational communication and connections, improvement of skills and qualifications for multicultural workplaces, enhancement of independence and confidence, development of open-mindedness, intercultural empathy, and critical thinking (Alberts, 2007; Gu & Schweisfurth, 2015; Heng, 2020; Obst & Forster, 2007; Urban & Bierlein Palmer, 2014; Yusoff, 2012). Such benefits have been a major motivation for international mobility among students. Nevertheless, motivations for international mobility are not solely derived from the potential benefits from IHE. Students' perceptions and attitudes toward internationalization may equally influence their decisions to study in a different country. How they perceive internationalization and how their perceptions and socialization influence their decisions of studying abroad may provide critical insights for those who have been impacted the most by IHE.

Chinese students have been the major recipients of the internationalization, regardless of whether they are the "consumers" or "beneficiaries"; to date, there is limited research on Chinese students' perspectives of IHE and what impacts their perceptions, particularly on those students who are still at universities but expecting to study abroad. Examining their perceptions and voices enables us to understand the impact of the reasoning process of these Chinese students on internationalization and how their personal experience contributes to their conceptualization of internationalization. The inclusion of students' perceptions will provide policy-makers and educators with a nuanced understanding of IHE. To the extent that it helps expand or reframe policies and models that guide international education and collaboration, capturing these consumer voices could significantly influence its future direction. The information gained through this study may also enhance students' sense of ownership of the internationalization of higher education and have significant implications in enriching their future social and academic experience.

This research, as part of a larger international project on IHE, focuses on the views of students at two universities in China. This study aims at seeking the "recipient" students' perceptions of or attitude toward IHE in China. The research explores the factors that impact their perceptions, and the ways in which their socialization relates to their perceptions of internationalization in higher education. This article commences with the context and literature review on the internationalization, followed by the sociocultural framework and cognitive research that guides the inquiry, and then reports the research process and results.

CONTEXT

International student mobility is fast-growing globally and it is becoming a distinctive feature of contemporary tertiary education. Up to 2018, more than 5 million higher education students studied abroad all over the world (Institute of International Education [IIE], 2018). This trend is more salient in China. According to the data compiled by the National Bureau of Statistics of China (NBSC), there were 662,100 Chinese students studying abroad until 2018 (National Bureau of Statistics of China [NBSC], 2020), accounting for about 13% of the total number of international students in the world. This means that one out of every eight international students around the world hails from China. According to the statistics from the OECD. Stat (OECD Stat, 2021), the outbound mobility ratio of China's higher education was 2.2% in 2019. Chinese students occupy a significant position in the global mobility of international students.

The internationalization of China's higher education can be traced back to the second half of the 19th century. Students were sent with public funding to developed countries such as Britain, Germany, France, and Japan (Huang, 2003). Since the founding of the People's Republic of China, China was the first country to send its students to study in the Soviet Union. In the early 1960s, policies were made to support students studying in the West. These policies laid a foundation for the management of students studying abroad.

In recent years, major actions to accelerate the internationalization of China's higher education are particularly reflected in the formulation and implementation of a series of national education policies. For example, the "Middle-and Long-term Education Reform and Development Plan Outline (2010–2020)" (Ministry of Education [MOE], 2010) states:

> Innovate and improve the mechanism of government-sponsored study abroad … with the principles of 'support studying abroad, encourage returning to China, and come and go freely' … and expand the scale of foreign students in the future. … Strengthen international understanding of education, promote cross-cultural exchanges, and enhance students' knowledge and understanding of different countries and different cultures. (item 48–50)

In August 2018, policy-makers announced the "Guiding Opinions on Accelerating the Construction of 'Double First Class' in Higher Education Institutions" (Ministry of Education, Ministry of Finance, National Development and Reform Commission [MOE, MOF, ND and RC], 2018), which aims to: "vigorously promote high-level substantive international cooperation and exchange, and play the role as a participant, promoter, and leader of world higher education reforms." (item 11)

As a result, Chinese students are given more opportunities for overseas exchange and learning, either self-funded or funded by scholarships from the nation or higher education institutions (Liu, 2016). A survey extending over 34 provinces in China by the New Oriental Vision Overseas Consulting Co., Ltd. and The Kantar Group (TKG) found that 73% of overseas Chinese students are in higher education and undergraduate students account for 57% (New Oriental Education & Technology Group [NOE & TG], 2020). As the economy is developing in China, more and more families are able to afford having their children study abroad, especially those with only one child (Wang, 2020). Students from middle-class families are increasing tremendously year by year (NOE & TG, 2020).

Since 2009, China has gradually implemented policies and guidelines to support students to study abroad on a larger scale (Liu, 2016). Studying abroad becomes more acceptable by the public in China (Liu, 2016). The number of students and the wide range of disciplines they are undertaking have reached an unprecedented level. Since 2000, there has been a substantial increase in the number of overseas students and returning students, through a series of programs by the government (Ryan, 2011) (see Figure 1 below).

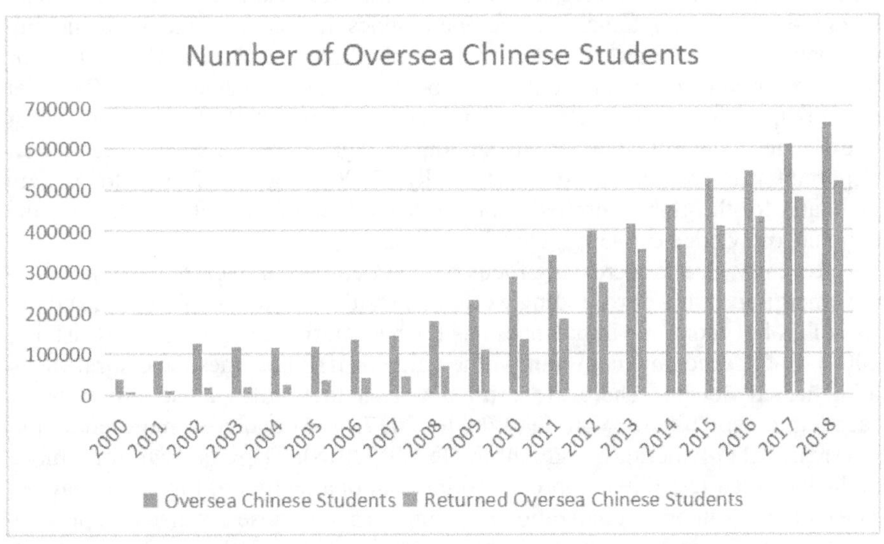

Figure 1: Number of Oversea Chinese Students

Source: China Statistical Yearbook 2020, National Bureau of Statistics Database. http://www.stats.gov.cn/tjsj/ndsj/2020/indexch.htm (accessed 16 January 2021)

LITERATURE REVIEW

Conceptualization of Internationalization

Internationalization is a broad concept and it gained popularity in education in the early 1980s. In the 1990s, the discussion on international education centered on differentiating it from comparative education, global education, and multicultural education (Knight, 2004). Until the 21st century, there was much discussion on transnational education, borderless education, multi-nationalization, and regionalization (e.g., Knight, 2008). To date, internationalization has been considered a global, strategic, and mainstream factor in higher education (Knight & De Wit, 2018). In addition, the mobility of students, scholars, and programs (e.g., Gao, 2020; Greek & Jonsmoen, 2021; Gu & Schweisfurth, 2015; Teichler, 2015); reputation and branding (manifested by global and regional rankings, such as QS and the Times Higher Education World rankings) (Lo, 2011; Stein, 2018); and a shift in paradigm from cooperation to competition (Van der Wende, 2001) have been the main manifestations of IHE over the past 30 years. Aigner et al. (1992) stated that maintaining global security, enhancing national economic strength, and promoting understanding among countries are the three main factors for the realization of internationalization in higher education.

Some scholars adopt a broader view of internationalization, including politics (e.g., national security, investment for diplomatic relations), economy (e.g., income-generation, international competitiveness), academic factor (achieving international academic standards, institution building), and cultural/social factor (e.g., preservation of national culture, respect of cultural diversity) (e.g., Castro et al., 2020; Knight, 2013; Olson et al., 2015; Zha, 2003). In the context of knowledge economy, internationalization in higher education has become an important way to generate revenue (Kelly, 2000; Teichler, 2010), to prepare graduates for the global competitive labor market, and to attract top talent for the national knowledge economy (De Wit et al., 2015).

Recently, due to increasing focus on competition, anti-globalization voices are emerging. Issues surrounding exclusion resulted from globalization, and the risk of global economic imbalances has further reinforced such voices (Castells, 2000). In the academic community, the value of IHE becomes the central focus of a heated debate. There are critical voices that are against any form of "academic capitalism" (Van der Wende, 2017, p. 6) and seek more equitable international collaboration (Knight & De Wit, 2018). There is a call for a more inclusive and a less elitist approach to internationalization of higher education. The call views internationalization not simply as a purpose but also as a process toward comprehensive equality development for all stakeholders (De Wit, 2019, 2020; De Wit et al., 2015). Led by Brandenburg et al. (2019), the "Internationalization in Higher Education for Society" (IHES) proposes a comprehensive inclusive vision of internationalization based on the unity of the world community (Leask & de Gayardon, 2021).

Internationalization and Its Impact on Students

Why does internationalization of higher education matter for students? Through the lens of students' mobility, Tran and Vu (2018) reveal in their study that IHE not only enhances students' educational experiences but also develops their cross-cultural understanding and relationships with different communities. Students with international learning experiences can develop a new social network and acquire extracurricular skills, such as personal development, as well as linguistic and cultural competence (Green, 2019; Krzaklewska & Krupnik, 2006; Wiers-Jenssen, 2003). For many students, international mobility is also driven by "credential inflation" (Wadhwa, 2016, p. 230). International experience and credentials may enhance their employment opportunities after graduation and put them in a more competitive position for high-status jobs (Fielden, 2007; Punteney, 2012). Particularly in Asia, there is a general belief that international higher education would enhance students' competitiveness in the global and local labor markets (Berling, 2018; Mok, 2018). Mok et al. (2020) stated that high-quality education, the reputation of the host country/university, greater acquisition of English proficiency, and the recognition of their diplomas/certificates for future careers are the main drivers for student mobility.

However, studying abroad also comes with challenges: language barriers, cultural conflicts, stereotypes, etc. All of these make it difficult to live in a foreign environment. In a survey among Canadian international students conducted by Guo and Guo (2017), respondents reported that they felt it was difficult to make local friends and communicate with their supervisors. They indicated that their home culture was not well respected, and they experienced racial discrimination. Another formidable challenge is severe financial difficulties, which can cause some mental and psychological problems, such as anxiety and stress, and eventually lead to poor academic performance (Nyland et al., 2013). Based on students' perspectives, Li and Collins (2014) explored Chinese students' experiences in American doctoral education and the challenges in their socialization, including communication barriers and negative feelings. Heng (2017) interviewed Chinese undergraduate students on their aspirations for living and studying in the United States and found that better support is needed for these students to navigate the education system.

In general, previous studies tend to focus on international higher education at the macro or meso level, examining its definitions, rationales, collaboration strategies, and pedagogical implications. Studies that have explored students' perceptions of international experiences mainly focus on overseas students. Little research has been done on students who are expecting or planning to study abroad and their perceptions of internationalization in relation to their backgrounds, socialization, and lived experiences. How do they perceive internationalization and what influences their perceptions that may affect their decisions on overseas study?

Students' Perception of Internationalization

In the context of internationalization, globalization means not only multicultural exchanges, but also mutual understanding and cooperation. In 1948, UNESCO advocated education for sustaining peace in the world by interactively understanding people of different sociocultural environments. For supporting education for global citizenship, United Nations Educational Scientific and Cultural Organization [UNESCO] (2015) has produced documents with key aims, including "develop values of fairness and social justice, and skills to critically analyze inequalities … " (p. 16). According to Clarke (2004), global education focuses mostly on the global awareness of students with respect to international matters, and their attitudes toward internationalism, and aims at preparing students to be world citizens.

In modern China, *International Understanding Education* is popular in elementary, junior high, and high school (Qin, 2013). Preparing students for global citizenship is an essential component of the international agenda for higher education institutions (Leask & Bridge, 2013). There is still space to develop in Chinese college students' international education (Gao et al., 2014). A survey of students in a Chinese university found that students present a one-sided understanding of internationalization. Most students tend to view global issues from a national perspective, and there is a lack of understanding of "global citizenship" (Gao, 2010).

CONCEPTUAL FRAMEWORK

This research explores how Chinese university students' diverse social backgrounds affect their international perceptions. It employs a sociocultural framework that is based on the recent development in socialization theory, combined with the psychological and anthropological cultural perspectives. According to Vygotsky's (1978) sociocultural psychology, social conditions and actions are primary to the formation of humans' consciousness. Changes in social conditions and the basis of consciousness can lead to the development of new thinking and actions. People's learning, behavior, and development are shaped by their sociocultural contexts and their interactions with their sociocultural medium. Changes in individuals' sociocultural circumstances throughout the life cycle, such as a specific family, a neighborhood friendship group, a school classroom, an adult work setting (Lave & Wenger, 1991), may help them develop different capabilities as a member of society and repertoires of multicultural competence (Goodenough, 1976). The complexity and dynamic in such changes are a crucial focus of educational practices in schools (Erickson, 2009, 2011; Gutiérrez & Rogoff, 2003). In general, personal development, including people's perceptions of a particular phenomenon, is shaped by diverse social conditions, as well as by dynamic changes in communities and social relationships (Heng, 2017, 2018).

Teichler (2014) also argues that cognitions and attitudes toward internationalization are important concepts in discussing internationalization in higher education. There are programs (such as Lisbon Convention, 1997) that have been set up to support mobility and cross-border knowledge transfer and to improve stakeholders' cognitive orientation to internationalization. These programs aim at enhancing stakeholders' "global understanding," to help them think critically of global or other countries' issues, and to promote respect of other cultures. Students' global awareness of internationalism is about what they know about other cultures, how the world systems operate, how they empathize with the values of other cultures, and what kind of standpoint they take on global issues (Díaz et al., 1999). Being a "global citizen" means expanding the boundaries of "citizenship" beyond the nation-state level and assuming responsibilities for human rights promotion (Dower, 2003).

Nevertheless, studies show that international mobility is largely driven by "added value," such as extracurricular skills, foreign linguistic and cultural competence for successful employment (Findlay et al., 2012). Such added value also includes building social networks, enhancing cosmopolitan competence, increasing independence, and bettering communication skills (Gu & Schweisfurth, 2015). There are variables that might affect the students' perspectives on internationalization of higher education and global citizenship. Trilokekar and Rasmi (2011) conducted a comprehensive analysis on the factors that affect students' desire to study abroad and identified two major sets of factors: the external environment factors, such as institutional and program characteristics, faculty involvement, and course contents; and internal subjective factors, including preferences for study abroad, demographic and psychosocial characteristics, psychological well-being, etc. They especially mentioned that an individual's social networks (including institutional, peer, and family) may affect their decisions to study abroad. However, such variables have not been fully considered. The domestic students who study at institutions of their home country may hold different views toward overseas studies and what it means to be a "global citizen." This study examines their diverse socialization backgrounds that can influence students' views on IHE. The study draws on an assumption that students' diverse socialization may influence their perceptions of IHE, their overseas study plans, and their understanding of being global citizens.

RESEARCH METHODOLOGY

This study is part of a larger international comparative study on the ethics of internationalization. The research project—Ethical Internationalism in Higher Education (EIHE), funded by the Academy of Finland (2012–2015)—examines the ethical issues arising from internationalization processes in higher education. This interdisciplinary, international mixed-methods research project involves 20 universities around the world. It explores ethical internationalism in higher education by comparing official university policies and the perceptions of faculty, students, and managers engaged with internationalization processes. This study focuses primarily on surveys in two universities in China to investigate the perceptions of college students on the internationalization of higher education.

Data Source and Sample

International education in China is developing rapidly, particularly in the coastal areas, such as southern and eastern China, where economic prosperity has led to more students studying abroad (Qin, 2013). This study draws on the survey data ($N = 511$) collected in 2014 from two universities, located in the South (SU, $N = 269$) and the West (WU, $N = 242$) of China, with the purpose of investigating their perceptions of internationalization and the influence of their own social background on their cognition. The following table provides a brief summary of the sample (unit: percentage):

University	SU (52.6%)		WU (47.4%)	
Gender	Female (77.9%)		Male (19.8%)	
Year of birth	1987–1997 (25.7%)		1992–1995 (74.3%)	
Year of study	First year (33.8%)	Second year (41.7%)	Third year (17.3%)	Fourth year (0.9%)

Note: There are 6.7% invalid cases.

This study aims at exploring whether diverse socialization or experiences socializing with people of diverse backgrounds impact students' critical awareness of the changing nature of internationalization. The study specifically used the following variables to explore the diverse socialization that students have and how it impacts their perceptions of internationalization:

Neighborhood where I grew up
My school experiences
My friends growing up
My friends at this university
My online friends
My romantic relationship

This research also measures students' perceptions of the internationalization of higher education, such as the importance of universities to society at large; opportunities that the internationalization of universities can offer; challenges posed by the internationalization of universities, etc.; and what is important to develop or learn about in the study of academic disciplines, such as skills and dispositions, global themes, social and political issues, etc. Students' demographic information has also been considered, especially the degree of their social diversity. A Likert scale was used to measure their diverse socialization:

All or nearly all from my own background
Mostly people from my own background
About half and half

Mostly people from a background different from mine
All or nearly all people from a background different from mine

Data Analysis

Student t-tests were used to investigate whether there is a statistical difference between students who mainly interact with people of their own background and those who interact with people from a different background. The comparison aims at exploring how students' socialization in the neighborhood where they grew up, through their school experience and friends, affects their perception of internationalization.

- Group 1: Less diverse socialization group—participants who interact with mostly people, all or nearly all from their own background
- Group 2: Diverse socialization group—those who interact with mostly people, all or nearly all from a different background

Thematic analysis is also conducted on students' attitudes toward the impact of internationalization on society between the two groups of students.

Inspired by De Wit (2020)'s proposition of a new approach to observe internationalization, this study also employs open-ended questions to gain a detailed understanding of students' perceptions of the topic.

RESEARCH FINDINGS

The study results show that there is a significant difference among Chinese college students in their perceptions of IHE in relation to their diverse socialization and lived experiences. Their experience and social backgrounds shape their worldviews and perspectives, expand their thinking over the processes and the implications of internationalization in higher education, and change their expectations and goals toward overseas studies.

Independent-samples *t*-tests were conducted to compare students who interact mostly with people, all or nearly all from a different background from them (Group 2) and those who interact mostly with people, all or nearly all from their own background in neighborhoods where they grew up (Group 1). Analysis results suggest that a significant statistical difference exists between Group 1 and Group 2 students in terms of the following perceptions: Internationalization of universities can offer students the opportunity to learn from other students from different countries (t (390) = 2.59, p = .01) and to critically analyze global issues (t (390) = 1.99, p < .05). Students who are used to interacting with people of diverse backgrounds are more likely to believe that internationalization could enable them to learn from others and to develop the capacity to analyze global issues. The experience of diverse interactions enables students to have a better understanding of different cultures and to become adaptable when facing changes resulting from transnational mobility.

Further analysis shows that Group 1 and Group 2 students differ in their views of skills and dispositions relevant to their field of study, in particular the skills of working well with people from a different culture (t (392) = 2.03, $p <$ .05) and making ethical decisions that benefit society (t (93) = 2.56, $p =$ .01). Group 2 students emphasize more on working well with people from a different culture ($M =$ 2.87, $SD =$ .83) and making ethical decisions that benefit society ($M =$ 2.95, $SD =$ .74). Students with a diversification of social capital are more likely to adapt to different modes of learning, living, and behavior. They have a greater potential to contribute to the intercultural process and to the new academic community.

A significant difference has also been found between these two groups in terms of what they value in their courses. Unlike Group 1, Group 2 students indicated that they attach more value to learning about how poorer countries can be helped to develop (t (106) = 2.83, $p =$ .01), debating course ideas (t (105) = 3.92, $p =$ .00), and learning from people who have experienced injustice (t (99) = 2.47, $p =$ .02). Students in Group 2 who tend to interact with people of diverse backgrounds demonstrate greater concerns with poverty and justice issues and are more likely to engage with issues in the global communities. They tend to identify themselves as global citizens with a greater sense of social responsibility and a mission in the understanding of and engaging with global issues.

A thematic analysis was conducted on 281 students (more than half of the sample) who responded to the open-ended questions on the impact of internationalization on society. The analysis results support our assumption. Students who responded thoughtfully to the open-ended questions in general had a rather balanced perception of the impact of internationalization in higher education, seeing internationalization as a double-edged phenomenon. It is noteworthy that students with diverse socialization backgrounds tend to respond to the open-ended questions (64.4% of the 281 who responded). They tend to have a more balanced and critical view of IHE than those without diverse socialization backgrounds. On the one hand, students see internationalization mainly as conducive to cultural exchange and development. For example, students commented:

> Internationalization can promote development, innovation, and interest integration (10001ED)

> Nations realize cultural enrichment through mutual exchanges (10080ED)

> For students, international learning can make them understand different cultures and then rethink other countries' or global issues in an inclusive way (10151HU)

These students believe that internationalization can strengthen exchanges and cooperation between different countries and promote sharing of the advanced scientific and technological achievements. It can also help students develop an inclusive understanding of different cultures and expand their thinking over other countries' and global issues.

On the other hand, students see internationalization mainly as impacting local cultural, social security, in addition to social conflict as well as social and economic polarization. One student expressed his concern that "internationalization increase the risk of neocolonialism and terrorism, exacerbating the gap between the East and the West/ the North and the South" (10146HU).

According to the surveyed students, global citizens need to deal with global issues from a holistic and multiple perspectives, be open-minded to different countries, and show respect to other cultures. What is important is to take the critical issues in mind, such as poverty, discrimination, and fairness, and assume the responsibility of building a better world, as one student indicated: "A good global citizen is one who is empathetic to others and responsible to make a better global society" (10248SC). Some students also feel they should have the ability to overcome the challenges of social division and difference: "As a global citizen, the key mission is to build an inclusive and diverse world" (10149HU).

Students look forward to increasing international understanding and learning about various cultures by participating more actively in overseas learning. Simultaneously, challenges and opportunities coexist. The surveyed students are also concerned with communication barriers and the social, cultural, or academic isolation led by the cultural divergence that they have to face. One student stated:

> Given the limited internationalization of my university, it is necessary to enlarge support networks to enhance activities for students to experience IHE, such as close relationship between domestic students with foreign ones to know the diverse culture and practice language skill. (11084ED)

Students see the benefits of being exposed to different cultures and how such exposure can enhance their understanding of people from other cultures and help them better integrate into an environment that is culturally diverse.

DISCUSSION

This research reveals that students are differentially positioned in relation to their social experience. Students with diverse socialization tend to have a stronger sense of global citizenship and are more concerned with global issues, social justice, equity, and power relations. Their concerns reflect the current ethically driven agenda of internationalization as suggested in recent studies (e.g., Andreotti, 2013; Guo & Guo, 2017; Khoo, 2011). These studies explored global citizenship by highlighting not only the economic but also the ethical implications of internationalization.

The students' perceptions of internationalization in this study represent a shift from the liberal model that emphasizes self-development in international education to a social transformation model that aims at strengthening students' awareness of international and intercultural matters related to equity, justice, human rights, and environment. Such an understanding equips them with critical thinking toward social transformation (Delanty, 2009). What is evident is that students' diverse experience in their social lives potentially contributes to the development of their critical thinking to diverse views of knowledge and skills, competence in ethical decision making, acceptance of diverse people, cultures and values, and better resilience in the multicultural overseas environment. It also helps them improve their intercultural capacity and remain competitive in the global workplace (Weenink, 2008).

Some students who experience socialization with people from diverse backgrounds also tend to have a strong sense of entrepreneurship in the context of neoliberalism. They believe that internationalization accelerates economic cooperation and the sharing of advanced scientific and technological ideas. Internationalization simply means the competitiveness of students, higher education institutions, and nations in the global economic marketplace (Fielden, 2007; Punteney, 2012; Wadhwa, 2016).

On the other hand, students with less diverse socialization are more concerned with issues at the national and societal levels, such as whether advanced technology can bring about the economic development of the nation, whether certificates or diplomas from an overseas university are conducive to providing them better career opportunities. In other words, they tend to focus more on personal gains in the labor market or national competitiveness brought about by the internationalization of higher education. In other words, they prefer to view international experiences as the "symbolic capital in elite competitive games of distinction" (Yemini et al., 2014, p. 307).

This study also raises the question of class participation of Chinese students. In Western colleges, the inquiry-based dialogic teaching method is used widely to cultivate students' critical thinking skills by interactive and cooperative communication (Holmes, 2005). Due to a lack of English proficiency and unfamiliarity with the native culture, Chinese students usually tend to be inactive in classroom participation. This results in the marginalization of Chinese students in classrooms (Holmes, 2005; Tian & Lowe, 2009). However, in this study, students with diverse socialization show a stronger democratic awareness of global issues and are more likely to actively participate in classroom discussions and debates.

Thus, critical global citizenship education is needed to help learners move toward a deeper understanding of global issues and world cultures (Andreotti, 2011). In order to achieve this goal, "internationalization efforts should be collaborative with each culture mutually enhancing and enriching a global curriculum" (Pitts & Brooks, 2017, pp. 257–278). Particularly in China, there is a strong need to develop students' critical thinking and reflection skills, which would enable them to challenge power relations and cultural stereotypes and break cultural fascination and exoticism (Brooks & Pitts 2016; Pitts & Brooks, 2017).

More importantly, students are not passive recipients of internationalization but are the core stakeholders. It is critical to highlight their voices, especially the voices of those who study in their home country while preparing for overseas studies. This study foregrounds the voices of Chinese students by sharing how they view the internationalization of higher education and what they value in the global context. It challenges the common observation that Chinese students tend to be passive participants who are unwilling or cannot express their thoughts and opinions (Ruble & Zhang 2013; Zhu & Bresnahan, 2018). On the contrary, this study showcases how Chinese students would like their domestic or host institutional community to support their international experiences.

CONCLUSION

In the context of globalization, this research examines the differences in the perceptions of internationalization of higher education in relation to students' socialization background from a micro perspective. Their diverse socialization pushes their thinking over internationalization in a more comprehensive and ethical manner. Students' perceptions suggest that internationalization should not be driven by economic or financial gains or lead to a new mode of cultural domination/imperialism. Instead, it needs to be an inclusive process that cultivates their sense of global citizenship and cultural understanding/communication. Higher education institutions need to rethink how they can better support students through diversifying students' social experiences and enriching their learning, for example, through the creation of various programs, including summer schools in which students can talk and share ideas; create diverse social experiences with people from different cultural backgrounds; integrate international elements into the curriculum and encourage students' active participation in discussions and debates with others; and cultivate students' sense of global citizenship.

REFERENCES

Aigner, J. S., Nelson, P., & Stimpfl, J. R. (1992). *Internationalizing the university: Making it work.* CBIS Federal.

Alberts, H. C. (2007). Beyond the headlines: Changing patterns in international student enrollment in the United States. *GeoJournal, 68,* 141–153. http://doi.org/10.1007/s10708-007-9079-7

Andreotti, V. (2011). (Towards) decoloniality and diversality in global citizenship education. *Globalisation, Societies and Education, 9*(3–4), 381–397. http://doi.org/10.1080/14767724.2011.605323

Andreotti, V. (Ed.). (2013). *The political economy of global citizenship education.* Routledge.

Berling, J. A. (2018). *Confucianism.* https://asiasociety.org/education/confucianism

Brandenburg, U., De Wit, H., Jones, E., & Leask, B. (2019). *Defining internationalisation in HE for society.* University World News. https://www.universityworldnews.com/post.php?story=20190626135618704

Brooks, C. F., & Pitts, M. J. (2016). Communication and identity management in a globally-connected classroom: An online international and intercultural learning experience. *Journal of International and Intercultural Communication, 9*(1), 52–68. https://doi.org/10.1080/17513057.2016.1120849

Castells, M. (2000). *The rise of the network society.* Blackwell.

Castro, P., Lundgren, U., & Woodin, J. (2020). *Educational approaches to internationalization through intercultural dialogue: Reflections on theory and practice*. Routledge.

Clarke, V. (2004). Students' global awareness and attitudes to internationalism in a world of cultural convergence. *Journal of Research in International Education, 3*(1), 51–70. https://doi.org/10.1177/1475240904041461

Council of Europe. (1997). *Convention on the recognition of qualifications concerning higher education in the European Union (ETS, No. 165)*. Strasbourg: Council of Europe.

De Wit, H. (2019). Internationalization in higher education, a critical review. *SFU Educational Review, 12*(3), 9–17. https://doi.org/10.21810/sfuer.v12i3.1036

De Wit, H. (2020). Internationalization of higher education: The need for a more ethical and qualitative approach. *Journal of International Students, 10*(1), i–iv. https://doi.org/10.32674/jis.v10i1.1893

De Wit, H., Hunter, F., Egron-Polak, E., & Howard, L. (Eds.). (2015). *Internationalisation of higher education: A study for the European parliament*. http://www.europarl.europa.eu/RegData/etudes/STUD/2015/540370/IPOL_STU(2015)540370_EN.pdf

Delanty, G. (2009). *The cosmopolitan imagination*. Cambridge University Press.

Díaz, C., Massialas, B., & Kantholpoulos, J. (1999). *Global perspectives for educators*. Allyn & Bacon.

Dower, N. (2003). *An introduction to global citizenship*. Edinburgh University Press.

Erickson, F. (2009). Culture in society and in educational practices. In J. Banks & C. Banks (Eds.), *Multicultural education: Issues and perspectives* (7th ed., pp. 32–57). John Wiley & Sons, Inc.

Erickson, F. (2011). Culture. In B. A. U. Levinson & M. Pollock (Eds.), *A companion to the anthropology of education* (pp. 25–33). Blackwell.

Fielden, J. (2007). *Global horizons for UK universities*. Council for Industry and Higher Education.

Findlay, A. M., King, R., Smith, F. M., Geddes, A., & Skeldon, R. (2012). World class? An investigation of globalisation, difference and international student mobility. *Transactions - Institute of British Geographers (1965), 37*(1), 118–131. https://doi.org/10.1111/j.1475-5661.2011.00454.x

Gao, C. (2010). Investigation of college students' international understanding education and cultivation strategies. *School Party Building and Ideological Education, 34*, 85–87. 高翠欣.(2010).大学生国际意识状况调查与培养策略. 学校党建与思想教育 *34*, 85–87. doi:CNKI:SUN:XXDJ.0.2010-34-039.

Gao, C. X., Zhang, J. G., & Jiang, W. (2014). The policy features and implementation ways of international understanding education for college students since the founding of new China. *School Party Building and Ideological Education, 17*, 82–84. 高翠欣, 张锦高 & 姜伟.(2014).新中国成立以来大学生国际意识教育的政策特点及实施途径. 学校党建与思想教育 *17*, 82–84. doi:CNKI:SUN:XXDJ.0.2014-17-031.

Gao, Y. (2020). How transnational experiences and political, economic policies inform transnational intellectuals' identities and mobility: An autoethnographic study. *Higher Education Policy, 3*, 1–18. https://doi.org/10.1057/s41307-020-00187-w

Goodenough, W. H. (1976). Multiculturalism as the normal human experience. *Anthropology & Education Quarterly, 7*(4), 4–7. http://www.jstor.org/stable/3216509

Greek, M., & Jonsmoen, K. M. (2021). Transnational academic mobility in universities: The impact on a departmental and an interpersonal level. *Higher Education, 81*(3), 591–606. https://doi.org/10.1007/s10734-020-00558-7

Green, W. (2019). Engaging "students as partners" in global learning: Some possibilities and provocations. *Journal of Studies in International Education, 23*(1), 10–29. https://doi.org/10.1177/1028315318814266

Gu, Q., & Schweisfurth, M. (2016;2015;). Transnational flows of students: In whose interest? For whose benefits? In S. McGrath, & Q. Gu (Eds.), *Routledge handbook of international education and development.* (pp. 359–379). Routledge.

Guo, Y., & Guo, S. B. (2017). Internationalization of Canadian higher education: Discrepancies between policies and international student experiences. *Studies in Higher Education (Dorchester-on-Thames), 42*(5), 851–868. https://doi.org/10.1080/03075079.2017.1293874

Gutiérrez, K. D., & Rogoff, B. (2003). Cultural ways of learning: Individual traits or repertoires of practice. *Educational Researcher, 32*(5), 19–25. https://doi.org/10.3102/0013189X032005019

Heng, T. T. (2017). Voices of Chinese international students in USA colleges: "I want to tell them that…". *Studies in Higher Education, 42*(5), 833–850. https://doi.org/10.1080/03075079.2017.1293873

Heng, T. T. (2018). Different is not deficient: Contradicting stereotypes of Chinese international students in US higher education. *Studies in Higher Education, 43*(1), 22–36. https://doi.org/10.1080/03075079.2016.1152466

Heng, T. T. (2020). Chinese students themselves are changing: Why we need alternative perspectives of Chinese international students. *Journal of International Students, 10*(2), 539–545. https://doi.org/10.32674/jis.v10i2.958

Holmes, P. (2005). Ethnic Chinese students' communication with cultural others in a New Zealand university. *Communication Education, 54*(4), 289–311. https://doi.org/10.1080/03634520500442160

Huang, F. (2003). Policy and practice of the internationalization of higher education in china. *Journal of Studies in International Education, 7*(3), 225–240. https://doi.org/10.1177/1028315303254430

Institute of International Education. (2018). *Project Atlas 2018: Infographics.* https://www.iie.org/Research-and-Insights/Project-Atlas/Explore-Data/Infographics/2018-Project-Atlas-Infographics

Kelly, P. (2000). Internationalizing the curriculum: For profit or planet. In S. Inayatullah & J. Gidley (Eds.), *The university in transformation: Global perspectives on the futures of the university* (pp. 161–172). Bergin & Garvey.

Khoo, S. (2011). Ethical globalisation or privileged internationalisation? Exploring global citizenship and internationalisation in Irish and Canadian universities. *Globalisation, Societies and Education, 9*(3–4), 337–353. https://doi.org/10.1080/14767724.2011.605320

Knight, J. (2004). Internationalization remodeled: Definition, approaches, and rationales. *Journal of Studies in International Education, 8*(1), 5–31. https://doi.org/10.1177/1028315303260832

Knight, J. (2008). *Higher education in turmoil: The changing world of internationalization.* Sense Publishers.

Knight, J. (2013). The changing landscape of higher education internationalisation - For better or worse? *Perspectives (Association of University Administrators (U.K.)), 17*(3), 84–90. https://doi.org/10.1080/13603108.2012.753957

Knight, J., & De Wit, H. D. (2018). Internationalization of higher education: Past and future. *International Higher Education, 95,* 2–4. https://doi.org/10.6017/ihe.2018.95.10715

Krzaklewska, E., & Krupnik, S. (2006). *The experience of studying abroad for exchange students in Europe.* Research Report, Erasmus Student Network Survey 2005.

Lave, J., & Wenger, E. (1991). *Situated learning: Legitimate peripheral participation.* Cambridge University Press.

Leask, B., & Bridge, C. (2013). Comparing internationalisation of the curriculum in action across disciplines: Theoretical and practical perspectives. *Compare, 43*(1), 79–101. https://doi.org/10.1080/03057925.2013.746566

Leask, B., & de Gayardon, A. (2021). Reimagining internationalization for society. *Journal of Studies in International Education, 25*(4), 323–329. https://doi.org/10.1177/10283153211033667

Li, W., & Collins, C. S. (2014). Chinese doctoral student socialization in the United States: A qualitative study. *FIRE: Forum for International Research in Education, 1*(2), 32–57. Retrieved from http://preserve.lehigh.edu/fire/vol1/iss2/3

Liu, Y. (2016). *Researching on oversea study policy change of The People's Republic of China (1949–2014)* [Doctoral dissertation, Northeast Normal University]. https://kns.cnki.net/KCMS/detail/detail.aspx?dbname=CDFDLAST2017&filename=1016109888.nh 刘艳. (2016). *新中国出国留学政策变迁研究（1949–2014）*(博士学位论文, 东北师范大学).

Lo, W. Y. W. (2011). Soft power, university rankings and knowledge production: Distinctions between hegemony and self-determination in higher education. *Comparative Education, 47*(2), 209–222. https://doi.org/10.1080/03050068.2011.554092

Mertkan, S., Gilanlioglu, I., & McGrath, S. (2016). Internationalizing higher education: From grand plans to evolving responses. *Journal of Organizational Change Management, 29*(6), 889–902. https://doi.org/10.1108/JOCM-10-2015-0185

Ministry of Education (2010). *Middle- and long-term education reform and development plan outline (2010–2020).* http://www.gov.cn/jrzg/2010-07/29/content_1667143.htm. *国家中长期教育改革和发展规划纲要 (2010–2020)*

Ministry of Education, Ministry of Finance, National Development and Reform Commission (2018). *Guiding opinions on accelerating the construction of 'double first class' in Higher Education Institutions.* 关于高等学校加快"双一

流"建设的指导意见. http://www.moe.gov.cn/srcsite/A22/moe_843/201808/t20180823_345987.html

Mok, K. H. (2018). Does internationalization of higher education still matter? Critical reflections on student learning, graduate employment and faculty development in Asia. *Higher Education Quarterly, 72*(3), 183–193. https://doi.org/10.1111/hequ.12170

Mok, K. H., Lang, S., & Xiao, H. (2020). The quest for global talent for changing economic needs: A study of student mobility and job prospects for returnees in China. *Globalisation, Societies and Education, 18*(1), 79–96. https://doi.org/10.1080/14767724.2019.1690734

National Bureau of Statistics of China. (2020). *2020 China statistical yearbook.* China Statistics Press.

New Oriental Education & Technology Group. (2020). 2020 *Report on Chinese students' overseas study (Chinese Edition).* Vision Overseas. 新东方前途出国图书编委会. 2020中国留学白皮书（中文版）.

Nyland, C., Forbes-Mewett, H., & Charmine E. J. H. (2013). Governing the international student experience: Lessons from the Australian international education model. *Academy of Management Learning & Education, 12*(4), 656–673. https://doi.org/10.5465/amle.2012.0088

Obst, D., & Forster, J. (2007). *Perceptions of European higher education in third countries: Country report: USA.* Institute of International Education.

OECD. Stat. (2021). *International student mobility: Share of national students going abroad.* https://stats.oecd.org/index.aspx?queryid=85226

Olson, J., Biseth, H., & Ruiz, G. (2015). *Educational internationalisation: Academic voices and public policy.* Sense Publishers.

Pitts, M. J., & Brooks, C. F. (2017). Critical pedagogy, internationalisation, and a third space: Cultural tensions revealed in students' discourse. *Journal of Multilingual and Multicultural Development, 38*(3), 251–267. https://doi.org/10.1080/01434632.2015.1134553

Punteney, K. (2012). International careers: The gap between student interest and knowledge. *Journal of Studies in International Education, 16*, 390–407. https://doi.org/10.1177/1028315311430354

Qin, L. (2013). Issues and solutions of international understanding education in china. *International Education Studies, 6*(11), 100. https://doi.org/10.5539/ies.v6n11p100

Quacquarelli Symonds. (2021). Studying abroad again: How do current and prospective international students feel about the return of studying overseas? *2021 International Student Survey.* London. UK.

Ruble, R. A., & Zhang, Y. B. (2013). Stereotypes of Chinese international students held by Americans. *International Journal of Intercultural Relations, 37*(2), 202–211. https://doi.org/10.1016/j.ijintrel.2012.12.004

Ryan, J. (Ed.). (2011). *China's higher education reform and internationalization.* Routledge.

Stein, S. (2018). National exceptionalism in the 'EduCanada' brand: Unpacking the ethics of internationalization marketing in Canada. *Discourse (Abingdon, England), 39*(3), 461–477. https://doi.org/10.1080/01596306.2016.1276884

Teichler, U. (2010). Internationalising higher education: Debates and changes in Europe. In D. Mattheou (Ed.), *Changing educational landscapes: Educational policies, schooling systems and higher education - A comparative perspective* (pp. 263–83). Springer.

Teichler, U. (2014). Opportunities and problems of comparative higher education research: The daily life of research. *Higher Education, 67*(4), 393–408. http://doi.org/10.1007/s10734-013-9682-0

Teichler, U. (2015). Academic mobility and migration: What we know and what we do not know. *European Review, 23*(1), 6–37. https://doi.org/10.1017/S1062798714000787

Tian, M., & Lowe, J. (2009). Existentialist internationalisation and the Chinese student experience in English universities. Compare: A Journal of *Comparative and International Education, 39*(5), 659–676. https://doi.org/10.1080/03057920903125693

Tran, L. T., & Vu, T. T. P. (2018). Beyond the 'normal' to the 'new possibles': Australian students' experiences in Asia and their roles in making connections with the region via the new Colombo plan. *Higher Education Quarterly, 72*(3), 194–207. https://doi.org/10.1111/hequ.12166

Trilokekar, R. D., & Rasmi, S. (2011). Student perceptions of international education and study abroad: A pilot study at York University, Canada. *Intercultural Education (London, England), 22*(6), 495–511. https://doi.org/10.1080/14675986.2011.644951

United Nations Educational Scientific and Cultural Organization. (1948). *Art. 26 of the Universal Declaration of Human Rights.* https://www.un.org/en/universal-declaration-human-rights/

United Nations Educational Scientific and Cultural Organization. (2015). *Global citizenship education: Topics and learning objectives.* http://unesdoc.unesco.org/images/0023/002329/232993e.pdf

Urban, E. L., & Bierlein Palmer. L. (2014). International students as a resource for internationalization of higher education. *Journal of Studies in International Education, 18*(4), 305–324. https://doi.org/10.1177/1028315313511642

Van der Wende, M. C. (2001). Internationalisation policies: About new trends and contrasting paradigms. *Higher Education Policy, 14,* 249–259. https://doi.org/10.1016/S0952-8733(01)00018-6

Van der Wende, M. C. (2017). *Opening up: Higher education systems in global perspectives* (Working Paper No. 22). UCL Centre for Global Higher Education.

Vygotsky, L. (1978). Mind in society: The development of higher psychological processes. In M. Cole, V. John-Steiner, S. Scribner, & E. Souberman. (Eds.), *Mind in society: The development of higher psychological processes* (pp. 19–105). Harvard University Press.

Wadhwa, R. (2016). New phase of internationalization of higher education and institutional change. *Higher Education for the Future, 3*(2), 227–246. https://doi.org/10.1177/2347631116650548

Wang, X. (2020). Capital, habitus, and education in contemporary China: Understanding motivations of middle-class families in pursuing studying abroad in the United States. *Educational Philosophy and Theory, 52*(12), 1314–1328. https://doi.org/10.1080/00131857.2020.1767074

Weenink, D. (2008). Cosmopolitanism as a form of capital: Parents preparing their children for a globalizing world. *Sociology-The Journal of the British Socio-logical Association, 42*, 1089–1106. https://doi.org/10.1177/0038038508096935

Wiers-Jenssen, J. (2003). Norwegian students abroad. Experiences of students from a linguistically and geographically peripheral European country. *Studies in Higher Education, 28*(4), 391–411. https://doi.org/10.1080/0307507032000122251

Yemini, M., Holzmann, V., Fadilla, D., Natur, N., & Stavans, A. (2014). Israeli college students' perceptions of internationalisation. *International Studies in Sociology of Education, 24*(3), 304–323. https://doi.org/10.1080/09620214.2014.950493

Yusoff, Y. M. (2012). Self-efficacy, perceived social support, and psychological adjustment in international undergraduate students in a public higher education institution in Malaysia. *Journal of Studies in International Education, 16*, 353–371.

Zha, Q. (2003). Internationalization of higher education: Towards a conceptual framework. *Policy Futures in Education, 1*(2), 248–270. https://doi.org/10.2304/pfie.2003.1.2.5

Zhu, Y., & Bresnahan, M. (2018). "They make no contribution!" versus "we should make friends with them!"--American domestic students' perception of Chinese international students' reticence and face. *Journal of International Students, 8*(4), 1614–1635. https://doi.org/10.5281/zenodo.1467817

ZHENG REN currently is a doctoral student at the Institute of Higher Education, Beihang University. She majors in higher education, internationalization of higher education, doctoral education. Email: lzrqg98@163.com

Dr. FEI WANG is an associate professor at the Faculty of Education in the University of British Columbia. His research interests include educational leadership and administration, social justice and diversity, educational organization and policy studies, and international and comparative education. Email: fei.wang@ubc.ca

Research Article

© *Journal of International Students*
Volume 12, Issue 3 (2022), pp. 756-776
ISSN: 2162-3104 (Print), 2166-3750 (Online)
doi: 10.32674/jis.v12i3.3996
ojed.org/jis

学霸Academic Hero: An Investigation of an Informal Bilingual Volunteer Peer Teaching Model in Supporting Chinese International Students' Learning

Jinqi Xu[1, 2]
*Office of Deputy Vice Chancellor - Education,
Enterprise & Engagement, The University of Sydney, Australia*

Lynne Keevers
*Faculty of the Arts, Social Sciences and
Humanities, University of Wollongong, Australia*

ABSTRACT

The growth in the number of Chinese students in Western universities has prompted academics to explore different pedagogical practices that are suitable for diverse classrooms. Some persisting contradictions between Western and Eastern conceptions of education exist in the practices and institutional structures that students encounter daily. Designing appropriate curricular and learning activities is crucial to the embedding of Chinese international students' learning experience in the West. Adopting a practice-based approach, this ethnographic study investigates how an informal bilingual volunteer peer teaching model, entailing a mix of pedagogical practices, contributed toward improving Chinese international students' learning experience in a Western context. This paper advocates a movement beyond the boundaries and the limits of the fixed pedagogies and turns toward diverse pedagogical practices in teaching Chinese students. This paper also provides new insights about the curricular design for

---

[1] We have no conflicts of interest to disclose.
[2] Correspondence regarding this article should be addressed to jinqi.xu@sydney.edu.au.

academic and institutional practices in order to further develop Chinese students' positive learning experiences in the West.

Keywords: bilingual teaching, Chinese students, diversity, higher education, international students, peer teaching, practice-based

The increasing numbers of Chinese international students enrolled in Western higher education institutions are creating opportunities and challenges for both academics and students because of the diversity in tertiary classrooms (Heng, 2021; Kimmel & Volet, 2010; Leask, 2009; Wu, 2015). Some Chinese international students experience academic stress (Heng, 2019; Yan & Berliner, 2010) and struggle to adjust to the Western learning environment and to make a successful transition from the Chinese education system and pedagogical practices to Western tertiary classrooms (Jiang & Smith, 2009). Western teachers may encounter difficulties when addressing Chinese international students' learning needs and concerns (Cruickshank et al., 2012; Summers & Volet, 2008). Some Western teachers may have limited exposure and understanding of the nuances of Chinese learning practices, which can result in these students being categorized as rote learners (Watkins & Biggs, 1996), passive learners (Jiang & Smith, 2009), with "lacks" or "deficits" (Clark & Gieve, 2006) and as a "problematic" group (Tan, 2011). Nevertheless, over the past decade, a large and diverse number of studies have been conducted to enhance the learning experience for Chinese international students. For example, studies have been conducted in the areas of learning strategies and pedagogy (Chen & Bennett, 2012), intercultural pedagogies (Wu, 2015), constructive alignment (Biggs & Tang, 2011), intercultural competency (Leask, 2009), academic performance (Crawford & Wang, 2015), curriculum internationalization (Cheng et al., 2018; Leask, 2012), learning behaviors (Kang & Chang, 2016), learning experience (Heng, 2019; Su & Harrison, 2016), anxiety and social communication barriers (Andrade, 2006; Marginson et al., 2011), difficulties in developing friendships with domestic students, and a lack of sense of belonging (Campbell & Li, 2008; Cruickshank et al., 2012; Volet & Ang, 2012). However, limited studies have been conducted with a practice-based approach to examine what practices and institutional arrangements can support their learning. Accordingly, this paper investigates how an informal bilingual volunteer peer teaching model, entailing a mix of pedagogical practices, supports Chinese international students' learning experience in the Western context.

PEDAGOGICAL CHALLENGES IN TEACHING CHINESE INTERNATIONAL STUDENTS IN WESTERN CLASSROOMS

Education systems in Australia and China are characterized by different social and cultural contexts, and each system is defined by its own contradictions and tensions in teaching and learning (O'Connor, 2020; Ryan, 2010a). The implications of pedagogical and curricular differences in both systems demand further investigation to elucidate this complex situation in Australian tertiary education (Chen, 2014; Floyd, 2011). It can be challenging dealing with the diverse learning needs in classrooms and promoting student engagement and advancement of skills and knowledge (Hornsby & Osman, 2014; Summers & Volet, 2008).

The Chinese education system entails a complex mixture of ideological, political, and economic factors, educational policies, and Confucian philosophical, social, and family influences (Heng, 2018; Yu, 2009). The Confucian tradition has been embedded in the Chinese culture for around 2,500 years and influences most aspects of Chinese culture, including the education system (Jin & Cortazzi, 2006; Watkins & Biggs, 1996). Traditional Chinese education is described as "teacher-centered," "classroom-centered," and "textbook-centered" (Hua et al., 2011) and the acquisition and transmission models are often adopted in teaching. Globalization, as well as the sheer size of the Chinese population and the education system drive the need for standardization and efficiency in pedagogy.

In contrast, Western culture often promotes collaborative-based constructivism and fosters critical thinking skills in educational approaches and teaching practices (Chiu, 2009; Kang & Chang, 2016). Asking questions and challenging teachers and peers are seen as signs of deep learning, which leads to group construction of knowledge (Liu et al., 2010; Thompson & Ku, 2005). However, teaching practices are not homogenous and educational concepts sometimes contradict each other (Cousin, 2011; Floyd, 2011; Hager & Hodkinson, 2011); for example, a significant increasing reliance on prerecorded online lectures coexisting with an emphasis on engaged participative learning environments. In western classrooms, transmission-based, participative, and constructivist models of learning coexist (Biggs & Tang, 2011; Porcaro, 2011; Prosser & Trigwell, 2014); tensions and contradictions exist between the process of massification and its effects, and the pedagogical requirements for quality control (O'Connor, 2020; Ryan, 2010b). For example, achieving learning outcomes in large classes, which is a feature of higher education, is challenging for academics and institutions (Hornsby & Osman, 2014).

Despite broad endorsement of constructivism within the higher education literature, there is little agreement about what constructivism is and should do within this context (Kirschner et al., 2006; O'Connor, 2020; Van Bergen & Parsell, 2019). Some argue that the Western constructivism approach assumes a prescriptive, outcome-orientated approach (as seen in Biggs and Tang's work 2011). Such an approach positions core curriculum knowledge as settled and unproblematic (O'Connor, 2020) and neglects the epistemic questions in knowledge (Goodson, 2008). Unsurprisingly, teaching Chinese international students in a diverse Western tertiary classroom can be difficult. Some academics struggle to help their Chinese international students and, therefore, tend to oversimplify these students' approaches to learning due to the lack of a deep understanding of their practices and constructivist learning practices (Kirschner et al., 2006).

Peer Teaching

Peer teaching has spread, is accepted in higher education, and has become embedded in certain education communities (Rees et al., 2016). Peer teaching is reported positively in the literature, with advocates suggesting that it enhances learning (Kassab et al., 2005), relieves exam-related stress (Kommalage & Thabrew, 2011), and serves as a helpful adjunct to the curriculum teaching (Naeger et al., 2013). Similarly, research shows that, in a peer-teaching relationship, the peer teachers fulfills roles such as that of an information giver and a facilitator as well as provides a role model for their peer learners (Bulte et al., 2007; Ma et al., 2010). Peer teaching offers opportunities for new knowledge and skills to be learned by students and enriches cognitive and social congruence (Lockspeiser et al., 2008). Cognitive congruence is achieved because of the similarity of tutor and student not only in social standing, where peer teachers seem to express a better understanding of students' needs and concerns, but also in intellect and thought processing, where a similar educational level leads to greater cognitive congruence compared with faculty-led teaching (Lockspeiser et al., 2008; Schmidt & Moust, 1995). As such, peer teachers may express complex topics in ways that increase learners' receptiveness and understanding (Lockspeiser et al., 2008; Rees et al., 2016).

Sense of Belonging

We need to belong to learn, and this belonging is an intrinsic condition for the creation and sharing of knowledge (Lave, 2019). Accordingly, developing peer relationships and friendships is essential to support international students' learning (Guan et al., 2008; Montgomery & McDowell, 2009; Sawir et al., 2008) and student success and retention (O'Keeffe, 2013). International students may feel anonymous in an unfamiliar crowd and experience the context as a lack of social belongingness (Arkoudis et al., 2019), and isolation or distancing (Gomes & Tran, 2017; Hockings, 2011; Mann, 2001). Consequently, international students may feel reluctant to participate in classroom activities such as discussions when they do not experience the classroom as inclusive (Tatar, 2005). Students' relationships with teachers and peers and their overall feelings of belongingness may support their positive learning experiences (Arkoudis et al., 2019), and such relationships significantly impact their educational persistence (Cooper, 2009). A sense of belonging through social networks enables students to feel empowered to contribute to learning conversations (Thomas, 2002; Zepke, 2013) and generates connections that create propensity for learning (Keevers & Abuodha, 2012).

There is no simple answer to the complexities in teaching Chinese students in a Western university classroom. Thus, exploring different teaching practices, pedagogy and moving beyond a fixed view of pedagogical concepts and practices becomes meaningful for higher education (Löytönen, 2017). This view invites us to engage with the complexity and open the possibilities in understanding pedagogies through multiplicities, such as connections, experiences, and contextual factors instead of compartmentalization (Löytönen, 2017). The informal bilingual peer teaching model, that is the focus of this paper, is a response to this call as it connects the differences between pedagogies, sociocultural background, parental influence, and Confucian educational beliefs to the context of Chinese international students studying in a Western learning environment. This study, underpinned by practice theory, aims at exploring how this teaching model enhances Chinese international students' learning experiences in Western classrooms.

PRACTICE-BASED APPROACH

Practice-based theories are prominent in educational literature, including in the area of learning in professional practice (Green & Hopwood, 2019; Hager & Beckett, 2019; Kemmis et al., 2012) and higher education (Keevers et al., 2014; Sykes et al., 2014). A practice-based approach focuses on a relational perspective (Barad, 2007; Haraway, 2008), emphasizing the relationships among people, and the material world that is continuously changing (Hager et al., 2012). Such an approach highlights the connectiveness and entanglement of one's past, present, and future, "everything that is has no existence apart from its relation to other things" (Langley & Tsoukas, 2010, p. 3). Practice-based studies comprise a diverse body of work that has developed explanations of social, cultural, and material phenomena based on the notion of practices (Barad, 2007; Schatzki, 2019). Schatzki (2019) describes practices as the complex interactions of a temporarily evolving, open-ended set of sayings, doings, and relating between people, other beings, and material artifacts. These practices are linked through a "teleoaffective structure," that is, "range of normativized and hierarchically ordered ends, projects and tasks, to varying degrees allied with normativized emotions and even moods" (Schatzki, 2002, p. 80). This normative conception of practice emphasizes that practices are constituted by the mutual accountability of their performances to what is at issue and at stake in a practice (Rouse, 2007). Therefore, practice-based approaches view learning as socially, collectively, and normatively constituted rather than individually constituted (Ray et al., 2020). This approach offers a good fit to study Chinese students' learning in an informal bilingual peer teaching program at an Australian university, as it stresses the importance of context and culture.

STUDY SITE AND METHODS

The Chinese Commerce Academic Development (CCAD) is an informal, voluntarily organized, bilingual, peer teaching program for Chinese international students that is mainly used for accounting and finance subjects in the Business Faculty, at a regional university in NSW. All the CCAD leaders are high-achieving students in the Faculty of Business, and they include Higher Degree Research (HDR) students, Dean's scholars, and casual academic tutors. Their practices were recognized by the faculty through the formation of CCAD; however, they are still largely based on voluntary work. The CCAD classes are bilingual and are conducted in English and Mandarin, with Mandarin being the principal language used.

This practice-based study employed ethnographic methods and was conducted for 18 months, over three consecutive semesters between 2013 and 2014. The researcher shadowed five participant students weekly; observed and interviewed three CCAD leaders and seven faculty members. Ethics approval (HE14/079) was granted prior to the data collection. The five participating students in CCAD programs were aged between 20 and 23 years of age, and they held student visas. None had experience studying outside of China prior to their enrollment in the commerce undergraduate degree. The data collection included formal semi-structured and informal interviews with the students and their CCAD leaders and faculty members. The research project also entailed observations of the students in lectures, tutorials, Peer Assisted Study Sessions (PASS), CCAD workshops, and library studies. The researcher took fieldnotes during the observation and interviews and wrote reflective notes after collecting the data (Schwartz-Shea, 2006). The process enabled the researcher to "zoom in" on the entwined practices and generate the sensitizing research questions to identify the practices that students employed in their learning journey (Nicolini, 2013).

The data were collected in Mandarin to enable the students to think deeply and discuss freely (Wu, 2015) in constructing their social worlds (Silverman, 2011). The interviews were audio-recorded and transcribed. The data were coded and reported in this paper with the participant students, CCAD leaders, and faculty member's pseudonym. Samples of translation and the observation notes were shared and checked by the participant students to ensure the accuracy of the data.

The data analysis required studying the practices at hand, engaging with the "messiness" of the data, tracing connections, and reinterpreting the findings in the light of the insights provided from different angles or positions of the data (Nicolini, 2009). The data were analyzed in a multilayered process involving various stages: transcribing, translating, exacting and categorizing key points, generating provisional themes, mapping clusters of practices, and selecting data evidence. The categorization and generation of themes were discussed with and confirmed by both Ph.D. supervisors. All the data were processed from an initial Word document to a spreadsheet, and they were then colored and organized with separate Excel workbooks. Through this process, extraction, and analysis of the related CCAD, data were consolidated and categorized; interconnections and inconsistences in students' learning experiences and practices were then revealed.

RESULTS

The following section presents six results of this study, including the hybrid–bilingual pedagogical approach; Jason Xueba (学霸)–Jason; Confucius' dialogic practices in asking questions; prompting higher level of cognitive skills; linking and summarizing; and meeting social needs and concerns and teaching academics' concerns.

Hybrid–Bilingual Pedagogical Approach

The description of the arrangement in two CCAD classes illustrates how distinctive its pedagogical approach was in the context of the business faculty. The overcrowded CCAD classroom and the pedagogical practices are unlike anything the researcher had previously experienced at the Business faculty in this university:

> It is a normal tutorial classroom, full of students (about 80 students in a standard tutorial room of 40) and students have moved extra desks and chairs from other classrooms. The desks are allocated next to each other, and there is no gap in between, with one little aisle left to one side. Everyone is very keen to learn, and the atmosphere is intense. The leader uses Chinese slang and some key English concepts words and drew diagrams on the whiteboard in both Chinese and English. The examples used are in the Chinese context ... students are chatting and giggling because of the humorous approach. (Fieldnotes, 0906: 30)

The CCAD setting offers students an opportunity to "hang together" to learn in the rare tutorial arrangements. A second observation with a smaller group has a different arrangement but some similarities:

> It is a standard lecture/tutorial room, and students sit in a circular classroom, and the leader, Jason, uses predesigned slides. The way he conducted the class is not like a peer-learning format, as it is more like a lecture. Students take notes or take photos of the slides. He asks questions to encourage students to participate. Students were involved intensively. They are busy, taking notes, looking at Jason, or talking with friends about what they are doing. They are active participants, which is in contrast to what I observed in normal lectures and tutorials, they were not so active and did not show much interest in the teaching most of time. The atmosphere is also light, as from time to time, his humour triggers some laughter. (Fieldnotes 1505: 5)

It is observed that the atmosphere of the CCAD workshop is different from that of the normal lecture/tutorial in the university. The CCAD leaders adopt a hybrid pedagogical approach by combining constructivism and transmission models in the teaching, by presenting the lecture slides, and by encouraging students to join the discussion. The students participate in the discussion and respond to the teacher's questions actively. The communication between the teachers and students is informative and effective because students engage with the teaching materials and teachers in the situated space of the CCAD classes.

Another key aspect of CCAD is that it is conducted mainly in Mandarin and partially in English. Students report that the bilingual pedagogical technique helps them overcome language and cultural barriers and understand the subject content in Chinese and English. Lin says:

> The key is that the classes are conducted in Chinese and therefore there is no language barrier. The students can think in the "Chinese way." The CCAD leaders explain the key concepts in plain Chinese. (Lin, 1406: 3)

In the observation of a CCAD workshop, I note,

> It is so interesting to see that Jason uses a Chinese business case study to explain an accounting concept. The case studies link to the students' background knowledge and the example given makes sense to students and is much easier to understand as students are familiar with the context. In this class, they responded to questions asked and joined the discussion actively. (Fieldnotes, 1505: 10)

Through CCAD's practice, a shared schema is achieved between teacher and learners. Similarly, Su mentions that " … Sunny uses Chinese in teaching and some Chinese examples when she explains the difficult concepts. It is very helpful for me" (Su, 2008: 11).

Jason Xueba (学霸)–Jason

The observations and interviews show that the sessions conducted by the CCAD leaders involved much more than peer teaching, learning, and tutoring. The seemingly contradictory combination of different approaches includes the way that they put together disparate sociocultural pedagogical and institutional practices, roles, and personal characteristics. For example, the leader Jason, similar to other leaders in CCAD, has a number of roles, including Dean's Scholar, Ph.D. student, and tutor. His Chinese background, sense of humor, age (he is older than the students), use of Chinese slang and case studies examples from Chinese context to make them easier to understand. He also has studying experience in Australia and he is familiar with institutional practices and Australian culture. His classroom' practices such as drawing diagrams in Chinese and English, use of illustrations from Chinese contexts, fluency in accountancy and finance practices and theories and in English and Chinese pedagogy all play a role in his ability as a leader. His strong, embedded social and cultural understanding is evident in his sense of humor and the way that he interacts with students. For example, Jason alludes to filial practices by teasing the students, ironically suggesting that they spend their time watching movies rather than studying and that if their parents knew they would be in trouble. Although Jason is not a lecturer, he is highly respected by students, who called him Xueba (学霸), or in English "academic hero."

Confucius' Dialogic Practices in Asking Questions

CCAD leaders' understanding of Chinese Confucius and Australian pedagogies is illustrated in the way they ask questions. As the participants report, their approaches are different from the way their lecturers and tutors usually ask questions because CCAD leaders not only focus on explaining concepts but also focus on triggering them to think about the reasons why the lecturers choose to use the specific concepts. It also appears to be dialogic in the Confucian sense of trying to engage students more deeply. Chinese students are familiarized with such an approach in the past; therefore, they can establish the connections between the past and the present when learning new concepts (Langley & Tsoukas, 2010). This approach encourages students to inquire about the meaning in the context of relationships by asking specific types of questions. Ting says:

> [CCAD] helps me to know the internal relationship [between the concepts] to cope with the change in the exam questions … CCAD helps to set up the relationship between concepts, even if the exam questions are changed, I still know how to relate the concepts and know how to do it … the teacher often asks, *do you know why? Do you know why the teacher talked about this concept? I will show you something to make it clear*. Then he shows the relationships in between, step-by-step, until we understand. (Ting, 2808: 5)

The leaders purposely ask questions and help the students link the concepts together by showing the connection between different concepts and how they are used in different accounting subjects. Ting's view is in line with the researcher's observations that "Lucas (CCAD leader) uses a process map on the white board to show the connection between different terms in both languages to help students recognize the relations between the key academic concepts" (Fieldnotes 1505: 16), it appears that the established connections help students to see the big picture and to identify topics that might appear in exams.

Prompting Higher Level of Cognitive Skills: Linking and Summarizing

From an academic practice perspective, bundles of practices utilized by CCAD facilitate students' learning, prompting them to identify the key difficult concepts and demonstrating how to set up links between concepts. As such, students focus on comprehending the concepts and theories; consequently, this improves their higher level of cognitive skills. Su works out which classes to attend and which teachers can assist her to learn effectively. She describes:

> Before I went to Sunny's class [CCAD workshop], I felt like I was in the clouds, and all seemed puzzling. After the workshop, I feel that there is a clear path in front of me. (Su, 2008, p. 7)

Clearly, the class helps her clarify the confusion in her mind. In Su's view, Sunny helps her to eliminate unimportant things, so she can focus on relationships between concepts and answer exam questions effectively:

> Sunny uses the diagrams to show their relationship and how they affect each other, and then explains and links the concepts together to make the relationship clear. He is very good at linking the concepts … there

are many concepts, which I have not thought through, but after he discussed them, they become clear to me. (Su, 2008, p. 8)

In one of the interviews, Su says she was sent by her father to study in Australia and her focus is always on how to pass exams, so she can obtain the graduation certificate. She reflects that the CCAD approach not only helps her to understand the difficult concepts but also provides strategies to prepare for exams. Lin compares the different approaches between CCAD and PASS. He also articulates that the CCAD leader, Joe's approach identifies the key confusing concepts that help him prepare for exams. Lin says,

> I attend the CCAD workshop. Joe summarises and connects the links from two topics.... Which is different from the PASS leader's approach. The approach is similar to a normal lecture. ... is more useful as it helps to discover which some concepts I still do not understand. (Lin, 0416: 2)

Meeting Social Needs and Concerns

Students participate in CCAD workshops for academic and social needs. In the group, all the students face similar issues in adapting to the foreign learning environment. For example, Lin is disappointed that he has few friends and that the different institutional practices and arrangements at the university make it difficult for him to develop friendships with other students.

> I have to find new friends each session, as I have never met most of students in my class before. To connect with other Chinese students and communities is an easy option to meet people and make friends. (Lin, 1909: 5)

Lin's experience shows that institutional practices can produce a different learning environment and experiences for students.

> I do not feel a strong sense of belonging to the new learning environment as no one knows me or cares about me much as they did before in China. I do not feel embarrassed if I make mistakes in answering the questions or if I cannot answer the teacher's questions in the class ... they are just strangers around me. (Lin, 1909: 5)

Lin manages to connect with other Chinese students by becoming active in Chinese student groups:

> I ask questions to other Chinese students; we share study materials. I join some Chinese student groups, such as CCAD, and this Chinese students' learning research. (Lin, 1408:3)

Lin joins the Chinese student groups, has more connection with peers, and feels like he belongs. Students become emotionally connected with peers through familiar sociocultural practices on a daily basis (Rouse 2007). Similarly, Chuchu has a clear motivation similar to Lin, lives in the university's accommodation, joins the international students' clubs, and participates in activities to create her social networks. The social networks open new opportunities for students' learning because though the networks students can share their study experience.

Teaching Academics' Concerns

The hybrid pedagogy used in CCAD helps students deal with the challenges associated with learning about complex English concepts by combining academic and sociocultural practices in the teaching. Although both the faculty executive and teaching academics acknowledge CCAD's contribution to learning and teaching, they also express potential concerns. Some academics express concerns, as Terisa explains,

> The main concern is that Chinese students use CCAD as an alternative to formal teaching hours (lecture and tutorial). Consequently, it reflects in the low attendance and student engagement rates in formal teaching hours. (Terisa, 1305:5)

She continues,

> The focus on students' exam performance enables students to practise short-cuts that may be unhelpful in their long-term development of important study practices that also may support student learning. The implicit contradiction is also evident in that student learning may be traded off for exam performance. (Terisa, 1305: 6)

Some academics also expresses concern that it is unfair that other international students do not have similar opportunities. Even though the concerns are understandable, potentially the lecturers and tutors could learn from the practices of CCAD to enhance engagement in the formal lectures and tutorials.

DISCUSSION

This study investigates how an informal voluntary peer-led model offers an alternative bilingual and culturally sensitive hybrid pedagogy entailing educational, sociocultural, and institutional practices to assist Chinese students face the challenges in learning in Western tertiary classrooms. Students' learning is intertwined with practices of their peers, the CCAD leaders, faculty members, and institutional structures (Schatzki, 2019). Although this study was conducted in one regional university in Australia, the findings of this research reveal a number of wider benefits and implications as follows.

First, the bilingual peer teaching method enabled students to express themselves freely in group discussions using their mother language (Cui et al., 2015). This bilingual approach helps to interpret subject materials for Chinese students in their first language, and this is perceived to offer great comfort to students who feel unsure and/or anxious about subject materials, assessment tasks, and exams. The CCAD leaders skillfully apply Chinese examples and strategically use Mandarin in teaching and communicating the complex concepts and meanings in core subjects to ensure students' understanding (Littlewood & Yu, 2011). Such an approach addresses the challenges that Chinese international students face in learning, which are caused by a lack of English academic literary and specialized disciplinary knowledge. Further, this approach also tackles the issues that Chinese students have due to the norms and conventions that are embedded in Western cultural values and beliefs (Wang, 2012), such as how to ask questions and join discussions. These difficulties cause stress and anxiety for students and contribute to them avoiding joining discussions with local students, asking questions, and engaging with their teachers in classes (Yan & Berliner, 2010).

Second, CCAD provides alternative pedagogical practices in teaching Chinese international students, which help them to navigate courses and overcome the barriers and differences between two educational systems. CCAD acts as a bridge that enables students to have a transitional pathway into the Western learning environment. The CCAD leaders capably employ the hybrid approach that not only includes Confucius pedagogy, but also includes the fundamental elements of acquisition, transmission, and constructivist approaches. The Confucius pedagogy inspires students with dialectic questions that help them understand the concepts and disciplinary knowledge. The acquisition and transmission approach can be seen in how the students are explicitly taught how to answer exam questions. The constructivist approach is evident in the ways that the leaders ask the students questions that push them to relate the concepts to everyday accounting and finance practices by using Chinese examples.

Third, the CCAD leaders and Chinese international students co-construct this model, which builds strong connections and establishes trust-based relationships between the leaders and the students in the situated learning environment (Yakhlef, 2010). Students' learning is intertwined with the practices of their peers and CCAD leaders, and it also indirectly connects to Chinese culture, community, and the education system. Students' educational and sociocultural practices become entangled with their peers and teachers in this environment and are socially and collectively construct and co-construct in their learning (Xu, 2019). The CCAD environment not only enables students to have the opportunity to connect with other students and support each other through familiar sociocultural practices (Montgomery & McDowell, 2009), but also softens culture shock and smooth intercultural adjustments (Lin, 2006). Such a space assists students in creating a sense of belonging through their daily practices and establishes constructive social relationships with peers from similar backgrounds (Keevers & Abuodha, 2012). Having close relationships with their peers assists students in navigating the transition to a Western learning environment. Students' learning is inseparable from interactions and relationships in every aspect of student life (Reich & Hager, 2014; Langley & Tsoukas, 2010). There is no clear line between Chinese students' study practices and social practices in this learning process.

Fourth, it is evident that tensions exist within and between the practices and institutional structures that students encounter as part of their journey in the university. The faculty may need to consider legitimating the CCAD model by endorsing it officially and including it in the formal curriculum. It helps the institution not only with the ongoing challenges they face with large and diverse classrooms and reduces the pressure arising from the limited resource and increased international student populations (Marginson, 2014; Stigmar, 2016). Such an approach further facilitates collaboration and builds a two-way learning role in which faculty members may have opportunities to learn from CCAD leaders to enhance their cultural humility and cross-cultural capabilities (Foronda et al., 2016; Tinkler & Tinkler, 2016). The process enables the faculty members to examine their own identity and biases and assists them to recognize the hidden curriculum (Lee & Lund, 2016), and it acknowledges individual limitations in knowledge and skills, thereby establishing a growth mindset of lifelong (Tinkler & Tinkler 2016). This process also calls forth teacher's practicing self-awareness and self-reflection when interacting with others to ensure them to be attentive to culture, power, and privilege (Foronda et al., 2016).

Significance of This Study and Conclusion

The findings of this study illustrate how the CCAD leaders have developed a method in assisting Chinese international students to bridge gaps between transmission, acquisition, and constructivism, and they support student engagement in learning. The pedagogical practices adopted by leaders help to address issues of high failure rates among Chinese students in core subjects. This informal, primarily voluntary peer teaching model is a practical example of designing curriculum and pedagogical methods of peer learning programs to improve international students' experience in a Western University (Leask, 2009). The strategy of developing bilingual lectures and academic support programs in core subjects and conducting Western pedagogical practices workshops could potentially make the first-year transition less complicated for Chinese international students (Kift et al., 2010). Institutional practices could legitimize, support, and develop peer teaching/learning programs to facilitate students learning at the start of their courses, thereby enhancing students' learning experiences and success at university. This study suggests that universities need to pay more attention in supporting the students' collaboration and developing a sense of belonging and community. A further qualitative longitudinal study to follow up students' learning across their entire degree would provide insight into how their study practices have changed over time with the CCAD support they received.

ACKNOWLEDGMENTS

This paper is based on my Ph.D. thesis. I would like to express my deepest thanks to my Ph.D. supervisor: Dr Christopher Sykes for his support and encouragement in the Ph.D. journey. I would also like to express my special thanks to Professor Lorraine Smith for her critical comments on this paper.

REFERENCES

Andrade, M. S. (2006). International students in English speaking universities: Adjustment factors. *Journal of Research in International Education, 5*(2), 131–154. https://doi.org/10.1177/1475240906065589.

Arkoudis, S., Dollinger, M., Baik, C., & Patience, A. (2019). International students' experience in Australian higher education: Can we do better? *Higher Education, 77,* 799–813. https://doi.org/10.1007%2Fs10734-018-0302-x

Barad, K. (2007). *Meeting the universe halfway: Quantum physics and the entanglement of matter and meaning.* Duke University Press.

Biggs, J., & Tang, C. (2011). *Teaching for quality learning at university: What the student does* (4th ed.). Open University Press.

Bulte, C., Betts, A., Garner, K., & Durning, S. (2007). Student teaching: Views of student near-peer teachers and learners. *Medical Teacher, 29*(6), 583–590. https://doi.org/10.1080/01421590701583824

Campbell, J., & Li, M. (2008). Asian students' voices: An empirical study of Asian students' learning at a New Zealand university. *Journal of Studies in International Education, 12*(4), 375–396. https://doi.org/10.1177/1028315307299422

Chen, R. T.-H. (2014). East-Asian teaching practices through the eyes of Western learners. *Teaching in Higher Education, 19*(1), 26–37. https://doi.org/10.1080/13562517.2013.827652

Chen, R. T.-H., & Bennett, S. (2012). When Chinese learners meet constructivist pedagogy online. *Higher Education, 64*(5), 677–691. https://doi.org/10.1007/s10734-012-9520-9

Cheng, M., Adekola, O., Shah, M., & Valyrakis, M. (2018). Exploring Chinese students' experience of curriculum internationalisation: A comparative study of Scotland and Australia. *Studies in Higher Education, 43*(4), 754–768. https://doi.org/10.1080/03075079.2016.1198894

Chiu, J. (2009). Facilitating Asian students' critical thinking in online discussions. *British Journal of Educational Technology, 40*(1), 42–57.

Clark, R., & Gieve, S. N. (2006). On the discursive construction of 'The Chinese Learner'. *Language, Culture and Curriculum, 19*(1), 54–73. https://doi.org/10.1080/07908310608668754

Cooper, R. (2009). Constructing belonging in a diverse campus community. *Journal of College and Character, 10*(3), 1–10. https://doi.org/10.2202/1940-1639.1085

Cousin, G. (2011). Rethinking the concept of 'Western'. *Higher Education Research & Development, 30*(5), 585–594. https://doi.org/ 10.1080/07294360.2011.598449

Crawford, I., & Wang, Z. (2015). The impact of individual factors on the academic attainment of Chinese and UK students in higher education. *Studies in Higher Education, 40*(5), 902–920. https://doi.org/10.1080/03075079.2013.851182

Cruickshank, K., Chen, H., & Warren, S. (2012). Increasing international and domestic student interaction through group work: A case study from the humanities. *Higher Education Research & Development, 31*(6), 797–810. https://doi.org/10.1080/07294360.2012.669748

Cui, J., Huang, T., Cortese, C., & Pepper, M. (2015). Reflections on a bilingual peer assisted learning program. *International Journal of Educational Management, 29*(3), 284–297. https://doi.org/10.1108/IJEM-12-2013-0175

Floyd, C. (2011). Critical thinking in a second language. *Higher Education Research & Development, 30*(3), 289–302. https://doi.org/10.1080/07294360.2010.501076

Foronda, C., Baptiste, D. L., Reinholdt, M. M., & Ousman, K. (2016). Cultural Humility: a concept analysis. *Journal of Transcultural Nursing, 27*(3), 210–217. DOI: 10.1177/1043659615592677

Gomes, C., & Tran, L. T. (2017). International students (dis)connectedness and identitiesIdentity: Why these matter and the way forward. In L. T. Tran & C. Gomes (Eds.), *International student connectedness and identity: Transnational perspectives* (1st ed.). Springer https://doi.org/10.1007/978-981-10-2601-0_16

Goodson, I. (2008). *Schooling, curriculum, narrative and the social future.* Routledge.

Green, B., & Hopwood, N. (2019). *The body in professional practice, learning and education body/practice.* Springer International Publishing.

Guan, J., Tregonning, S., & Keenan, L. (2008). Social interaction and participation: Formative evaluation of online CME modules. *Journal of Continuing Education in the Health Professions, 28*(3), 172–179. https://doi.org/10.1002/chp.174

Hager, P., & Beckett, D. (2019). *The emergence of complexity: Rethinking education as a social science.* Springer.

Hager, P., & Hodkinson, P. (2011). Becoming as an appropriate metaphor for understanding professional learning. In L. Scanlon (Ed.), *"Becoming' a professional - An interdisciplinary analysis of professional learning* (pp. 33–56). Springer.

Hager, P., Lee, A., & Reich, A. (2012). *Practice, learning and change: Practice-theory perspectives on professional learning.* Springer.

Haraway, D. (2008). *When species meet.* University of Minnesota Press.

Heng, T. T. (2018). Different is not deficient: Contradicting stereotypes of Chinese international students in US higher education. *Studies in Higher Education, 43*(1), 22–36. https://doi.org/10.1080/03075079.2016.1152466

Heng, T. T. (2019). Understanding the heterogeneity of international students' experiences: A case study of Chinese international students in U.S. universities. *Journal of Studies in International Education, 23*(5), 607–623. https://doi.org/10.1177/1028315319829880

Heng, T. T. (2021). Socioculturally attuned understanding of and engagement with Chineseinternational undergraduates [Advance online publication]. *Journal of Diversity in Higher Education,* 1–14. https://doi.org/10.1037/dhe0000240.

Hockings, C. (2011). Hearing voices, creating spaces: The craft of the 'Artisan Teacher' in a mass higher education system. *Critical Studies in Education, 52*(2), 191–205. https://doi.org/10.1080/17508487.2011.572831

Hornsby, D., & Osman, R. (2014). Massification in higher education: Large classes and student learning. *Higer Education, 67*, 711–719. https://doi.org/10.1007/S10734-014-9733-1

Hua, Z., Harris, A., & Ollin, R. (2011). Student autonomy and awareness: Vocational education and student - centred learning in China. *Journal of Vocational Education and Training, 63*(2), 191–203. https://doi.org/10.1080/13636820.2011.566346

Jiang, X., & Smith, R. (2009). Chinese learners' strategy use in historical perspective: A cross-generational interview-based study. *System, 37*(2), 286–299. https://doi.org/10.1016/j.system.2008.11.005

Jin, L., & Cortazzi, M. (2006). Changing practices in Chinese cultures of learning. *Language, Culture and Curriculum, 19*(1), 5–20. https://doi.org/10.1080/07908310608668751

Kang, H., & Chang, B. (2016). Examining culture's impact on the learning behaviors of international students from confucius culture studying in western online learning context. *Journal of International Students, 6*(3), 779–797. https://doi.org/10.32674/jis.v6i3.356

Kassab, S., Abu-Hijleh, M., Al-Shboul, Q., & Hamdy, H. (2005). Student-led tutorials in problem-based learning: Educational outcomes and students' perceptions. *Medical Teacher, 25*, 521–526. https://doi.org/10.1080/01421590500156186

Keevers, L., & Abuodha, P. (2012). Social inclusion as an unfinished verb: A practice-based approach. *Journal of Academic Language and Learning, 6*(2), A42–A59.

Keevers, L., Lefoe, G., Leask, B., Fauziah, K. P., Sultan, D., Ganesharatnam, S., Loh, V., & Lim, J. (2014). 'I like the people I work with. Maybe I'll get to meet them in person one day': Teaching and learning practice development with transnational teaching teams. *Journal of Education for Teaching: International Research and Pedagogy, 40*(3), 232–250. https://doi.org/10.1080/02607476.2014.903024

Kemmis, S., Edwards-Groves, C., Willkinson, J., & Hardy, i. (2012). Ecologies of practice. In P. Harger, A. Lee, & A. Reich (Eds.), *In practice, learning and change* (pp. 33–49). Springer.

Kift, Nelson, K., & Clarke, J. (2010). Transition pedagogy: A third generation approach to FYE: A case study of policy and practice for the higher education sector. *The International Journal of the First Year in Higher Education, 1*(1), 102–111. https://doi.org/10.5204/intjfyhe.v1i1.13

Kimmel, K., & Volet, S. (2010). University students' perceptions of and attitudes towards culturally diverseGroup work: Does context matter? *Journal of Studies in International Education, 14*(1), 157–181. https://doi.org/10.1177/1028315310373833

Kirschner, P. A., Sweller, J., & Clark, R. E. (2006). Why minimal guidance during instruction does not work: An analysis of the failure of constructivist, discovery, problem-based, experiential, and inquiry-based teaching. *Educational Psychologist, 41*(2), 75–86. https://doi.org/10.1207/s15326985ep4102_1

Kommalage, & Thabrew, H. (2011). Student-led peer-assisted learning: the Kuppi experience at the medical school of the University of Ruhuna in Sri Lanka. *Education for Health, 24*(2), 516–516.

Langley, A., & Tsoukas, H. (2010). Introducing "perspectives on process organization studies". In T. Hernes & S. Maitlis (Eds.), *Process, sensemaking, and organization* (pp. 1–26). Oxford Univeristy Press.

Lave, J. (2019). *Learning and everyday life: Access, participation and changing practice.* Cambridge University Press.

Leask, B. (2009). Using formal and informal curricula to improve interactions between home and international students. *Journal of Studies in International Education, 13*(2), 205–221. https://doi.org/10.1177/1028315308329786

Leask, B. (2012). Comparing internationalisation of the curriculum in action across disciplines: Theoretical and practical perspectives. *Compare, 43*(1), 79–101. https://doi.org/10.1080/03057925.2013.746566

Lee, L., & Lund, D. (2016). Infusing service-learning with social justice through cultural humility. In A. S. Tinkler, B. Tinkler, V. M. Jagla, & J. R. Strait (Eds.), *Service-learning to advance social justice in a time of radical inequality* (p. 359–382). Information Age Publishing.

Lin, C. (2006). Culture shock and social support: An investigation of a Chinese student organization on a US campus. *Journal of Intercultural Communication Research, 35*(2), 117–137. https://doi.org/10.1080/17475750600909279

Littlewood, W., & Yu, B. (2011). First language and target language in the foreign languageclassroom. *Language Teaching, 44*(1), 64–77. https://doi.org/10.1017/S0261444809990310

Liu, A., Hodgson, G., & Lord, W. (2010). Innovation in construction education: The role of culture in e-learning. *Architectural Engineering and Design Management Learning, 6*, 91–102. https://doi.org/10.3763/aedm.2009.0109

Lockspeiser, T., O'Sullivan, P., Teherani, A., & Muller, J. (2008). Understanding the experience of being taught by peers: The value of social and cognitive congruence. *Advances in Health Sciences Education Theory Practice, 13*(13), 361–372. https://doi.org/10.1007/s10459-006-9049-8

Löytönen, T. (2017). Educational development within higher arts education: An experimental move beyond fixed pedagogies. *International Journal for Academic Development, 22*(3), 231–244. https://doi.org/10.1080/1360144X.2017.1291428

Ma, I. W., Roberts, J. M., Wong, R. Y., & Nair, P. (2010). A procedural teaching tree to aid resident doctor peer-teachers. *Medical Education, 44*(11), 1134–1135. https://doi.org/10.1111/j.1365-2923.2010.03809.x

Mann, S. (2001). Alternative perspectives on the student experience: Alienation and engagement. *Studies in Higher Education, 26*(1), 7–19. https://doi.org/10.1080/03075070020030689

Marginson, S. (2014). Student self-formation in international education. *Journal of Studies in International Education & Training, 18*(1), 6–22. https://doi.org/10.1177/1028315313513036

Marginson, S., Kaur, S., & Sawir, E. (2011). *Higher education in the Asia-Pacific : Strategic responses to globalization.* Springer.

Montgomery, C., & McDowell, L. (2009). Social networks and the international student experience: An international community of practice? *Journal of Studies in International Education, 13*(4), 455–466. https://doi.org/10.1177/1028315308321994

Naeger, D., Conrad, M., Nguyen, J., Kohi, M., & Webb, E. (2013). Students teaching students: Evaluation of a ''near-peer'' teaching experience. *Academic Radiology, 20*(9), 1177–1182. https://doi.org/10.1016/j.acra.2013.04.004

Nicolini, D. (2013). *Practice theory, work & organization.* Oxford University.

O'Connor, K. (2020). Constructivism, curriculum and the knowledge question: Tensions and challenges for higher education. *Studies in Higher Education.* https://doi.org/10.1080/03075079.2020.1750585

O'Keeffe, P. (2013). A sense of belonging: Improving student retention. *College Student Journal, 47*(4), 605–613.

Porcaro. (2011). Applying constructivism in instructivist learning cultures. *Multicultural Education & Technology Journal, 5*(1), 39–54. https://doi.org/10.1108/17504971111121919

Prosser, M., & Trigwell, K. (2014). Qualitative variation in approaches to university teaching and learning in large first-year classes. *Higher Education, 67,* 783–795. https://doi.org/10.1007/s10734-013-9690-0

Ray, N., Keevers, L., & Chen, Y.-Y. (2020). It's the news of difference that makes the difference: Witnessing social action through an international collaboration between Australia and Taiwan. *Advances in Social Work and Welfare Education, 22*(1), 34–37. https://doi.org/10.3316/aeipt.227205

Rees, E., Quinn, P., Davies, B., & Fotheringham, V. (2016). How does peer teaching compare to faculty teaching? A systematic review and meta-analysis. *Medical Teacher, 38*(8), 829–837. https://doi.org/10.3109/0142159X.2015.1112888

Reich, A., & Hager, P. (2014). Problematising practice, learning and change: Practice-theory perspectives on professional learning. *Journal of Workplace Learning, 26*(6/7), 1–15. https://doi.org/10.1108/JWL-02-2014-0016

Rouse, J. (2007). Social practices and normativity. *Philosophy of the Social Sciences, 37*(1), 46–56. https://doi.org/10.1177/0048393106296542

Ryan, J. (2010a). *China's higher education reform and internationalisation.* Routledge.

Ryan, J. (2010b). "The Chinese learner": Misconceptions and realities. In J. Ryan & G. Slethaug (Eds.), *International education and the Chinese learner* (p. 37–56). Hong Kong Univerisity Press.

Sawir, E., Marginson, S., Deumert, A., Nyland, C., & Ramia, G. (2008). Loneliness and international students: An Australian study. *Journal of Studies in International Education, 12*(2), 148–180. https://doi.org/10.1177/ 1028315307299699

Schatzki, T. (2002). *The site of the social - A philosophical account of the constitution of social life and change*. Pennsylvania State University Press.

Schatzki, T. (2019). *Social change in a material world*. Routledge.

Schmidt, H., & Moust, J. (1995). What makes a tutor effective? A structural equations modelling approach to learning in problem-based curricula. *Academic Medicine, 70*, 708–714. https://doi.org/10.1097/00001888-199508000-00015

Schwartz-Shea, P. (2006). *Judgying quality: Evaluative criteria and epistemic communites*. M.E, Sharpe, Inc.

Sierk Ybema, Dvora Yanow, Harry Wels, & Frans Kamsteeg. (2009). Zooming in and Zooming Out: A Package of Method and Theory to Study Work Practices. In *Organizational Ethnography: Studying the Complexities of Everyday Life* (p. 120–138). SAGE Publications Ltd. https://doi.org/10.4135/9781446278925.n7

Silverman, D. (2011). *Interpreting qualitative data: A guide to the principle of qualitative research* (4th ed.). Sage Pulications Ltd.

Stigmar, M. (2016). Peer-to-peer teaching in higher education: A critical literature review. *Mentoring & Tutoring: Partnership in Learning, 24*(2), 124–136. https://doi.org/10.1080/13611267.2016.1178963

Su, M., & Harrison, L. M. (2016). Being wholesaled: An investigation of Chinese international students' higher education experiences. *Journal of International Students, 6*(4), 905–919. https://doi.org/10.32674/jis.v6i4.325

Summers, M., & Volet, S. (2008). Students' attitudes towards culturally mixed groups on international campuses: Impact of participation in diverse and non-diverse groups. *Studies in Higher Education, 33*(4), 357–370. http://dx.doi.org/10.1080/03075070802211430

Sykes, C., Moerman, L., Gibbons, B., & Dean, B. (2014). Re-viewing student teamwork: Preparation for the 'real world' or bundles of situated social practices? *Studies in Continuing Education, 36*(3), 290–303.https://doi.org/10.1080/0158037x.2014.904784

Tan, P. L. (2011). Towards a culturally sensitive and deeper understanding of "rote learning" and memorisation of adult learners. *Journal of Studies in International Education, 15*(2), 124–145. https://doi.org/10.1177/ 1028315309357940.

Tatar, S. (2005). Classroom participation by international students: The case of Turkish graduate students. *Journal of Studies in International Education, 9*(4), 337–355. https://doi.org/10.1177/1028315305280967

Thomas, L. (2002). Student retention in higher eduation: The role of institutional habitus. *Journal of Educational Policy, 17*(40), 423–442. https://doi.org/10.1080/02680930210140257

Thompson, L., & Ku, H. (2005). Chinese graduate students' experiences and attitudes toward online learning. *Educational Media International, 42*(1), 33–47. https://doi.org/10.1080/09523980500116878

Tinkler, A. S., & Tinkler, B. (2016). Enhancing cultural humility through critical service-learning in teacher preparation. *Multicultural Perspectives, 18*(4), 192–201. https://doi.org/10.1080/15210960.2016.1222282

Van Bergen, P., & Parsell, M. (2019). Comparing radical, social and psychological constructivism in Australian higher education: A psycho-philosophical perspective. *The Australian Educational Researcher, 46*, 41–58. https://doi.org/10.1007/s13384-018-0285-8

Volet, S. E., & Ang, G. (2012). Culturally mixed groups on international campuses: An opportunity for inter-cultural learning. *Higher Education Research & Development, 31*(1), 21–37. https://doi.org/10.1080/07294360.2012.642838

Wang, Y. (2012). Mainland Chinese students' group work adaptation in a UK business school. *Teaching in Higher Education, 17*(5), 523–535. https://doi.org/10.1080/13562517.2012.658562

Watkins, D., & Biggs, J. (1996). *The Chinese learners: Cultural, psychological and contextual Influences*. Australian Council for Educational Research.

Wu, Q. (2015). Re-examining the ''Chinese learner'': A case study of mainland Chinese students' learning experiences at British Universities. *Higer Education, 70*, 753–766. https://doi.org/10.1007/s10734-015-9865-y

Xu, J. (2019). A practice-based study of Chinese students' learning – Putting things together. *Journal of University Teaching & Learning Practice, 16*(2). https://doi.org/10.53761/1.16.2.5

Yakhlef, A. (2010). The three facets of knowledge: A critique of the practice-based learning theory. *Research Policy, 39*, 39–46. https://doi.org/10.1016/j.rcspol.2009.11.005

Yan, K., & Berliner, D. C. (2010). Chinese international students in the United States: Demographic trends, motivations, acculturation features and adjustment challenges. *Asia Pacific Education Review, 12*(2), 173–184. https://doi.org/10.1007/s12564-010-9117-x

Yu, J. (2009). The influence and enlightenment of confucian cultural education on modern European civilization. *Frontiers of Education in China, 4*(1), 10–26. https://doi.org/10.1007/s11516-009-0002-5

Zepke, N. (2013). Student engagement: A complex business supporting the first year experience in tertiary education. *The International Journal of the First year in Higher Education, 4*(2), 1–14. https://doi.org/10.5204/intjfyhe.v4i2.183

JINQI XU, Ph.D., is a lecturer in interdisciplinary education, Deputy Vice-Chancellor (Education), Education, Enterprise & Engagement Portfolio, at the University of Sydney, Australia. Her major research interests span Chinese international Students in Higher Education, diversity in education, interdisciplinary education, and Confucius education. She develops these interests through a focus on practice theory and practice-based studies using collaborative methodologies, for example, ethnography, participatory action research and grounded theory. Email: jinqi.xu@sydney.edu.au.

LYNNE KEEVES, Ph.D., is associate professor in Social Work at the University of Wollongong. Social Justice is the connecting thread of Lynne Keever's research. She has a professional and research interest in the practices of social justice in civil society organizations and higher education. She develops this interest through a focus on practice theory and practice-based studies using collaborative methodologies such as participatory action research, collaborative ethnography, and feminist-informed participatory research. Email: lkeevers@uow.edu.au

Research Article

© *Journal of International Students*
Volume 12, Issue 3 (2022), pp. 777-793
ISSN: 2162-3104 (Print), 2166-3750 (Online)
doi: 10.32674/jis.v12i3.3493
ojed.org/jis

Investigating the Benefits and Challenges of Workplace Volunteering Experiences for International Students' Employability Literacies

Georgina Barton
Marie Kavanagh
Marthy Watson
University of Southern Queensland, Australia

Kay Hartwig
Yijun Hu
Griffith University, Australia

ABSTRACT

For many international students the prospect of employment in overseas locations post-study is a strong desire. The concept of employability has infiltrated the literature, but little is known about how volunteering experiences might impact international students' preparedness for work placement during their programs of study. Using theoretical framing related to types of employability literacy, this paper shares data from interviews with international students who volunteered. Findings revealed several themes aligning with linguistic proficiency, cultural awareness, attitudes and mindset, and vocational literacies. Additional themes such as hospitable relationships and building trust were also revealed, which could relate to sustainable citizenship. Many benefits result from volunteering experiences for both international students and their hosts; however, more work is needed to support hosts through cultural awareness programs and international students due to their study commitments and limited time.

Keywords: employability literacies, industry partner hosts, international students, volunteering

INTRODUCTION

International students are a priority to higher education and workplace sectors, as they contribute significantly to cultural diversity in many countries (Spencer-Oatey & Dauber, 2019). International students can provide opportunities to build international networks, contribute to the diverse employability of graduates, and improve intercultural understanding (Trice, 2003). In Australia, for example, international students are reported to be the third-largest export area next to coal and iron ore (Universities Australia, 2019). The Australian Government reported "758,154 full-fee paying international students in 2019, an increase 10% on the previous year" (Australian Government, 2019, p. 1). It is, therefore, essential that international students are supported throughout their study, ensuring success for all stakeholders.

In response to the significance of international students across the globe, many internationalization policies outline several focus areas for universities to best support international students, including intercultural understanding and learning and teaching approaches related to curriculum and pedagogy (Galligan, 2008). In addition, universities must consider effective strategies to support international students before, during and after core or mandatory workplace components within study programs (Barton et al., 2017). Many international students are required to undertake a work placement, internship, practicum, and/or work-integrated-learning (WIL); however, although there is wide-ranging research on such experiences for university students generally, limited research exists on international students' workplace experience specifically (Barton et al., 2017).

This paper reports on a study exploring the benefits and challenges related to a group of international students who voluntarily participated in a workplace environment prior to core or mandatory workplace experiences in their study programs. Two questions are posed to reveal the complex issues that shape international students' workplace experiences: What are the benefits and/or challenges experienced by international students during volunteering opportunities? How do these relate to specific employability literacies? For the purpose of this paper, volunteering is defined as meeting three conditions: There is no financial gain for the volunteer, it is undertaken at the volunteer's free will, and it has potential to benefit both the volunteer and third party (Petriwskyj & Warburton, 2007). Having a deeper understanding of how volunteering experiences might benefit or challenge international students' employability literacy is critical as international students report their desire to find employment post-university studies (Garrett, 2014). These volunteering opportunities may include cocurricular work at universities such as in societies, clubs, and events, and/or in community organizations or workplace environments. They can provide international students the chance to familiarize themselves with local work, culture, and language (Finn & Green, 2009).

A REVIEW OF THE LITERATURE

Themes Related to International Student Experience in Higher Education

Moving to another country to study is both daunting and exciting. Not only do international students have to leave their family and friends and organize their travel and accommodation, but they also need to adjust to a new cultural context, where often an additional or second language is spoken (Barton et al., 2017). It is unsurprising then that the research literature extensively reports on issues and concerns associated with such change (Abu-Araba & Parry, 2015; Baker, 2017; Sawir, 2013; Sherry et al., 2010; Wong, 2004).

In 2000, Mori categorized the issues faced by international students as academic, financial, interpersonal, intrapersonal, and linguistic. Language is, by far, the most reported issue for international students who are English as second language speakers (Carty et al., 1998; Crawford & Candlin, 2013; Greenberg, 2013). However, it is important to note that international students are a diverse group, and it is important to consider educational mobility, pedagogic variation, and differences in their English proficiency (Jones, 2017). Further, most international students are required to pass strict language assessment regimes to qualify to enroll in foreign study, for example, the International English Language Testing System (IELTS) (Ata, 2015). Nevertheless, language support is necessary, especially if academic requirements and expectations differ from what international students have previously experienced (Crawford & Candlin, 2013; Li et al, 2010).

Studying in another country is expensive, and the stress of finance on international students is significant (Sherry et al., 2010; Temple et al., 2016). International students must also comply with the rules and regulations of visa requirements. International students regularly experience these issues, so universities must ensure the necessary support systems are available. In relation to interpersonal and intrapersonal skills, it has been reported that international students tend to socialize with other international students, in particular peers from their own home countries, rather than seek out involvement with others (Tran & Pham, 2016). The same study noted that universities and other external organizations need processes to support and increase international students' confidence in meeting new people.

Each of these themes directly relates to workplace experiences. The next section, therefore, outlines relevant literature that shows how these themes impact international students before, during, and after such workplace experiences as well as other issues that may arise.

Themes Related to International Student Workplace Experience

The workplace experience for international students is generally assessed and therefore places pressure on students to pass their studies. Consequently, when the workplace experience is not a positive one, it can seriously impact whether international students continue with their study programs. International students are required to socialise into their new country and university life. If they are then doing work placement this 'multi-socialisation' can put extra pressure on them (Barton et al., 2017, 2019). It is, therefore, important that these experiences are set up for success despite such challenges.

Issues related to language proficiency, with particular focus on professional communication skills, and understanding new cultural contexts, were highlighted in the literature. It was noted that both language and cultural concerns become more complex when considering workplace environments (Spooner-Lane et al., 2009; Welch et al., 2012). International students need to utilize effective communication and vocabulary from the profession in which they study. They also need to understand and negotiate within the "culture" of that workplace context (Lilley et al., 2008).

Other concerns reported in the literature include the communication channels between the university, workplace, and international student before, during, and after the work placement (Newton et al., 2016). The study reported that communication with students was obstructed by their limited proficiency in English, but that an improvement was noted when students made attempts to improve their language skills by using "local dialect and colloquial terms" (Newton et al., 2016, p. 1495). Often, there is miscommunication and differing expectations that could be solved relatively quickly, ensuring success for the international student and benefits for the workplace supervisor (Ozek, 2009; Panos, 2005).

In addition, it has been noted that international students are often not aware of the support systems available or do not access these when needed before, during, or after work placement (Barton & Hartwig, 2017; Billett, 2011; Celik, 2008). Issues such as not being able to rely on their usual support networks, such as family and friends during work placement (particularly due to time differences and proximity), were raised in the literature. On the other hand, several benefits are provided in the literature for all parties (Doyle et al., 2010; Jackson & Greenwood, 2015). Many have noted how the supervisor/s or hosts of international students value the richness that international students bring to the work context. This includes incorporating their language and diversity skills while working with clients, for example, translating business transactions, different approaches, etc.

THEORETICAL FRAMEWORK

The employability of international students after their study programs is a critical indicator of the success of higher education. Countries such as Australia have now introduced Post-Study Work Visas to encourage international students to seek employment after graduation. Successful employment also highlights the personal and professional capacities of individual students, including their disposition and discipline-specific knowledge, understanding, and application within a workplace context. Therefore, workplace experience as under- or postgraduate students can instrumentally contribute to such success, with many employers noting the need for highly nuanced possession of interpersonal skills such as communication, teamwork, and flexibility and adaptability (Koo et al., 2008). Further, Koo et al. (2008) offer a conceptual framework related to pluriliteracy that supports students' preparation for post-university employment. The model includes eight kinds of literacy that change depending on changes in workplace contexts. These are linguistic proficiency, communicative literacy, culture awareness, content literacy, sustainable citizenship, attitudes and mindset, vocational literacy, and critical literacy (Lie et al., 2009).

According to Lie et al. (2009), *linguistic proficiency* relates to the abilities and skills needed to use a particular language such as written and oral argument capacities and the use of generic conventions, including circumstance, authorship, textual production, and intended audience. It also includes the ability to apply these skills in a range of contexts. *Communicative literacy* involves face-to-face communication and the effective use of digital tools such as computers and mobile devices. Communication in today's world also involves multimodal and multimedia literacy more than ever before (Barton, 2020). According to The United Nations Educational, Scientific and Cultural Organization (UNESCO, 2005), all stakeholders, including business and the higher education sector, should promote the acknowledgment of cultural diversity. This awareness includes aspects such as age, ethnicity, gender, region, class, and lifestyle (Lie et al., 2009). *Cultural awareness* is described as the "predisposition, ability and willingness to suspend judgement on others especially if their way of being, attitude and/or practice differs" (Lie et al., 2009, p. 4). Koo et al. (2008) acknowledge this capacity as being necessary for graduates to be competitive in the employment market.

Given that workplace experiences require international students to understand professional knowledge in context, content and professional literacy are important for success. Much research in the field of literacy has explored the notion of content area literacy, with Bean et al. (2011) noting that it should support learning about the content to be learned as well as the processes that students apply when acquiring, organizing, and integrating content. *Content literacy* is achieved when students possess skills and strategies to master a subject. It is also acquired when the ability to manipulate and generalize that content to other learning situations is mastered (Bean et al., 2011).

Sustainable citizenship refers to "attitudes and practices of social responsibility towards sustaining democratic and ecological environments" (UNESCO, 2016, p. 2). Sustainable citizenship includes ethics and values that support and sustain culturally diverse communities through democratic thinking and action. Such action requires relevant *attitudes and mindsets*. These include openness and curiosity, problem-solving skills, the capacity for teamwork, and high ethical standards in personal and professional life that are underpinned by a capacity for self-directed activity (as cited in Lie et al., 2009, p. 4). Professional development and socialization literature often discuss the notion of individual traits needed for positive workplace environments. Billett (2011), for example, describes dispositions, including people's own personal agency to enact change. These skills are important for professional satisfaction and, hence, success.

Vocational literacy relates to content literacy, specifically industry skills and knowledge that support students' career development in a global context (Bates,

2002). Vocational literacy includes the concept of entrepreneurialism in a rapidly changing world. Finally, *critical literacy* supports students' ability to question the status quo by interrogating textual and other forms of communication that they receive at work. This may include reflective and reflexive reasoning by considering alternative perspectives and the ability to "adapt and transfer the critical methods of the discipline to a variety of working environment" (Lie et al., 2009, p. 5).

METHODOLOGY

The nature of the data presented in this paper is qualitative, even though data from this entire research project included both qualitative and quantitative information. International students were invited to participate in the study through an email invitation as per our ethics approval. We then organized for consenting students to participate in an initial interview about their career, cultural and study backgrounds. We also identified a potential host for their volunteering experiences through various business and community contacts. The international students participated in these opportunities (between 2 and 4 weeks in total).

Participants

Eight international students participated in the entire study. Three of the students were undertaking Business Studies at a regional university in Queensland, Australia and five were completing a Master of Education at a metropolitan university in Brisbane, Australia. Table 1 outlines the students' country of origin and study programs.

Table 1: International Students' Demographic Information

Students' name (pseudonym)	Study program	Country of origin
Evelyn	Master of Professional Accounting	Iraq
Sunil	Master of Professional Accounting	Nepal
Raj	Master of Professional Accounting	India
Armina	Master of Education	Russia
Lily	Master of Education	Vietnam
Hernando	Master of Education	Colombia
Ilai	Master of Education	Fiji
Calli	Master of Education	Indonesia

Limitations

There were several limitations to this project. First, the sample was small; however, the team found it quite difficult to recruit students due to their busyness and the assessment load they experienced. Unfortunately, four extra students interviewed prior to the volunteering placement were unable to attend the workplace due to other competing pressures. We acknowledge that students sometimes feel stressed about their studies, particularly closer to the end of each semester. Many international students have families and other work commitments, so another commitment just proves too much for them.

FINDINGS

To gauge the impact of volunteering experiences on international students' employability and other skills related to work placements, several interviews were carried out. Three students from the University of Southern Queensland's School of Commerce's Master of Professional Accounting program accepted to participate, and five students from Griffith University's Master of Education program accepted to participate.

After all the interviews were transcribed, the team identified the codes and themes common across each transcript. This process involved the researchers first manually coding and then recoding. The codes were any blocks of information that stood out from the interview and focus group transcripts. Once this part of the coding and recoding process was completed, we aligned these original themes (shown in brackets below) with the employability literacy outlined by Koo et al. (2008). The themes identified included:

- Linguistic proficiencies (language barriers)
- Cultural differences (cultural awareness)
- Attitudes and mindset (value of assistance and approachability of coworkers)
- Vocational literacy (value of work experience)
- Sustainable citizenship (building trust and eliminating prejudice)

The following discussion shares information related to each of these themes, including data from the student interviews.

Linguistic Proficiencies

In general, the international student volunteers had trouble understanding the Australian accent in any context they encountered. However, they indicated that they were very determined to learn English to the best of their ability. The international students also shared that if they did not understand what someone was saying to them, they would ask for clarification as well as use body language to help them understand.

> English is a second language for us, and sometimes it's hard to find the
> proper words to explain what you are thinking. No, it is the feelings that
> we can't able to communicate with each other, and it is easy to mess up
> that and to understand each other. (Sunil)

> You know that I discover the different cultures is really interesting for
> us. Even that we have a barrier with the language, but you know I think
> that I can assist them. I use the body language when I need something.
> (Lily)

Our data pointed to the fact that the language barrier made it difficult for our
volunteers to express their feelings and they, therefore, could make mistakes
because of misunderstandings. In previous research (Barton et al., 2017),
international students found it difficult to ask for further clarification or negotiate
the workplace expectations placed on them. However, in this study, one student
combated this challenge by seeking support from others in the Nepalese
community by asking them to help him explain his feelings. These community
members also assisted in helping him with his difficulty with professional
language.

> Mainly they are talking on the professional way so it's the accounting
> terms. I just got the theoretical knowledge, but just half of the way. They
> use the same language as well. Like soft form, they speak in the soft
> form. It's very difficult to find what they ask. (Sunil)

For Sunil, explaining how people in his chosen profession use language—in soft
form—enabled him to conceptualize the meaning behind intended
communication.

Cultural Awareness and Differences

In relation to cultural differences, the international students often commented
that expectations in the workplaces were different from what they experienced in
their home countries. As a result, the international students had to consider
different ways to behave in the workplace context, at least different to what they
were used to. They indicated that this was necessary so that they could fit in or
socialize positively with their workplace peers.

> People in Australia are straightforward. Nothing like in Indonesia, like
> in here, you just do your job description, do not do others job because
> sometimes I just can't help myself not to do, if there is a mess up in the
> kitchen or is it the other room, I just clean it up and then my assistant
> director or my director is like, that is not your job so you shouldn't do it.
> But I just can't help it. But, I'm just getting used to it and all. (Calli)

As such, trust needs to be built between workplace partners and the international
student volunteers because of the cultural differences that occur. In addition, the

international student volunteers implied that they also need to learn to listen, be patient, flexible and accept their point of view.

> I think that we also have to be flexible because we have to be flexible to adapt with the new environment. (Lily)

Interestingly, the international students mentioned the diversity of their workplaces and how this assisted with them socializing positively and finding people they could ask for help:

> Actually, here in the workplace people are from different countries, so, yeah, not from only one country, not only Australia. New Zealand, from Philippines, Naples. Yeah, yeah, quite a diversity here in my workplace. (Sunil)

Attitudes and Mindsets: Value of Assistance and Approachability of Their Co-workers

Related to the diversity of the workplaces, the international students commented on how it was important to work positively with other people. This meant that their work colleagues fostered collaboration and friendship. The international students all said that the workplace colleagues were supportive and friendly and that this helped them learn and fit into the environment.

> But when we work together, day by day, and through the many different activities, it could said that all of us really friendly. So yeah, I can feel better and yeah, can work with them effectively, yeah. That is a good way [to] make [a] friend. (Lily)

> Yes. I just wanted to learn and first looking, listening and I will analyse and acceptable with it. (Lily)

In addition, the international students commented that when the work colleagues were able to explain procedures clearly, then this assisted the volunteers in progressing in this learning. Some activities that helped included collaboration with team members, daily meetings, and interactions, which gave the volunteer a sense of belonging and structure.

> Actually, they all are friendly, and then what they are doing, and they explain pretty much work. (Sunil)

> And I like to learn whatever I can, so whenever I have a chance to learn something, I just do it … where my family comes from, we see work as something that is rewarding, and it does not matter whatever you do, you have to do it to the best of your abilities. So it is like we'll always take whatever job we're given and try to do it to our best. (Armina)

Vocational Literacy: Value of Work Experience

All international student volunteers valued the opportunity to work and learn new skills in the situations they were provided. This means that volunteering experiences can greatly benefit international students prior to work placements as part of their study programs. The international students said that observing procedures in the workplace was a positive and valuable experience. They were able to see how various companies operate, for example, working with the clients to do tax returns/payroll and invoices.

The international students also noted the importance of being able to do workplace experiences in Australia, as this may assist them in finding employment here.

> Actually, I do here and the people ask what I do? They explain pretty much. I do little different to capture what they are saying because I do not have any working experience, but I [have] material knowledge. And then, they do it different what we study in the union in college, and the work they we are actually performing in real life, real life work. (Sunil)

The international students believed that volunteering allowed them to learn without the pressures of assessment, but they needed to be aware of not enforcing their own opinions.

> That was sort of my eyes open maybe for the first time so I had to rethink a lot about my own argument. (Sunil)

Sustainable Citizenship: Building Trust and Eliminating Prejudice

The interview data also showed that building trust was critical for success for our international students in the workplace contexts. Trust needs to be built between all stakeholders, given the challenges that may be faced due to cultural differences and, consequently, experiences.

> And we have to like take times, patient, to listen and listen what they want and like accept that is a different culture. So we have to like definitely understand the situation, why they do not want to send the kids to the school. Because they're living the simple life. They do not want to live in other communities. They do not want to go outside their communities. We have to be patient and really a good listener. (Lily)

Sometimes when students did not feel safe in other contexts it was due to nonacceptance of their differences. They noted that this can also occur in the workplace because "you are an immigrant":

> But you speak very good English. It's like, you do not know. So they're expecting, usually people that are not from Australia, to have a heavy accent, or speak broken English I guess. So there is that part too in which they are a little bit prejudiced about it, to a potential immigrant I guess. (Hernando)

DISCUSSION AND CONCLUSION

Workplace experiences for international students can be challenging, especially if their hosts are unlikely to understand the distinct differences and needs that international students may have compared with domestic students. Our data showed a direct alignment with scholarly work carried out by Koo et al. (2008) that offered a conceptual framework for international student employability literacy. Their notion of pluriliteracy included linguistic proficiency, communicative literacy, culture awareness, content literacy, sustainable citizenship, attitudes and mindset, vocational literacy, and critical literacy. Even though our data revealed direct alignment with these literacies, it also highlighted that more attention needs to be paid to the support and training of employers in readiness to host international students in their workplace environments.

Therefore, in answering the questions: What are the benefits and/or challenges experienced by international students during volunteering opportunities? How do these relate to specific employability literacies? we have found that despite international students experiencing some challenges during volunteering, they are often resilient and seek out support regularly when needing advice or help. Our participants also commented on the many benefits of volunteering, including building positive relationships with employers, and learning more about the Australian culture within a professional context. This discussion will first summarize the findings related to each of the pluriliteracies identified by Koo et al. (2008) and second, share new insights into the experiences of international students while undertaking a short volunteering experience throughout their studies.

The challenge of, and anxieties associated with, learning a new language for international students has featured in the literature for some time (Cheng & Erben, 2012). Our data showed that this challenge related more specifically to the Australian accent as well as language related directly to the professional context (Kim et al., 2019). These issues also relate to communicative, content, and vocational literacies. Our participants were eager to improve their understanding of cultural colloquialisms as well as manage their response to their hosts' ways of discussing professions. Sunil shared the difficulty in not expressing herself clearly in context, and Lily discussed how she used body language and other cues to support her understanding. This emphasized that each participant had different experiences and approaches to learning the multiple literacies associated with communication.

In relation to attitudes and mindsets and cultural awareness, it was evident that the international students were generally positive about having the volunteering opportunities but felt that more experience in the profession would have been beneficial. They highlighted how they would like more responsibilities while volunteering. They showed their enthusiasm for learning more about work-related tasks in their allocated workplaces. However, they commented on how they were directed mainly to observe this practice rather than be given opportunities to carry out these tasks explicitly.

Cultural awareness, related to predispositions and willingness to accept difference, can empower students to learn and work in multicultural and diverse environments (Koo et al., 2008). This notion was also raised in terms of the international students observing how in their volunteering opportunities, workplaces often carried out tasks differently from how they would be done in their own home countries. One participant noted that the workforce in their context was diverse, so people already accepted any cultural differences between their colleagues and the international students.

Finally, sustainable citizenship and critical literacy showed that the partnerships built between the hosts and international students were crucial to success. Overall, our international students felt welcomed into the workplace and able to ask any questions they had regarding their learning as a volunteer. Our study showed the importance of building positive relationships between the university, international students, and the workplace. The conversations with the international students interestingly pointed to spaces where the hosts could have provided more culturally appropriate and responsive support for international students. With these opportunities offered to students, we argue that successful employability is more achievable if associated with literacies and cultural sensitivity. Having a deeper understanding of how volunteering experiences might benefit or hinder international students' employability literacy is critical as universities need to consider how best to support international students in gaining employment post-study. This will maximize the inclusion of volunteering opportunities (Chwialkowska, 2020). Our study showed that this inclusion in university study programs is warranted if the following recommendations are valued in the provision of such opportunities.

RECOMMENDATIONS

The study revealed that improved practice related to workplace volunteering experience for international students could be achieved when the following recommendations are considered. First, students should have regular access to language support. This needs to include not just learning English generally but also learning workplace-specific vocabulary (content/vocational literacies) as well as local jargon where appropriate. The understanding of communicative cues such as body language, different accents, and colloquialism plays an integral part in supporting awareness and acceptance in the workplace. Second, employers should be supported to understand that international students want to participate more fully in volunteering experiences, as students learn through participation and not only observation. In addition, employers should be attuned to cultural differences and accept, acknowledge, and learn how work might be carried out differently in different countries and different contexts. There should be a mutual synergy between students and employers to foster better relationships by understanding cultural differences. Lastly, opportunities should be created for employers to present information on campuses to engage international students and share ways to gain a positive work experience and increase their own productivity. This process should foster active and transparent communication prior to, during, and after the volunteering experience to build positive relationships with employers. This can ensure that both parties have a more inclusive and positive volunteering experience.

REFERENCES

Abu-Araba, A., & Parry, A. (2015). Supervising culturally and linguistically diverse (CALD) nursing students: A challenge for clinical educators. *Nurse Education in Practice, 15*(4), e1–e9. https://doi.org/10.1016/j.nepr.2015.02.006

Ata, A. W. (2015). Knowledge, education, and attitudes of international students to IELTS: A case of Australia. *Journal of International Students, 5(4)*, 488–500. https://doi.org/10.32674/jis.v5i4.410

Australian Government (2019). *End of year summary of international student Data 2019*. Department of Education Skills and Employment.

Baker, C. (2017). *Understanding the study abroad experience for international students from China at the University of Vermont*. UVM Honors College Senior Theses, 132.

Barton, G. M. (2020). *Developing literacy and the arts in schools*. Routledge Publishers.

Barton, G. M., & Hartwig, K. (Eds.). (2017). *Professional learning for international students: Exploring theory and practice*. Springer.

Barton, G. M., Hartwig, K., Bennett, D., Cain, M., Campbell, M., Ferns, S., Jones, L., Joseph, D., Kavanagh, M., Kelly, A., Larkin, I., O'Connor, E., Podorova, A., Tangen, D., & Westerveld, M. (2017). Work placement for international students: A model of effective practice. In G. M. Barton & K. Hartwig (Eds.), *Professional learning in the workplace for international students: Exploring theory and practice* (pp. 13–34). Springer Publishers.

Barton, G. M., & Hartwig, K., & Le, A.-H. (2018). International students' perceptions of workplace experiences in Australian study programs: A large-scale survey. *Journal of Studies in International Education*. https://doi.org/10.1177/1028315318786446

Bates, S. (2002). Literacy support in vocational training. *Literacy Today, 32*(2). Retrieved from: http://www.literacytrust.org.uk/Pubs/ltlineups.html#32

Bean, T. W., Readence, J. E., & Baldwin, R. S. (2011). *Content area literacy: An integrated approach*. Kendall Hunt Publishing Company.

Billett, S. (2011). *Guidelines for practice: Integrating practice-based experiences*. Australian Learning and Teaching Council (ALTC). http://espace.library.curtin.edu.au/R

Carty, R., Hale, J., Carty, G., Williams, J., Rigney, D., & Principato, J. (1998). Teaching international nursing students: Challenges and strategies. *Journal of Professional Nursing, 14*(1), 34–42. https://doi.org/10.1016/s8755-7223(98)80010-0

Celik, M. (2008). Pre-service EFL teachers' reported concerns and stress for practicum in Turkey. *Egitim ve Bilim, 33*(150), 97.

Cheng, R., & Erben, A. (2012). Language anxiety: Experiences of Chinese graduate students at US higher institutions. *Journal of Studies in International Education, 16*(5), 477–497. https://doi.org/10.1177/1028315311421841

Chwialkowska, A. (2020). Maximizing cross-cultural learning from exchange study abroad programs: Transformative learning theory. *Journal of Studies in International Education, 24*(6), 1028315320906163. https://doi.org/10.1177/1028315320906163

Crawford, T., & Candlin, S. (2013). A literature review of the language needs of nursing students who have English as a second/other language and the effectiveness of English language support programmes. *Nurse Education in Practice, 13*(3), 181–185. https://doi.org/10.1016/j.nepr.2012.09.008

Doyle, S., Gendall, P., Meyer, L. H., Hoek, J., Tait, C., McKenzie, L., & Loorparg, A. (2010). An investigation of factors associated with student participation in study abroad. *Journal of Studies in International Education, 14*(5), 471–490. https://doi.org/10.1177/1028315309336032

Finn, D., & Green, P. (2009). Global world: Global village? Impact of volunteering for international students. *Enhancing Learning in the Social Sciences, 2*(2), 1–36. https://doi.org/10.11120/elss.2009.02020007

Galligan, L. (2008). *Internationalisation of the curriculum: Learning and teaching support unit.* University of Southern Queensland.

Garrett, R. (2014). *Explaining international student satisfaction: Insights from the international student barometer.* https://www.i-graduate.org/assets/2014-Explaining-Satisfaction.Pdf

Greenberg, N. (2013). A project to increase faculty's cultural competence in mentoring English as a second language nursing students. *Teaching and Learning in Nursing, 8*, 128–135. https://doi.org/10.1016/j.teln.2013.07.003

Jackson, D., & Greenwood, K. (2015). *Enhancing work-integrated learning outcomes for international students in Australia.* Edith Cowan University Funded by the Australian Collaborative Education Network (ACEN).

Jones, E. (2017). Problematising and reimagining the notion of "international student experience". *Studies in Higher Education, 42*, 933–943. https://doi.org/10.1080/03075079.2017.1293880

Kim, R., Roberson, L., Russo, M., & Briganti, P. (2019). Language diversity, non-native accents, and their consequences at the workplace: Recommendations for individuals, teams, and organizations. *The Journal of Applied Behavioral Science, 55*(1), 73–95. https://doi.org/10.1177%2F0021886318800997

Li, G., Chen, W., & Duanmu, J. L. (2010). Determinants of international students' academic performance: A comparison between Chinese and other international students. *Journal of Studies in International Education, 14*(4), 389–405. https://doi.org/10.1177/1028315309331490

Lie, K. Y., Pang, V., & Mansur, F. (2009). Employer perceptions on graduate literacies in higher education in relation to the workplace. *English for specific purposes World, 4*(20), 1–15.

Lilley, M. K., Nulty, D. D., & Stewart, D. (2008). *Work-integrated learning (WIL): Developing an evidence-based support framework for international students*. In Paper (peer reviewed) presented at the 11th International Conference on Experiential Learning.

Newton, L., Pront, L., & Giles, T. M. (2016). Experiences of registered nurses who supervise international nursing students in the clinical and classroom setting: An integrative literature review. *Journal of Clinical Nursing, 25*(11–12), 1486–1500. https://doi.org/10.1111/jocn.13127

Ozek, Y. (2009). Overseas teaching experience: Student teachers' perspectives of teaching practicum. *Procedia-Social and Behavioral Sciences, 1*(1), 2541–2545. https://doi.org/10.1016/j.sbspro.2009.01.448

Panos, P. T. (2005). A model for using videoconferencing technology to support international social work field practicum students. *International Social Work, 48*(6), 834–841. https://doi.org/10.1177/0020872805057095

Petriwskyj, A. M., & Warburton, J. (2007). Redefining volunteering for the global context: A measurement matrix for researchers. *Australian Journal on Volunteering, 12*(1), 7–13. https://search.informit.org/doi/10.3316/ielapa.840215979693516

Sawir, E. (2013). International students and internationalisation of higher education. *Education Review, 9*(4), 448–463.

Sherry, M., Thomas, P., & Chui, W. H. (2010). International students: A vulnerable student population. *Higher Education, 60*(1), 33–46. https://doi.org/10.1007/s10734-009-9284-z

Spencer-Oatey, H., & Dauber, D. (2019). Internationalisation and student diversity: How far are the opportunity benefits being perceived and exploited? *Higher Education, 78*(6), 1035–1058. https://doi.org/10.1007/s10734-019-00386-4

Spooner - Lane, R., Tangen, D., & Campbell, M. (2009). The complexities of supporting Asian international pre - service teachers as they undertake practicum. *Asia - Pacific Journal of Teacher Education, 37*(1), 79–94.

Temple, P., Callender, C., Grove, L., & Kersh, N. (2016). Managing the student experience in English higher education: Differing responses to market pressures. *London Review of Education, 14*(1), 33–46. https://doi.org/10.18546/LRE.14.1.05

The United Nations Educational, Scientific and Cultural Organization (2005). *Promoting cultural diversity and intercultural dialogue.* https://en.unesco.org/creativity/policy-monitoring-platform/promoting-cultural-diversity

The United Nations Educational, Scientific and Cultural Organization (2016). *Education for people and planet: Creating sustainable futures for all.* Global Education Monitoring Report. UNESCO Publishing.

Tran, L. T., & Pham, L. (2016). International students in transnational mobility: Intercultural connectedness with domestic and international peers, institutions and the wider community. *Compare: A Journal of Comparative and International Education, 46*(4), 560–581. https://doi.org/10.1080/03057925.2015.1057479

Trice, A. G. (2003). Faculty perceptions of graduate international students: The benefits and challenges. *Journal of Studies in International Education, 7*(4), 379–403. https://doi.org/10.1177/1028315303257120

Universities Australia (2019). *Australia has one of the best higher education systems in the world: Data snapshot.* Australian Government.

Welch, B., Vo-Tran, H., Pittayachawan, S., & Reynolds, S. (2012). Crossing borders: Evaluating a work integrated learning project involving Australian and Vietnamese students. *Australian Academic & Research Libraries, 43*(2), 120–134. https://doi.org/10.1080/00048623.2012.10722265

Wong, J. K. K. (2004). Are the learning styles of Asian international students culturally or contextually based? *International Education Journal, 4*(4), 154–166.

Dr GEORGINA BARTON, PhD, is a professor of literacies and pedagogy at the University of Southern Queensland, Brisbane, Australia. She has experience as an Acting Head of School, Associate Head of School, Research and Program Director. She teaches English and literacy education courses in both under- and postgraduate programs. Before being an academic, Georgina taught in schools for more than 20 years; she had been an acting principal and a lead teacher in literacy. She has more than 130 publications in the areas of sociocultural theory and the arts and literacy, including an edited book titled: *Professional Experience for International Students.* Email: georgina.barton@usq.edu.au

Dr KAY HARTWIG, EdD, is adjunct at Griffith University, Brisbane, Australia. Dr Hartwig teaches in the discipline of music (undergraduate to Ph.D. level students) and is the director of internationalization for the School of Education and Professional Studies. In this role, she coordinates study tours for Australian student teachers internationally. Apart from music and arts education research, her research interests are currently centered around international education; internationalization of the curriculum; and work placements for international students. Email: k.hartwig@griffith.edu.au

Dr YIJUN HU, PhD, is an early career academic in the sociology of education and teacher education. With research experience in both Australia and China, she has developed a special interest in exploring knowledge dissemination, pedagogical recontextualization, and the professional identity construction of Asian academics when traveling between their home countries/cultures and the Western ones. Her recent research explores professional development of the in-service teachers in internationalized schools in China. Email: huyijun@beiwaiguoji.com; yijun.hu@alumni.griffithuni.edu.au

MARIE KAVANAGH, PhD, is a university professor of Accounting, with a diverse range of skills and expertise in business, governance, and management, and a national and international research profile in business education. Her main research focus is on business education where she is currently engaged in topics investigating the impact of factors such as authentic assessment, professional work experience, and the shift to online learning due to COVID-19 on the learning outcomes for both undergraduate and postgraduate domestic and international students. Marie has been successful in obtaining funding for, and leading, several large national projects to deliver business education and training to enhance employment opportunities, particularly in low SES and culturally diverse communities. Email: marie.kavanagh@usq.edu.au

Dr MARTHY WATSON, PhD, is a lecturer at the University of Southern Queensland, Brisbane, Australia. She has been an arts educator for more than 20 years and taught the arts in secondary and primary schools in South Africa, New Zealand, and Australia. Marthy has extensive experience in leading and developing course materials in the area of literacy and arts education. She has worked on numerous research projects supporting culturally and linguistically diverse communities. Her current research focuses on reflective practice thought arts-based learning. She strongly advocates for the arts and regularly presents at conferences and arts workshops in schools. Email: marthy.watson@usq.edu.au